ERKS ON HERCS

BY

ANDY MUNIANDY

Maiden flight of Lockheed's YC-130 Hercules on 23rd August 1954

This is Copy No. 980

in a Limited Edition of 2000 copies

The Author,

Andy Muniandy MBE, MISM
Associate Member of The Royal Aeronautical Society
Former Master Engineer, Royal Air Force

Published in 1995 by Hercules Publishing House,
18 St. Mary's Close, Bradenstoke, Chippenham, Wiltshire SN15 4ET.
Fax (01249) 8911145

© A. Muniandy 1995

All rights reserved. No part of this publication may be
reproduced, stored in a retrieval system or transmitted
in any form by any means, electronic, mechanical,
photocopying or otherwise, without first obtaining written
permission of the copyright owner.

ISBN 0 9522608 1 6

Edited and designed by A. Muniandy of Hercules Publishing House
Cover Design by J. A. Osborough and A. Muniandy
Proofreading by by J. A. Osborough
Word processing by Jane Wiseman
Auto CAD illustrations by Steve Bister
Illustrations by Sanon's graphic artist
Typesetting by Desktop Publishing & Design,
Chippenham, Wiltshire.

SANON
Printed by SANON PRINTING CORPORATION SDN BHD
Kuala Lumpur Malaysia. Fax:603-7809082

Colour Separation by C H COLOUR SCAN SDN BHD
Kuala Lumpur Malaysia. Fax:603-2419497.
Final proof DTP operators: Mr. Micheal Soon & team.

ERKS ON HERCS

BY

ANDY MUNIANDY

DEDICATION
This book is dedicated to all of Lyneham's Groundcrew – both past, present and future.
In an uncertain world one thing is certain, the groundcrew of the Royal Air Force are the envy of the world.

GROUNDCREW .... GOD BLESS 'EM

Here's a tribute to all of the groundcrew, whether First Line or others on Station too, To those great 'Erks who will go down in history as the "Fat Albert's" Herculean Groundcrew.

They are magnificent, handsome and stalwart – they are dedicated ones thru and thru,

Those fine young "Cat–Walk" look–a–likes, so smartly dressed in their Royal Air Force Blue.

As their team–work on the superstructure proves, there's nothing that they do not know,

When the tools of their trade are gripped tightly, it's then you'll see pure magic flow.

Tis true they do have to face danger. Maintaining aircraft all round the World.

From war–torn Bosnia, Ulster and the Falklands, their toolkits are always ready – unfurled.

Each man wields a real mean screwdriver, and with a "3–in One" oil can as well,

Can strip an Allison T56–A15 engine, down in seconds, to a mere basic shell.

Their hardest task comes when they try putting a Hamilton Standard Propeller back in place,

Why is it there's always one bit left over/ And of the hole where it goes, not a trace!

Tis no good, it's again they must do it, and make sure all those pieces will fit,

God alone knows what time they'll get finished. They wonder which one was "the Git!"

Much later when the groundcrew finally get home, they don't cease being an ordinary 'Erk,

For their partner is there waiting to greet them, with the poignant phrase – "This Bloody iron still doesn't work!"

Our 'Erk replies, "But my toolkit's in my locker, so I'm afraid there's nothing I can do"

It's then that the fur and saucepans really start flying, and the air turns a different Blue!

Alas life is not easy for the groundcrew, for each one has their own cross to bear,

And all this for a mere paltry pittance – I ask you, can this really be fair?

Isabel Hancock 1995

When man first started his labour
In his quest to conquer the sky
He was designer, mechanic, and pilot
And he built a machine that would fly.

But somehow the order got twisted,
And then in the public's eye
The only man that could be seen
Was the man who knew how to fly.

We all know the name of Lindbergh,
And we've read of his flight into fame,
But think, if you can, of his maintenance rnan,
Can you remember his name?

And think of our wartime heroes,
Bader and Guy Gibson's lot
Can you tell me the names of their crew chiefs?
A thousand to one you cannot.

Now pilots are highly trained people
And wings are not easily won
But without the work of the maintenance man
Our pilots would march with a gun.

So when you see mighty jet aircraft
As they carve their way through the air,
The grease-stained man with the wrench in his hand
Is the man who put them there.

Author Unknown

THE ROYAL AIR FORCE BENEVOLENT FUND

The "Herc" has been serving the Royal Air Force for more than a quarter of a century, but the RAF Benevolent Fund has served the RAF for three times as long! The fund has come a long way since Lord Trenchard set it up in 1919. The welfare expenditure for its first year was £919. The fund relieves distress or need among past and present members, irrespective of rank or sex, of Royal Air Force, the Womens' Services, the Royal Auxiliary Air Force and the Reserve Forces, including their widows, children and other dependants. In 1994, the welfare expenditure exceeded £9 million pounds while the fund's total expenditure since its inception in 1919 amounts to over £130 million, spent helping some 838,000 people. We need to raise an average of £33, 000 each day of the year to continue our work. Any contributions will be most gratefully accepted by the Director Appeals at 67 Portland Place, London WlN 4AR - and by all those who will benefit from your generosity.

THE PAHAR TRUST IN NEPAL

The "Pahar Trust" was created to provide schools for the children of the Nepalese mountain region. It operates through a self help programme o ex-Gurkha servicemen. The organisation of these much needed projects is the work of two ex-servicemen of the Brigade of Gurkhas, Mr Tom Langridge and Mr Chandrabahadur Gurung, both of whom served as Warrant Officers in the Queen's Gurkha Engineers. Other include ex-servicemen from various regiments of the Brigade of Gurkhas, as well as friends and local organisations. Although each project has a team of professional artisans, paid for by the "Pahar Trust", the work is still labour intensive due to difficult working conditions. For this reason the villagers themselves provide the labour necessary for collecting and carrying the building materials. The first school was completed in 1991 in the village of Pokhari Thok followed by Ghamrang in 1992 and Pasgaun and Sindi in late 1995. Tel: 01734-404004

Foreword by
The Station Commander
Royal Air Force Lyneham

In their 28 years service with the Royal Air Force, the Lockheed C–130 Hercules of RAF Lyneham have been involved operationally in every corner of the world, both in support of the UK government's foreign policy and in the delivery of humanitarian relief in its many forms. The Hercules has proved itself to be equally at home, whether dropping grain in Ethiopia from a height of 12 feet in 1985 or operating in the hostile airspace of the former Republic of Yugoslavia in support of the United Nations since 1993. Although many books have been written about the Hercules since it first flew in Aug 1954, no one book has been dedicated to the technical aspects of the aircraft and the personnel who maintain it.

In this book, a sequel to his first – "Hercules – The RAF Workhorse" – Andy Muniandy takes a detailed look at the aircraft, its systems and the personnel at RAF Lyneham who, either directly or indirectly, help to maintain it. Recently retired, Andy has served for the last 27 years as an Air Engineer on the aircraft and is thus in a unique position to write authoritatively and from personal knowledge. I commend this book, both as an entertaining and informative read and more especially because all the profits will be donated to two excellent charities: the RAF Benevolent Fund; and Gurkha Charities.

Group Captain D B Symes RAF
Station Commander
Royal Air Force Lyneham
June 1995

Foreword by
Officer Commanding Engineering Wing
Royal Air Force Lyneham

In common with a great many RAF personnel, the Hercules has occupied a special place in my life. I have flown as a passenger, both as an Air Cadet during summer camps at RAF Colerne, and during my days on the Harrier Force where every detachment was made possible by "Fat Albert". More recently, I have been fully involved with the maintenance of the aircraft at RAF Lyneham, first with Aircraft Engineering Squadron and now commanding Engineering Wing. I am proud to have played a small part in the Hercules story. It gives me great pleasure to contribute this preface to Andy Muniandy's latest book which details the technical aspects of the aircraft and introduces the men and women who maintain her.

Andy Muniandy's enthusiasm for flying, for the Hercules and for the RAF are evident in this book. His love affair with flying was kindled at an early age and, having decided to join the RAF, he set off by bicycle from his home in West Malaysia to cover the 15,000 miles to England. Eleven months later he reached these shores and was able to enlist, initially in the Supply trade, and later training as an Air Engineer. In addition to his flying, Andy became deeply involved in charities in the UK, in Nepal and in Belize. This selfless work was recognised in 1990 by his investiture in the Most Excellent Order of the British Empire. Andy, by now a Master Air Engineer, retired from the RAF in October 1994.

This is Andy's second book about the Hercules and in similar fashion to his first, "Hercules – The RAF Workhorse", all profits will be split between the RAF Benevolent Fund and Gurkha Charities. The work of the Benevolent Fund, relieving distress amongst past and present members of the RAF and its auxiliary forces, needs little introduction. The Gurkha Charities are perhaps less well known and it is worth recording that the previous book funded the building of Singdi School, shown in the photograph above, at Pokhara, 200 miles north west of Kathmandu. The school takes some 250 pupils and doubles as both a medical centre for the visiting doctor and as a weekend community centre. Classrooms in the school have been named after the Squadrons and sections at RAF Lyneham. Andy intends that "Erks on Hercs" should fund the building of a second, similar, school in north west of Nepal with the classrooms this time being named after sections within Engineering Wing.

After covering the history and flying achievements of the RAF C–130 in "Hercules – The RAF Workhorse", Andy has turned in this latest book to the technical side of the aircraft. The book takes the reader through a short but detailed ground school course and then turns its attention to the technicians themselves, looking at who they are, what they do and how they do it. I am delighted that the people and the work of RAF Lyneham's Engineering Wing have been recorded by such an enthusiastic author and I am grateful to him for highlighting so accurately and affectionately the often unsung specialists who keep "Fat Albert" in the air.

Wing Commander F M Church
MBE BSc CEng MIMechE RAF
Officer Commanding Engineering Wing
Royal Air Force Lyneham
June 1995

Author's preface

I first saw a C-130 Hercules in Kuching, Sarawak during my active service there in 1964. I was amazed at this gentle giant with its 4 massive propellers land on the short runway. Furthermore, the tactical take-off was spectacular. With its belly hugging close to the surface of the runway, it roared gently and took off using only a fraction of that runway. At that moment I did not even think that I was going to spend the major part of my service career on the flight deck of the Hercules, let alone writing 3 books about it(the hat trick is in the pipeline).

Over 65 countries operate this aircraft, and yet not one book has been written solely on the technical aspect or about the engineering ground crew. Very few service personnel even know what goes in the hangars or the flight line. Did you know that it takes 4 hours preparation(servicing) for a 5 minute flight from Lyneham to Brize Norton! The maiden flight of the YC-130 Hercules, serial number 53-3397, occurred on 23rd August 1954 from the Lockheed plant at Burbank, California. After two long runs along the runway, the most memorable moment came on the take-off as its wheels left the ground after reaching only 855ft of the long runway. Since 1954, the Hercules has been operating from military airfields, civil airports and rough unprepared landing strips alike at all hours of the day and night in all sorts of weather from the poles to the equator. This humane machine has alleviated the sufferings of many innocent people and children caught in war, flood and famine where the arrival of the Hercules has meant salvation.

The first Hercules CMk1 delivered to RAF Lyneham was on 1st August 1967 and the initial delivery was to No 36 Squadron, which was also my first squadron. RAF Lyneham came into being in May 1940. The station has been a terminal airfield for international flights, including a period between 1943 and 1945 when BOAC operated civil schedules from the base. In 1975 the Hercules deep servicing organisation moved in from Colerne. Since then Lyneham is the home to the entire Hercules Force- the 4 flying squadrons plus the OCU(replaced by No57(R) Squadron on 12th October 1992) together with the engineering support needed to maintain it. This included first and second line servicing, the training of the ground servicing personnel of the Engineering Wing together with all the supply, transportation and administration to operate the 60-strong Hercules fleet.

The Engineering Wing comprises some 1700 personnel, this is by far Lyneham's largest section. All servicing is centralised, and Lyneham also carries out second line servicing on the unique Meteorological Research Hercules-WMk2, operated by the MRF from Boscombe Down. The layout of Lyneham's airfield and the need to provide 24 hour, year-round coverage has necessitated the establishment of two entirely separate Line Servicing Squadrons. The flow chart on page 8 gives the breakdown of the Engineering Wing.

The following are some of the feats of the Mighty Hercules:

1. It can take-off from short unprepared runway. It can also take-off from an aircraft carrier.
2. It can snatch men and mail bags from the ground as in Vietnam and the Falkland Islands.
3. It can take-off with one of its 4 main wheels damaged/removed.
4. In an emergency it can lift more than twice its normal passenger load.
5. Takes-off with 2 operative engines! It cruises with only 2 operative engines.
6. In 1982 an RAF Hercules set the world record for the longest flight of 28 hours and 4 minutes from Ascension Island to the Falkland Islands and return.

The author

CONTENTS

TECHNICAL SECTION

CHAPTER 1	AIRFRAME	9
CHAPTER 2	PROPULSION	31
CHAPTER 3	ELECTRICS, AVIONICS AND INSTRUMENTS	51

ENGINEERING WING SQUADRONS

CHAPTER 4	A AND B LINE SERVICING SQUADRONS (LSS)	71
	After Flight (A/F) and Before Flight (B/F) Servicings	75
	Primary and Primary Star Servicings	81
	Engine Start Sequence	85
	Heavy Rectification (Heavy Wrecks!)	87
CHAPTER 5	AIRCRAFT ENGINEERING SQUADRON (AES) A AND B FLIGHTS	91
	Minor and Minor Star Servicings	93
	Aircraft Support Flight (ASF)	102
CHAPTER 6	MECHANICAL ENGINEERING SQUADRON (MES)	107
	Propulsion Repair Flight (PRF)	107
	Rebuilding the Allison T56–A–15 Engine	108
	Power Plant Bays and Sections	113
	Ground Engineering Flight (GEF) – Maintenance Bays and Sections	117
	Armoury	120
	Role Equipment Section (RES), Survival Equipment Section (SES) and Station Workshops (SWS)	121
CHAPTER 7	ELECTRICAL ENGINEERING SQUADRON (EES)	125
	Avionics Bay – Air Radar, Flight Systems, Aircraft Electrical Section	126
	Simulator Servicing Flight (SSF)	129
	Communication and Information Systems Engineering Flight (CIS)	130
CHAPTER 8	ENGINEERING PLANS FLIGHT	133
	Engineering Plans, Aircraft Ground Engineers	133
	Visiting Aircraft Section (VAS)	134
CHAPTER 9	MECHANICAL TRANSPORT (MT) SQUADRON	137
	MT Maintenance Flight (MTMF), MT Operating Flight (MTOF)	137
	Aircraft Support MT (ASMT)	138
CHAPTER 10	AIRCRAFT DEFENSIVE EQUIPMENT	141
	COLOUR SECTION	145
	ACKNOWLEDGMENTS	161

SQUADRON AND FLIGHT FLOW CHARTS 71, 91, 106, 125, 132, 136

ILLUSTRATIONS
  – Airframe 10, 14, 16, 18, 19, 21, 22, 23, 24
  – Propulsion 30, 31, 32, 34, 39, 40, 42, 43, 48, 50
  – Electrics, Avionics and Instruments 52, 66, 68

SPECIFICATIONS
  – Airframe 27, 28, 29
  – Propulsion 49
  – Electrics 70

ENGINEERING WING – ORGANIZATION LINE DIAGRAM

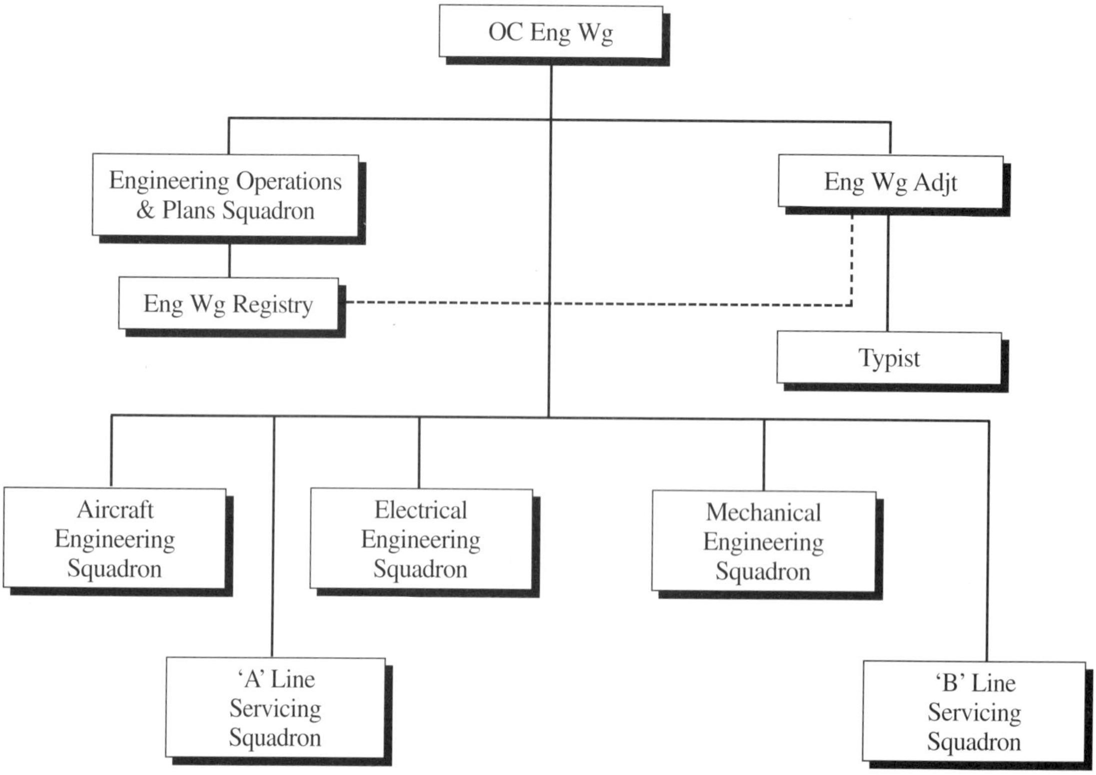

```
                          OC Eng Wg
                              |
      ┌───────────────────────┼───────────────────────┐
Engineering Operations                            Eng Wg Adjt
   & Plans Squadron                                    |
      |                                                |
Eng Wg Registry - - - - - - - - - - - - - - - - - - - -|
                              |                        |
                              |                     Typist
      ┌───────────────────────┼───────────────────────┐
   Aircraft              Electrical               Mechanical
 Engineering            Engineering              Engineering
   Squadron              Squadron                  Squadron
      |                                                |
  'A' Line                                         'B' Line
  Servicing                                        Servicing
   Squadron                                         Squadron
```

Wing Commander T Kirby MBE, RAF, Officer Commanding Engineering Wing (Nov 1992 – May 1995) with some of the engineering officers

CHAPTER ONE

C130K HERCULES

The Hercules is a high wing, long range, land based monoplane powered by four Allison turbo–prop engines each driving a constant speed, fully feathering, reversible pitch propeller.

It is a derivation of the long line of C130 aircraft built by the Lockheed company for many of the world's air forces, and known by the company for the RAF as the C130K.

The aircraft may be used both in the Strategic and Tactical roles. When used as a tactical transport, ground troops or paratroops may be carried and cargo may be transported for ground or air delivery. In order to make the aircraft fully self–supporting in this role, a fuselage mounted gas turbine compressor (GTC) supplies low pressure air for engine starting, operation of an air turbine motor (ATM) driven AC generator and for air conditioning. Stretchers can be installed to convert the aircraft for casualty evacuation. The CMK1K (tanker) can dispense fuel in flight to other aircraft.

The flight crew consists of two pilots, a navigator, a flight engineer and a loadmaster. Controls and instruments for the pilots are grouped on the main instrument panels, the centre console and on side shelves, whilst the engineer has an overhead panel. The navigator's controls and instruments are mounted above his table.

The Hercules is a versatile aircraft. The high–wing has a greater aspect ratio (to give maximum lift), and further lift is provided by fowler flaps. The high wing also allows the mounting of the Allison engine with its large 13 ft 6 ins Hamilton Standard propeller. The fuselage is made up of extruded longerons and formers and riveted together with skins to form sections which are then bolted together. The whole fuselage assembly resembles a long tube with a flat floor. The CMK3 is 15 ft longer than the CMK1. The floor consists of removable sheet aluminium panels which are secured to the longitudinal beams with cross–head screws. Drain holes beneath the floor on the bottom fuselage skin are covered by rubber flaps which close when the aircraft is pressurised. The centre wing section is part of the fuselage to which the port and starboard outer wings are bolted to. Removable leading edges are attached to the front beam (spar). The centre wing's trailing edge houses the 4 liferafts and the inner flap supporting tracks. The empennage section consists of the fin, rudder and elevator sections.

*High wing, propeller and engine.
Flaps extended to 100%*

*Stowage for the 2(port) liferaft shown.
2 on the opposite side*

AIRCRAFT STATIONS. In order to locate precisely the position of components, the fuselage, wings and empennage are divided into Flight

Stations (FS). On the fuselage, for instance, the line dividing the flight deck and the cargo compartment is FS 245. (All numbers being in inches.)

FLIGHT CONTROLS

FLAPS. Fowler flaps are fitted for additional lift. These are needed for take–off and landing and for flights at low speed. Two flaps (inboard and outboard) are fitted to the port and starboard wing. The flaps are of the high–lift type. The flap motion is a combination of an aft movement to increase wing area, (for additional lift), and a downward tilting movement to alter the aerofoil section. This provides less lift and more drag, used during the landing phase. When fully extended (100%), the flaps form an angle of 35° with the wing chord line. The flaps are operated by a reversible hydraulic motor through a gearbox, torque tubes and screwjacks. In an emergency, manual extension or retraction is made possible by operating the drive assembly with a hand crank. The utility hydraulic system pressure is used for normal operation, and selection of the flaps is controlled from the flight deck (centre pedestal) flap quadrant. The quadrant also houses a 70% micro switch (the warning horn will sound if the gear is not down) and a 15% switch which will energise the rudder diverter valves to provide reduced pressure to move the rudder. Some of the components used on the flap system are: flap motor brake, drive control unit, position transmitter and indicator, asymmetric brakes, flap actuator, flap control valves emergency flap brake, flow regulator and flow restrictor, surge damper, NRVs and a pressure relief valve.

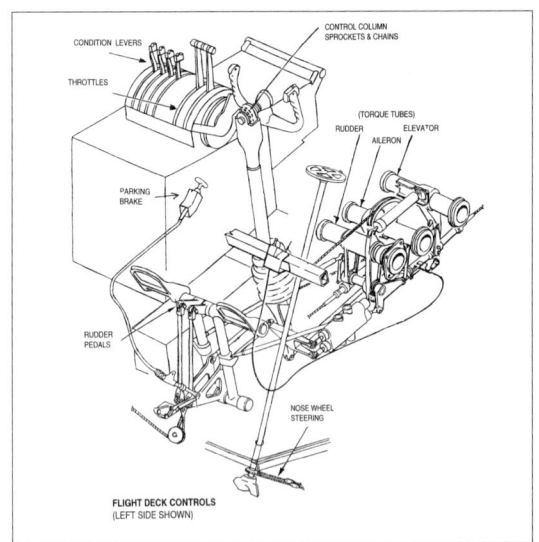

Pilot's controls

FLIGHT CONTROLS. The main surfaces, AILERON, RUDDER AND ELEVATOR, are controlled mechanically with hydraulic pressure. The trim tabs are operated electrically. The movement of these surfaces are controlled from the pilot's and co–pilot's control column with the yoke and the rudder pedals. The mechanical section includes cable, pulleys, pushrods, bellcranks and torque tubes. As the aircraft flies through extreme temperatures, its skin expands and contracts. Therefore, the control cables must have a coefficient of expansion as near to that of the aircraft's structure as possible. Hence LOCKLAD cable is used, as it is also more rigid than standard steel cable, thus needing fewer supports. Cable tension regulators are used on the cable runs. These are high lead screws

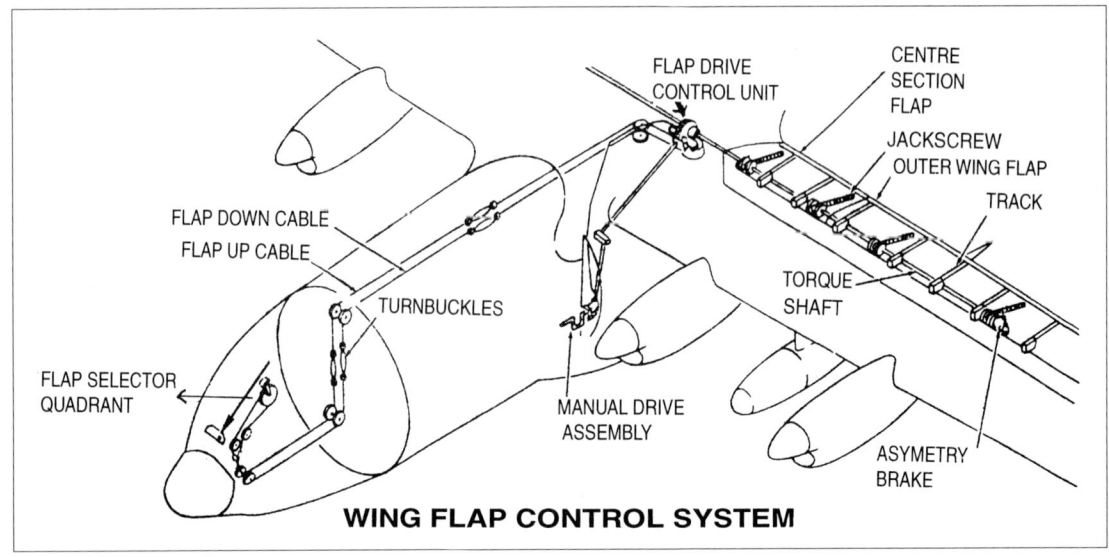

Flap control system

with opposing springs which will expand and contract with changes with temperature. However, for example, when the yoke is moved forward (to initiate a dive) the tension on the lead screw will be greater at one end and it will lock. This will provide positive motion to the hydraulic Booster Assembly to move the control surfaces.

AILERONS. Ailerons are fitted to each wing outboard of the outboard flaps to give roll control. The port and starboard ailerons are attached to the wings by hinge and bracket assemblies. They form the outer wing trailing edge. Mass balance weights are attached which protrude forward into the wings. The port aileron is fitted with a trim tab which can be operated from the flight deck. The one fitted to the starboard aileron is fixed and can only be adjusted on the ground.

Control column, rudder pedals, and the flight station torque tubes (foreground)

AILERON CONTROL. On the flight deck there is one control each for the pilot and co–pilot. A "U" shaped control wheel is mounted on the shaft at the upper end. The shaft has a sprocket, and attached to it is a roller chain which runs through each side of the column to the torque tube control cables. These connect to the flight station torque tube (under the flight deck floor). The co–pilot's system is also connected to the torque tube. The pilot's left hand grip on the control wheel contains 3 switches, and the same on the co–pilot's but on the right hand grip. The switches are: an auto pilot trip, a "Press to transmit" and a pair of elevator trim controls. The port and starboard dual control cables which run rearwards to the hydraulic booster assembly are connected to the flight station torque tube. Directional changes are made by pulleys and a cable tensioner is installed in each of the 4 cables. The booster assembly is mounted overhead on the aft of the wing rear face in the cargo compartment.

BOOSTER ASSEMBLY. This assembly is the link between the pilot's low mechanical input (via the cables) to the high power required to move the ailerons (via the large aileron push rod mechanism). Some of the components of this assembly are: the quadrant, the tandem actuator, Booster Manifold Assembly, Booster control valve, filters, Booster shut off valves, Pressure Reducing Valve (P Red V), Pressure Relief Valves (PRV), Booster Valve Viscous Damper (BVVD) and linkages input and output lever (and so on). The port and starboard dual control cables and the auto–pilot output cable are connected to the quadrant. The tandem actuator unit has 2 cylinders housed inside the actuator cylinder housing and 2 pistons with a common push rod. One end of this rod is free and the other is connected to the output lever. The Booster manifold assembly contains ports and passages for the hydraulic pressure and returns hydraulic fluid to and from the control valve and actuator. The control valve provides a pressure and return path to the tandem boost cylinders, causing the actuating cylinder rod to operate the output lever. The Booster shut off valves can isolate either the utility or Booster or both system pressures from their respective pistons. The P Red V reduces the hydraulic system pressures to 2050 ± 50 psi. This reduced pressure prevents over–stress due to rapid rate of roll. The PRV is set at 2300 psi. The BVVD prevents sudden input to, and oscillations of, the control valves.

OPERATION. Assume a left wing down roll is needed. The pilot moves the control wheel (yoke) in an anti– clock-wise direction. This will move the dual control cables and the quadrant, which will displace the control valve through a system of linkages, causing the tandem actuating rod to move the output lever (the port and starboard aileron push rods are connected to the output lever). As the

Port aileron deflected upwards

ailerons move, its output (via the output lever's feedback) will close the control valve ports. This will hold the ailerons in the selected position for a left wing bank (port aileron up and starboard aileron down). The reverse happens when the control wheel is re–selected clockwise for neutral or for a right wing bank. The aileron push rod contains an idler bell crank, and an aileron control bell crank. The former causes differential movement of the ailerons ie the upgoing one is deflected more (drag) than the downgoing one (lift), whilst the latter changes the output direction by 90° to give a fore and aft movement.

Port aileron control bell crank

RUDDER. The original short fuselage length of 99 ft 6 ins (CMK1) required a large rudder to provide stability and control. The rudder forms the trailing edge of the vertical fin from the tailplane upwards to the rudder tip. The structure is somewhat like the outer wing and is fitted on to the fin by 4 tapered hinge pins on brackets. The rudder's bottom end (base) pivots in a support bearing in the tailplane. The tip is filled with lead for mass balance. The control of the rudder is from the pilot's and co–pilot's rudder pedals which are mounted on the pedal shafts on the flight deck. By a system of linkages the fore and aft movement of these pedals are transmitted to the flight station torque tube, and by depressing the top, toe pressure will set the brakes (via different linkages). As no two pilots are of the same height, the rudder pedals can be adjusted with a pedal adjustment knob. From the flight station torque tube, only one pair of cables (continuous circuit) is connected to the rudder boost quadrant. A tension regulator and a turnbuckle are fitted to the cables. The booster assembly is installed on the forward face of the pressure bulkhead at the rear of the cargo door and its function is similar to the aileron booster assembly except for the following: diverter and PRedV, PRV, push rod pressure seal, rudder lower counter balance weight. When the flaps are selected to 15% or less the valves are diverted to give a pressure of 1275 ± 75 psi and full system pressure at all other times. The P Red V is set to 1600 psi. The output lever is connected to the push rod and it has to pass through the pressure bulkhead to move the rudder. The push rod pressure seal prevents loss of pressurisation.

OPERATION. When the pilot's or co–pilot's left pedal is pushed forward, the rudder moves to the left and vice–versa with the right pedal.

ELEVATOR. These are provided to give pitch control. The port and starboard elevators are constructed nearly like the rudder. Each elevator is connected separately to the port and starboard tailplane by horizontal hinge pins positioned in roller bearings, and by a torque tube assembly. The port and starboard inboard torque tubes are connected by a crank to which the push rods (from the elevator booster assembly) are attached. Balance weights are fitted to the inboard torque tubes and they protrude forwards.

The elevators are controlled from the flight deck by either of the 2 vertical control columns which are hinged at the flight deck floor. Below the hinge

Empennage showing elevators up and rudder to port

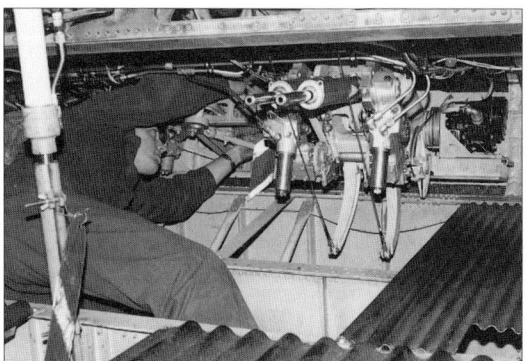
Elevator booster assembly (centre) and auto pilot servomotor (right)

point, the foot of the column is connected to the elevator flight station torque tube by a push rod. This arrangement gives the column a fore and aft movement and physical stops are incorporated to limit its movement. To improve the pitch stability a bobweight is attached to the torque tube. The port and starboard dual control cables are fitted to the torque tube and run rearwards to the Elevator booster assembly which is mounted at the rear pressure bulkhead. It is similar to the Aileron booster assembly but with slight differences. The booster assembly has dual cylinder actuators, side by side (ganged) which operate independently and not as a tandem. The two actuators are connected to a single output lever to which 2 push rods are fitted. It is these 2 rods that move the elevators up and down.

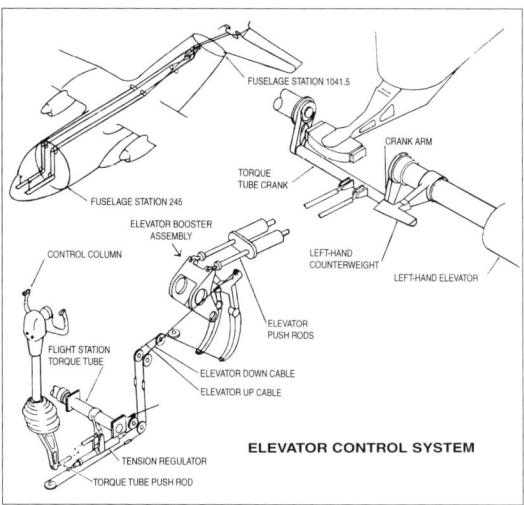
Elevator control system

OPERATION. For the aircraft to pitch up (climb), the pilot pulls the control column and through the system of linkages, cables and the quadrant, hydraulic power moves the actuators and the rods move the elevators up. The reverse happens when the column is pushed.

HYDRAULICS

GENERAL. There are 3 separate systems installed to operate such systems as the landing gear, flight controls and the cargo ramp and door.

BOOSTER SYSTEM. The system's reservoir is mounted forward of the starboard main wheel and its sole purpose is to provide hydraulic power to operate half of the tandem aileron and rudder, and one of the dual elevator booster cylinders. It holds 1.6 Imp gallons of OM15 hydraulic fluid when filled to the mark on the sight glass, and the AC electrical suction boost pump is attached below. A vent line (with a filter) vents into the cargo compartment and any fluid from it and the boost pump's drain, drips on to a tray below. The output from the pump is piped to a NRV, which is located in the output line above it. This primary NRV will maintain a head of fluid for repriming the Engine Driven Pumps (EDP). An accumulator is installed in the system pressure line (below the reservoir). One EDP is located on the No 3 engine reduction gearbox (RG), the other in No 4. The EDP is a variable volume pressure type which has a drive shaft at one end driven by the RGB gearing. It also incorporates a temperature sensor. Basically it is a cylindrical barrel containing 9 pistons (convential axial piston type) and a variable angle cam assembly. As the barrel rotates, the cam assembly causes the 9 pistons (these do not rotate) to move in and out within their bores. This action picks up the low pressure fluid from the intake and discharges it at a high variable pressure to the outlet. This pressure has to be controlled at 2900 to 3200 psi (normal system pressure). This is accomplished by the compensator spool valve which is part of the pump assembly. The spool senses the increased output pressure and moves against a reference spring to port this pressure to the stroking piston. This piston alters the angle of the variable cam unit and hence, the 9 pistons to vary the volume of the output thus maintaining 2900 to 3200 psi. The temperature sensor can also actuate the compensator spool. The following components are installed in the system: in line pressure filters, low pressure warning switches, pump and firewall shut–off valves, "Run Around" circuit, pressure transmitter, high pressure relief valve (HPRV) and ground test connections. When the suction boost pump's pressure drops to 20 psi, or the EDP's output drops to 1000 ± 100 psi, their associated warning lights located in the hydraulic panel will illuminate. The "Run Around" circuit is located between the 2 valves (pump shut–off and firewall shut–off) and protects the pump with its trapped fluid when these 2 valves are closed (pump switched off with the EDP's "on" and "off" switch). The pressure gauge indicates the system's pressure from the transmitter located near the reservoir. The HPRV starts to open at 3450 psi and fully open at 3850 psi. The ground test connection is for airframe technicians to use and is located externally forward of the starboard wheel well.

Booster system reservoir and components

UTILITY SYSTEM. The system reservoir is mounted forward of the port wheel well and contains 2.6 IMP gallons. It operates the other half of the flying controls, normal operation of the flaps, landing gear, nose wheel steering, and normal brakes. The EDPs from Nos 1 and 2 engines operate this system. It also has a ground test connection.

AUXILIARY SYSTEM. This system is slightly larger, containing 2.8 IMP gallons and is located aft of the port para door. It is primarily used for operations of the cargo ramp and door, emergency brakes and emergency lowering of the nose gear. On the ground this system can be connected for ground checks to the Utility System (prevents starting Nos 1 and 2 engines). An electrically driven pump or the hand pump provides pressure up to 2900 to 3300 psi. The electric pump is oil cooled and driven by 115V 3 phase AC. The following components are fitted to the system: pressure transmitter, direct reading gauge, NRV, oil cooler assembly and a high pressure relief valve.

OPERATION. One switch and gauge is on the flight deck (on the hydraulic panel) and another switch and the direct reading gauge are near the reservoir. Either switch can start the pump to pressurise the line. The pump will then run on no load until a service is operated. Both gauges indicate the pressure, however, when the hand pump is used, only the direct reading gauge will indicate.

HYDRAULIC SERVICES

LANDING GEAR. The system consists of 2 steerable nose wheels and 2 main wheels in tandem in the port wheel well and 2 in the starboard. Normal operation of retraction and lowering is with utility system hydraulic pressure. In an emergency the nose gear can be lowered by the auxiliary system pressure. It can also be lowered by "free fall" if no hydraulic pressure is available.

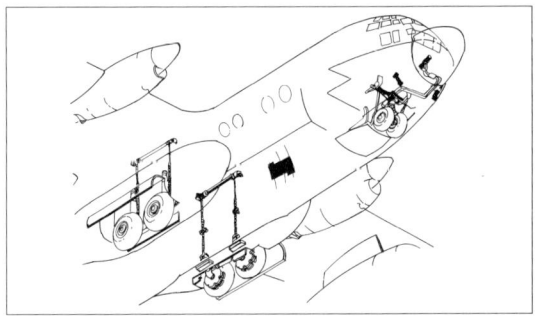

Landing gear location

MAIN LANDING GEAR. This consists of 4 wheels. Each wheel on the tandem configuration is attached to the bottom of a separate oleo strut by an axle and a horizontal strut maintains wheel alignment between them. The oleo strut's shoes runs

Port rear wheel oleo

Technician pointing to the reversible hydraulic motor

in the vertical tracks attached to the fuselage wall. On the lower end of the track is a shelf bracket through which runs the bottom of a screw jack (a lock nut attachment below the shelf bracket prevents it coming off). The top end passes through a ball nut attached to the lower mounting flange on the strut and connects to a swivel bracket. A vertical shaft is installed on the swivel bracket at its lower end and connected to the 90º gearbox at its top end. A reversible hydraulic motor (similar to the Booster hydraulic system EDP but using hydraulic pressure to provide a rotary mechanical output) is located above the forward strut and connected to a horizontal torque shaft. Mounted on the forward and rear of this shaft are the two 90º gearboxes to which the front and rear wheels' vertical torque shafts are connected. As the motor turns, the vertical torque shafts turn causing the screw jacks to turn. The ball nut moves the oleos up (gear up) or down (gear down). Down lock of the gear is provided by a friction washer installed between the locking nut and the lower shelf bracket. Uplock is provided by the spring loaded brake. When the gear is up, hydraulic pressure is removed from the hydraulic motor, causing its spring loaded brake to be applied. In an emergency the gear can be lowered manually. The doors are opened and closed mechanically, via linkages, when the wheels are lowered or raised.

NOSE LANDING GEAR (NLG). The twin wheels mounted on the single oleo strut retract into the nose wheel well by a hydraulic jack. It extends for NLG "up" and retracts for NLG "down". The 2 NLG doors operate mechanically by linkages attached to the NLG.

DOWNLOCK. The downlock is integral within the NLG hydraulic jack. When the jack retracts, a plunger operated by it and assisted by the downlock spring overcomes the downlock pawls' force. This causes the plunger to move and force an indicator pin which operates a micro switch. When hydraulic pressure is removed on shutdown, only the pawls and the downlock spring hold it in the downlock position. Hence a pip pin (ground safety lock) is inserted through a hole at the jack's forward end to prevent inadvertant operation.

UPLOCK. The uplock is a mechanically engaged (geometric uplock) and hydraulically (or manually) released assembly. It is secured to the forward top bulkhead in the nosewheel well. The nosewheel gear uplock link (NGUL) is part of the NLG's lower oleo strut and when it is extended (for gear up), it strikes the latch guide. This action causes the uplock latch's jaws to engage and lock the NGUL. When "gear down" is selected, the latch's jaws are removed by hydraulic pressure.

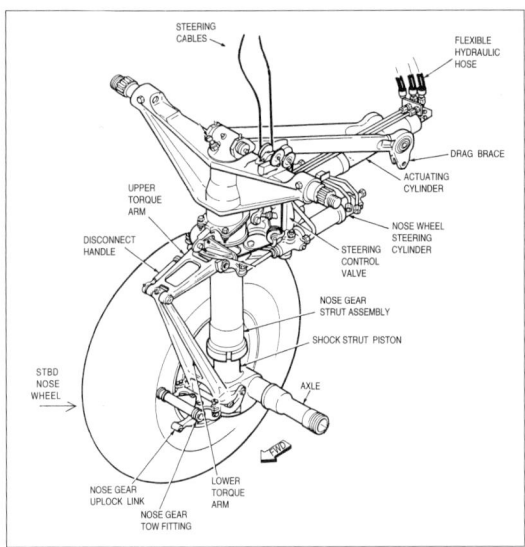
Nose wheel landing gear. Port wheel removed

NOSE WHEEL STEERING is made possible by the "steering wheel" (SW) and an indicator located to the left of the first pilot's position. A linkage connects it to the steering control valve (via the control cable and rocket arm). Two jacks and a follow up mechanism operate the steering system. When the SW is turned left, the control valve is positioned to route hydraulic pressure fluid to one of the port jack and to the opposite side of the starboard jack. The former retracts whilst the latter one extends. This motion (output) is transmitted through the steering assembly on the upper oleo strut steering collar to the upper torque arm. A disconnect handle connects this to the lower torque arm which is part of the wheel axle assembly and the wheels turn to the left. As it turns the feedback cable repositions the control valve. On the jacks hydraulic return line, a restrictor reduces the pressure to 70 psi to provide shimmy damping. Nosewheel steering is not available in the emergency extension position.

LANDING GEAR (MLG AND NLG) CONTROL AND OPERATION

GEAR UP. When "UP" is selected from the co–pilots instrument panel, the gear control valve (GCV) is positioned electrically to the "up" position. Hydraulic pressure is routed to the MLG reversible motor to release the uplock brakes and to retract the wheels. The GCV also routes the pressure to the NLG jack to release the downlock and extend the gear upwards to contact the uplock and the limit switch. When the port and starboard limit switches, (on the upper oleo strut) and the NLG switch are made, the GCVs solenoid is broken. This action puts the GCV into a neutral position to release the hydraulic pressure from the motors, allowing their brakes to apply to the MLG uplock.

GEAR DOWN. When "DOWN" is selected, the control valve ports hydraulic fluid to the down line – MLG motor brakes are released and gear extends. On the NLG, the uplock is released and the jack operates to lower the gear which is positively locked when it is fully down. However, the pressure is maintained to the gear system until the engines are shutdown.

NOTE: The forward wheel of the port and starboard MLG also actuate the touchdown switches. This allows certain systems to operate in the air and on the ground.

WARNING CIRCUITS AND INDICATIONS. On the landing gear control panel (LGCP), three visual electromagnetic indicators (VEI) operate to show the position of the gear. If there is no electrical power or if the gear is not locked, each VEI shows a striped display. When the gear is up the word "UP" is displayed, whilst the display shows a wheel and tyre for the gear down. The landing gear warning system consists of an audible horn (in the flight deck roof), a silence switch and a red warning light will illuminate when the "PRESS TO TEST" button is pressed or when the landing is in transit. When the flaps are selected beyond 70% and the gear is not locked down, the horn will sound. The horn and light operate when the gear is not locked down and the throttles are moved to below the 34° position.

MLG BRAKE AND ANTI–SKID. Each main wheel brake system consists of multiple disc brake, operated by a high pressure and low displacement. "Normal" brake operation is from the utility system pressure whilst the auxiliary system is used for "Emergency". The anti–skid facility is only available in the "Normal". The parking brake is from the 'T' shaped handle in front of the captain's seat. The following are the components that make up the brake system: Brake system accumulator, NRVs, Brake pressure transmitter and receiver (gauge), brake control panel, brake selector valves, brake shuttle valves, brake control valves, parking brake, brake assembly.

OPERATION. The brakes are actuated by depressing the rudder pedals from either of the 2 pilots' positions. Differential braking is avoided due to the tandem wheel arrangement, except in an emergency.

Port MLG multiple disc brakes and hubs

"NORMAL" BRAKE SYSTEM. When the pedals are depressed they open the port and starboard control valves. If the selector valve switch is in the "Normal" position, (on the co–pilot's hydraulic panel), utility system pressure will be supplied to the multiple disc self adjusting brakes and with "anti–skid" selected, a smooth deceleration is made. If emergency is selected anti–skid is not available and the auxiliary system pressure takes a different route to the brake unit. For parking, the rudder pedals are depressed first and the parking 'T' handle is pulled. The pedals are released slowly and this action locks the brake pressure.

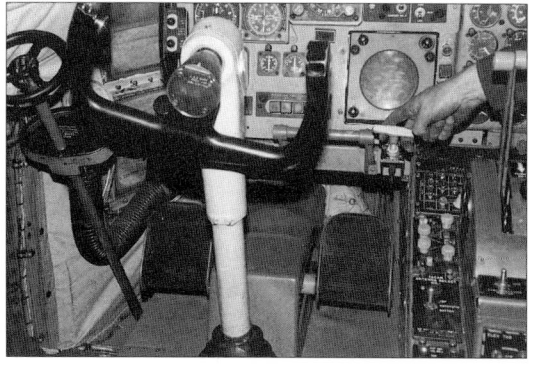
The two rudder pedals (brake pedals when depressed) and the parking brake 'T' handle

ANTI–SKID MK II. The system's components are: a transducer in each wheel hub, control box (electronic brain) located in the cargo compartment roof rack (hogg's trough), the control valve above the booster system reservoir and one adjacent to the utility system reservoir. These 2 valves control the brake pressure supplied to each wheel. The MK II system provides an anti–skid facility for each wheel independently and the brake pressure is dumped proportionally to the intensity of the skid. The system has only one moving part – the pulse generator (transducer) in each wheel hub and, therefore, more reliable.

POWER SUPPLIES AND TEST PANEL. The system uses 26V AC and MAIN DC. The DC power supply is routed through the "Normal" brake selector and anti–skid "Inoperative" switch. Then through the MLG "UP" limit micro switches, the "parking" brake switch and the touchdown switches before power is applied to the control box and valves. Switching off any of the above inhibits the system. The test panel has 4 green lights and a 3 position switch located adjacent to the top left side of the overhead panel.

OPERATION. Whilst taxying, the system is inoperative below 15 KTS, for normal braking and parking. After take–off (as the wheels leave the ground) the touchdown switches allow release of the brake pressures. When the gear is selected "DOWN" for landing this empty brake pressure system prevents braking immediately after landing until the wheels have spun for 2 seconds or 25 wheel RPM. If the pilot brakes harshly the wheels decelerate and the pulse generators (transducers) send the signals to the control box. The amplified signals will be sent to the correct anti–skid valves to release the brakes sufficiently to relieve the skid condition. In icy conditions the brakes could cause a "locked wheel" condition – full skid, in this case the system dumps the brake pressures. Hence, reverse thrust and gentle braking are used on contaminated runways.

TEST. The test panel provides a means of testing the system on the ground and in the air.

SUMMARY. The utility hydraulic system pressure is used to power half the flying controls, flaps, landing gear, nose wheel steering, brakes. The booster system operates the other of the flying controls. The Auxiliary system operates the ramp and door, the emergency brakes, nose wheel lowering and provides a means of connecting it to the utility system on the ground (via the ground test valve located behind the port MLG wheels).

TRIM TABS

AILERON. Trim tabs are fitted to the ailerons (one on each wing). The port one is operated from the flight deck, but the starboard one is fixed and adjusted on the ground for any trim problems. Essential AC is provided to operate an actuator, driven by a single phase motor assembly to move the tab up or down. The position transmitter sends its position to the receiver (gauge) located on the lower portion of the captain's instrument panel. DC power operates 2 relays (at FS 245) to allow AC power to the motor. When the aircraft is airborne, the pilot will feel whether it is left wing or right heavy. Assume the left wing is heavy, there will be a constant load on the ailerons to keep the aircraft level. Hence "right" is selected on the toggle switch, located on the trim panel on the centre pedestal, which will move the trim tab up to deflect the aileron down (gives lift to left aileron) to correct the imbalance. Maximum trim movement is 20° on either side.

ELEVATOR. The elevator trim tab is installed in each elevator's trailing edge. A gearbox (driven by either an AC or DC motor and installed on the aft face of the tail plane) drives the port and starboard flexible drive shaft. The tabs are actuated (up or down) by 2 screwjacks, which are connected to the flexible drive shafts. The position transmitter and receiver are the same as the ailerons. A three position NORMAL/OFF/EMERG power switch is located on the centre pedestal. When "Normal" is selected the AC power is routed to the AC motor and the control is from the 2 trim switches on the pilot's and co–pilot's control column yoke. In the "Emerg" (emergency) position, only DC power is routed to the emergency DC motor and the control is from the same toggle switch as the ailerons' trim tab control.

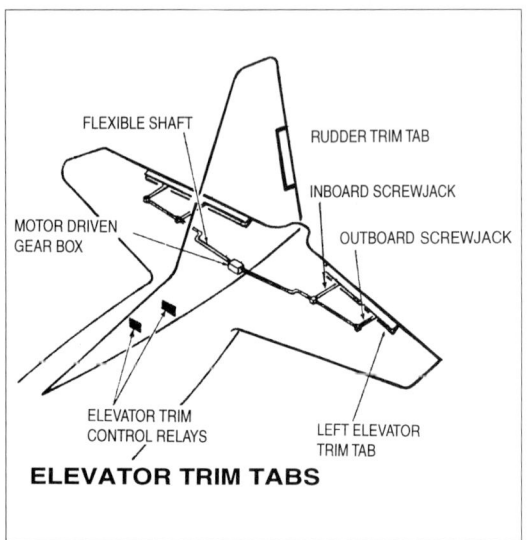

Elevator trim tabs

This switch is moved fore and aft. DC relays to control AC power to its motor are located in the overhead rack above the ramp door area. Maximum trim is 25° "Nose up" and 6° "Nose down". Assume the aircraft is on a normal route sortie with a full load. After take–off, if the pilot feels the nose is heavy, he needs to exert a force on the control column to offset this. He will move the trim switches to the desired position, which will move the trim tabs down and force the elevator slightly up. The aircraft will then fly "trimmed".

RUDDER. The trim tab is installed at the lower section of the rudder. The actuator assembly and position transmitter and gauge are the same as the aileron tab system. The control switch is a 3 position Nose Left/Off/Nose Right located on the trim panel. As no DC is used for the control an insulated control knob is mounted on the switch. The momentary contacts (for nose left or nose right) on this switch carries the single phase AC.

Note the 6 feet rudder trim tab

RAMP AND DOOR

The ramp and door provides entry and egress for large loads and wheeled vehicles. Control of the ramp and door is achieved electrically or manually from the "Ramp Control Panel", located aft of the port para door, or electrically from the ADS control panel on the centre pedestal (in the air only). Some of the components of this system are: the ramp manifold valve, 2 ramp jacks, ramp uplocks, aerial

Ramp and door open

delivery system ramp support arms (ADS arms), aft cargo door jack, aft cargo door down locks and uplock, ramp control switch, aft cargo door control switch, anchor cable support arms, ADSparachute ejectors and manual controls (aft cargo door manual control handle and ramp manual control knob). The ramp manifold valve itself contains the following components: 3 spool valves, 5 NRV, 6 solenoid operated valves, a 500 psi pressure reducing, and a 4100 psi PRV. On the opening cycle, the door is opened first, followed by the ramp which is closed first followed by the door on the closing cycle.

OPERATION. Electrically from the "Ramp Control Panel" the auxiliary pump is switched on (allows auxiliary hydraulic system pressure) and pressure builds up. To open the door, the door switch is held "open" and when the door uplock is made the switch is released. For the ramp, its switch is held in the "LOWER" position until the green "RAMP POSITION AIR DROP" light illuminates. To lower the ramp to the floor the ADS support arms must be disconnected. The ramp and door can be opened or closed manually using the hand pump, the ramp manual control knob and the aft cargo door manual control handle. On MSP supply drop the ramp and door is opened from the flight deck ADS panel and closed from the rear of the port para doors "Ramp Control Panel".

BLEED AIR

The source of bleed air is from the Gas Turbine Compressor (GTC), the engine compressor and an external mobile air start trolley. The output of the GTC is approximately 35 psi, 126 lbs/min at 435°F. The air trolley's output is similar to that of the GTC and the engine's is over 70 psi, 158 lbs/min at 635°F. The bleed air from each engine is tapped from the

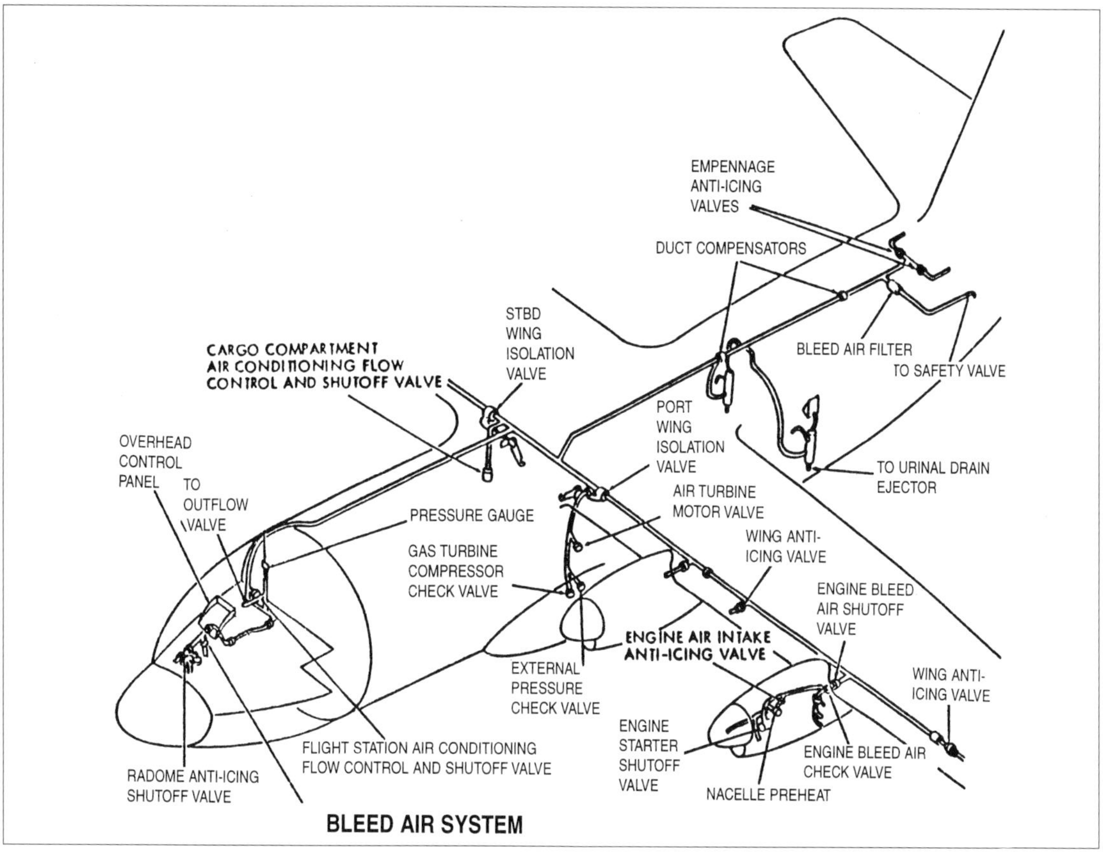

Bleed air manifold (stbd wing section omitted)

14th stage (diffuser) via NRV and fed to the centre bleed air manifold. It runs across the entire wing, forward of the box section. Other components such as the throttle cables and wiring looms also run parallel with the bleed air pipe. Hence this hot pipe is insulated and duct compensators fitted for expansion and contractions. Several valves are fitted to control the supply of the bleed air. In the cargo compartment overhead bleed air duct, one forward and one aft, tappings are taken via insulated pipes for the operation of many items. Two wing isolation valves are located in the centre manifold (at the extreme end where the wings join the fuselage). These are electro–mechanical type and operated from the flight deck. There is a continuous bleed through the rear urinal (drain ejector).

Bleed Air is used for the following systems: Engine starting, engine anti–icing, air turbine motor, wing and tail anti–icing, air conditioning and pressurisation, radome anti–icing, urinal drains and nacelle pre–heat.

ENGINE STARTING. The pneumatic starter is fitted to the rear of the reduction gearbox. It is driven by bleed air and through its gearing turns the engine via the reduction gearbox.

AIR TURBINE MOTOR (ATM). The ATM needs bleed air to turn its motor at approximately 43,000 RPM. Some of the components used are: an inwards flowing turbine, a housing assembly, reduction gearing and lubrication system and a control assembly. The generator is connected directly to the motor via the gearing and turns at about 8000 RPM. The motor and the generator are cooled by a fan driven electrically and directly by the latter.

OPERATION. The solenoid operated shut–off valve is controlled by a two position switch from the overhead panel. Switching it to RUN allows the bleed air to enter (via the solenoid valve) the diaphragm assembly whose actuator opens the shut–off valve. Further downstream is the modulating valve assembly. Its actuator opens the modulating valve and the ATM motor turns and hence the generator. The speed of the motor is controlled by the governor in the speed control assembly acting on the diaphragm assembly. Should an overspeed of 53,000 PRM occur, a trip mechanism (connected to the speed control assembly) allows controlling pressure to the diaphragm to close the modulating valve. This trip mechanism can only be reset on the ground.

WING AND TAIL ANTI–ICING. The leading edge of each wing is divided into 2 sections. One switch on the overhead panel controls this and another adjacent switch controls a further 2 sections in the empennage. The solenoid controlled Anti–Icing Shut–Off Valves (AI SOV), 4 for the wings and 2 for the empennage are interchangeable.

Fitting the stbd inner leading edge

Their control thermoswitches maintain the leading edge temperatures between 158ºF – 180ºF. This keeps the leading edges free of ice at the expense of a loss in engine power. Six leading edge temperature gauges located left and right of the 2 controlling switches indicate the temperature of their associate leading edges. These are 75ºF, 75ºF – 200ºF (normal operating range), 200ºF and above (overheat). Below the 6 gauges are 12 (6 on each side) overheat warning lights. These are only for the leading edges of the wing sections and operate when their sections leading edge temperature exceeds 215ºF – 235ºF. The 2 of the 6 gauges are for the tailplane and the rudder and are used as reference for normal and overheat conditions. Some of the components of the system are: the pipes, overheat warning thermostats, duct compensators, temperature bulbs, AISOVs, control thermostats and ejector assemblies. The ejector is fundamentally a tube with nozzles which face the leading edge of the sections. When the hot bleed air leaves these nozzles it mixes with the air within the leading edge. This, then circulates through an inner double skin, into the airspace between the leading edge and the front spar.

RADOME ANTI–ICING. The radome's outer layer and inner layer's space is supplied with controlled bleed air via a Shut–Off Valve (SOV) and an ejector assembly. The air then enters the supply plenum and exits through the return passages back into the top of the ejector assembly. A PRV maintains a constant pressure of 6 psi on the return plenum side by ejecting any used excess air to

Opening the radome

Large air intake

atmosphere. The control thermostat is also located on the return plenum side and set at 150°F. Above this it opens to reduce the diaphragm pressure and the actuator will move the SOV to reduce the flow of bleed air into the radome. The high limit thermostat operates at 275°F to chose the SOV completely.

OPERATION. A 3 position switch at the navigator's station operates the system. It comes on in the "MANUAL" position and also in the AUTO position, provided AUTO is selected on the anti–icing sub–panel of the engineer's overhead panel.

NACELLE PRE–HEAT. In temperatures below –18°C the engine nacelle needs to be warmed. A gate valve is located forward of the engine oil tank and the bleed air from it is tapped from the manifold. This warms the area within the nacelle.

OPERATION. One switch for each engine is located on the overhead panel and the system can only be used on the ground. When it is switched "ON" the valve opens and the hot air rushes through the spray.

ENGINE ANTI–ICING. The engine air inlet duct (intake) and the oil cooler inlet (scoop) can be anti–iced by bleed air from the aircraft bleed air manifold or hot air from its (the engine's own) diffuser section. But, the following vane anti–icing system can only be provided when its engine is running as the bleed air is drawn from its own diffuser assembly. These are: air inlet housing, 8 hollow struts, compressor inlet temperature and pressure probes (information from these goes to the Fuel Control Unit), lower half of the torquemeter shroud and the compressor inlet anti–icing vanes. Two anti–icing valves are located externally on the air inlet housing and fed by the bleed air from the

diffuser by 2 pipes. These two valves (connected by a balance pipe) control the flow of anti–icing to the 8 hollow radial struts, the temperature and pressure probes. A flexible pipe connected to the balance pipe directs bleed air to the torquemeter shroud. Another valve routes anti–icing to the intake and the oil cooler scoop.

OPERATION. Control is by the 4 engine anti–icing switches to "ON" and the single 3 position Reset switch to "MANUAL". The system comes on automatically if the above 4 switches are set to "ON" and the Reset Switch to "AUTO" and the auto system is activated (during icing conditions). The navigator's radome anti–icing is connected to the above "AUTO" system provided "AUTO" is selected on the radome control's 3 position switch.

AIR CONDITIONING AND PRESSURISATION.
There are two air conditioning units which use the bleed air from the aircraft bleed air manifold. These are the flight deck air–conditioner and the other, the cargo compartment air–conditioner. The flight deck's is located on the starboard side under the flight deck floor. Its system provides 30 lbs/min of conditioned air in flight. This quantity is made possible by the Flow Control Shut–Off Valve (FCSOV) controlling the air entering the refrigeration

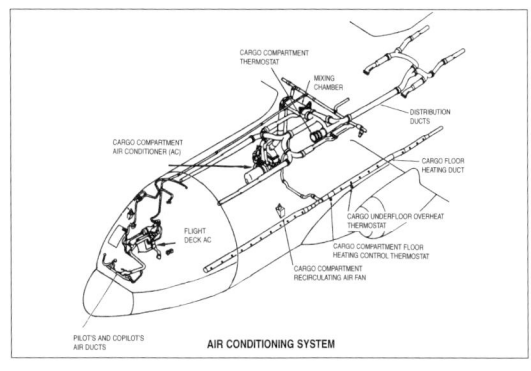
Air conditioners, overhead ducts and underfloor heating

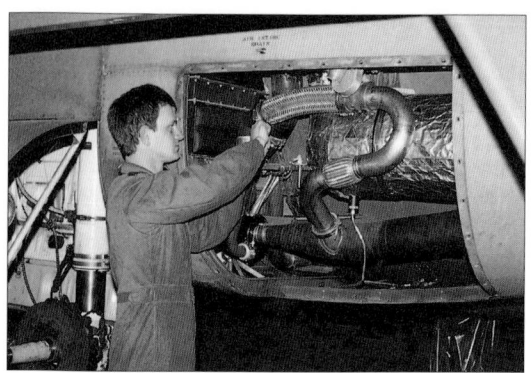

Securing the clamp on the cargo compartment air conditioner

unit. This hot air is warmed as it leaves the unit and takes 2 paths. One goes through the turbine assembly and joins the other (turbine by–pass), prior to entering the water separator together. Further moisture is removed and this cold air joins another quantity of hot air (refrigeration by–pass). The temperature is controlled by 2 valves located together on the refrigeration by–pass and the turbine by–pass pipes. The controlled air then enters the flight deck through louvres. The cargo compartment air–conditioner is larger and provides 70 lbs/min conditioned air. It is located outside the pressure hull, forward part of the starboard undercarriage blister. This system differs by a few components and: not all the cooled air goes through the water separator and under–floor heating is available. The conditioned air is routed through the overhead ducts. When underfloor heating is selected: the Floor Control Valve (FCV) situated after the FCSOV but before the diverter valve opens and the overhead recirculating starts. This hot bleed air flows through an ejector assembly and joins the cargo compartment's ambient air. The diverter valve allows up to 43 lbs/min through the floor out of the 70 lbs/min. This results in the loss of mass airflow from the overhead ducts. Hence, the recirculating fan is connected to the overhead duct. If an overheat of 180°F occurs under the floor, its thermo–switch will activate to close the FCV.

CONTROLS AND COMPONENTS. Both conditioners are controlled by their respective OFF/NORMAL switches (for the FCSOVs) and two temperature control knobs activated by their MANUAL/AUTO switches. The underfloor heating switch is located beside the left knob. A further centrally positioned 7 position Rotary Switch (RS) controls the air–conditioning and pressurisation. The following are some of the components. Two individually controlled refrigeration units, FCSOVs, FCV, ejector assembly, temperature control system (including thermostats in AUTO and MANUAL) overheating warning system, recirculating fan, overhead ducts, a mechanical over–ride lever for the flight station FCSOV, auxiliary vent valves and so on. Should an overheat warning occur within the cargo compartment housing area, the detectors here will illuminate the warning light on the overhead panel at temperatures between 215°F – 235°F.

PRESSURISATION. Some of the components are as follows: the Pressure Controller (PC) is located on the overhead panel and the outflow valve (adjacent to the starboard wall bulkhead near the navigator's station). The safety valve is situated in a circular aperture on the cargo door. The aux vent valves (one per air–conditioner) and the plumbing.

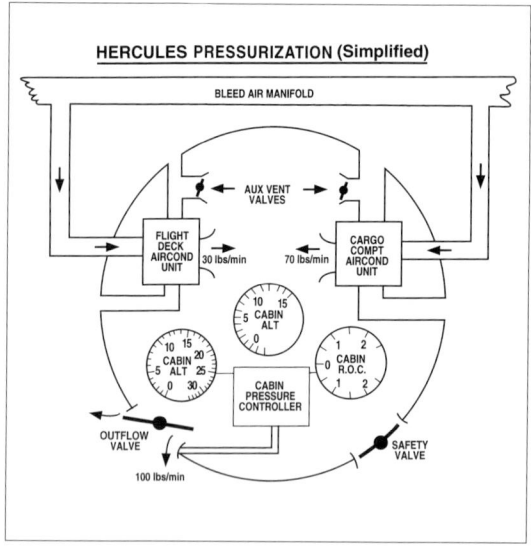

Pressurisation 'Noddy's diagram'

The controls are from the 7 position rotary switch and the PC. The air–conditioning and pressurisation system are inter–connected in many aspects. The pressurisation is maintained in AUTO by the pressure controller and the discharge of the 100 lbs/min air to the atmosphere by the outflow valve. If the AUTO system is unserviceable, it can be controlled manually by varying the position of the outflow valve. In an emergency the aircraft can be depressurised electrically. Power from the battery bus–bar closes both FCSOVs, and opens the outflow valve and the safety valve. Mechanical depressurisation is by a 'T' handle piece on the overhead panel. It is connected by a cable to the release mechanism of the circular door which is part of the centre escape hatch (aft of the centre wing section) when it is pulled the circular door is released outwards. Bungee cords hold it and it can be re–assembled on the ground.

OPERATION. The PC has 4 ranges of operation: unpressurised, rate, isobaric and differential. The unpressurised range is when the aircraft height is below or equal to the selected cabin altitude on the PC. The rate range occurs when the rate of climb of the aircraft exceeds that of the selected cabin rate. The isobaric range of operation occurs during the cruise when the selected cabin altitude is reached and maintained by the normal differential pressure. When the aircraft climbs higher, the PC's differential range operates to open the outflow valve to maintain the normal differential. This archaic system has been operating successfully for over 40 years, but it was a well advanced system in the early 50s.

OXYGEN

In an emergency, such as during depressurisation or a smoke and fume filled environment, oxygen is required by the crew. Gaseous oxygen in cylinders is heavy and occupies a large space. Hence, a Liquid Oxygen (LOX) system is utilised which consists of a LOX converter. It is basically a vacuum flask with heat exchanging coils and other components, located on the starboard side inside the nosewheel well. A small quantity of LOX produces a large quantity (850:1) of gas.

LOX flask

Some of the components used, in addition to the converter are: the Combined Fill and Vent Valve (CFVV), drain valve, shut–off valve, heat exchanger, 10 regulators, contents and warning indications, 4 re–charging points (for the portable oxygen bottles), pipes and so on. The servicing and charging of this system is hazardous and extra safety precautions are taken, including the wearing of protective clothing, gloves and masks. The aircraft is isolated of all

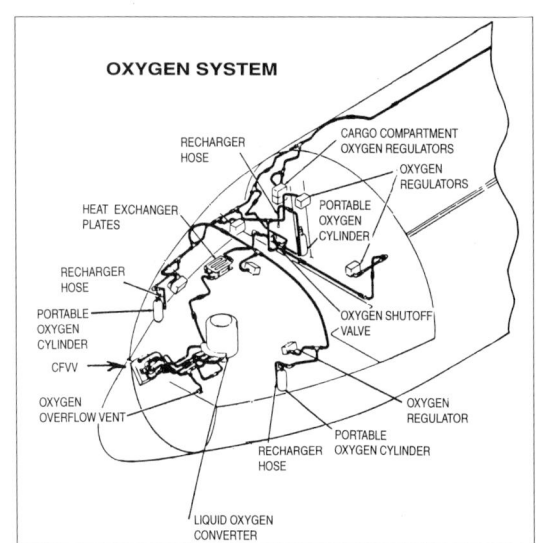

Oxygen System

electrics and any other hazardous materials. Two personnel are needed for charging the system. The hose from the charging trolley is connected to the CFVV, thereby allowing any gas from the top of the converter to vent. As the LOX enters the converter, the system will vent continually. The system is full when liquid oxygen flow from the vent pipe and the charging system is turned off. The aircraft electrical system is restored and the contents gauge is checked. The transmitter for this gauge is a capacitance type probe located within the converter. Beside the gauge (on the co–pilot's front panel) a test button and a caption warning light are located. The system contains 25 litres when it is full. When the button is pressed, the gauge's pointer decreases. This action (and also if the actual contents reaches 2.5 litres) illuminates the caption.

OPERATION. A head of pressure acts on the space on top of the LOX in the converter which is gaseous. This is made possible by a small amount of LOX entering the heat exchanger where it vaporises. This flows through the Pressure Closing Valve (PCV) and the CFVV to act on top of the LOX until the pressure builds to 300 psi. At this point the PCV closes to prevent any further LOX entering the heat exchanger. LOX also flows through an NRV in the distribution line where it is vaporised by another heat exchanger. The crew can use this gaseous oxygen via the regulators and masks. As the pressure drops, the NRV opens and a further small amount of LOX enters the distribution line and the NRV closes. The low pressure valve in the build up line and a high pressure one in the distribution line protects the system. Each crew member connects the mask (via

Portable Oxygen bottle and charging adapter

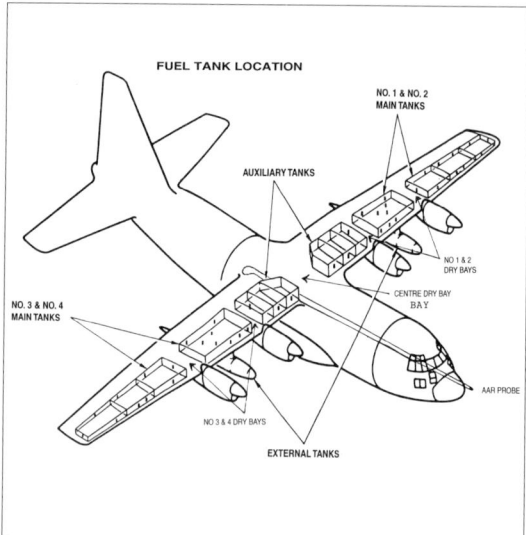

Fuel tanks and dry bays

a hose) to the regulator. This has a pressure gauge, 3 switches and a "dolls eye" indicator. There are 2 re–charging points on the flight deck and 2 in the cargo compartment. Adjacent to these are 4 Mk 4 portable oxygen bottles to which the masks can be connected (allows mobility for the crew). There is one portable Mk 9 stowed on the rear of FS 245. This is a gaseous type oxygen system, complete with a mask and once depleted it can only be charged on the ground.

FUEL SYSTEM

The fuel for the Hercules is carried in the wing sections and the external tanks. For the CMk1K (tanker) version 4 additional tanks are bolted to the cargo compartment floor, each holding 7000 lbs.

CMK1 AND CMK3. Four integral main wing tanks, two auxiliary tanks and two externally mounted pylon tanks carry a total usable fuel of 62900 lbs. The two pylon tanks (LH Ext and RH Ext) are fitted one on each side of the wings between the engine nacelles. A single pipe allows refuelling, defuelling, dumping and most of all to feed the engines. Each tank is made up of the forward, centre and rear sections. Two fuel pumps are mounted side by side, inside and a receptacle for overwing refuelling is in the centre section of each tank. The two auxiliary tanks (LH Aux and RH Aux) are located between the inboard engines and the fuselage and each is made up of 3 inter–connected bladder cells but has no overwing receptacle. One pump is located in the lower portion of the centre cell. The two inboard main tanks (Nos 2 and 3) occupy the box beam section (between the inboard and outboard nacelles) of the outer wing. The smaller of the 2 compartments of each tank has the fuel pumps. The two outboard tanks (Nos 1 and 4) occupy from each outboard dry bay to the wing tip. Due to the length of each tank, it is divided into 3 compartments, the inner one being the surge box and contains the fuel pumps. This division prevents surging and a "percolator" tube is routed between these for faster refuelling than the flapper valves located on the tank baffles. Each of the four wing tanks has a receptacle for overwing refuelling. The normal method of refuelling is from the single point refuelling (SPR) panel located behind the starboard rear wheel.

Numerous components for the fuel system are located inside the tanks, dry bays, engine nacelles, fuselage and the SPR area. The fuel pipes and associated plumbings are also found in the above areas. The following are worth noting.

INDICATION. On the engineer's overhead panel (flight deck) are all the gauges – fuel contents, totaliser and pressure, fuel low pressure warning lights, fuel booster pump switches (normal), dump valves and pump switches (dumping), crossfeed and fuel selector cocks, primer button, test button (for the gauges), and the tank empty warning lights (Ext and AUX tanks only). Above the navigator's station is the fuel air–to–air refuelling panel. This contains the switches and controls for air–to–air refuelling. Normal ground refuelling is via the SPR panel which is larger than the one at the navigator's station. It contains the refuelling hose adapter, 8 fuel quantity gauges, refuelling and ground transfer switches and a surge suppressor behind the SPR panel which absorbs the shock loading when the refuelling tank valves close.

Fuel tank gauges on the overhead panel

TANK PUMPS. The wing tanks (1, 2, 3, 4) have one boost pump each which can feed its engine or another via the fuel cross feed manifold. The aux tanks only pump and the external tanks' two pumps (one is termed the boost pump) have a high output pressure. There are 8 dump pumps – one in each wing tank, 2 in the aux and the 2 in the external tanks. The 2 external tank boost pumps can also be doubled as the dump pumps.

VENTING. Venting system is installed for all the tanks.

FUEL QUANTITY. Indicating system is of the capacitor type tank units (probes). A total of 50 probes and 8 (1 for each tank) density compensators are fitted to the 8 tanks. Multiple contact relays and 115V AC operates this indication system (the 8 in the SPR panel and the 8 plus one totaliser gauges in the flight deck).

FUEL PRESSURE AND WARNING SYSTEM for the pump's pressure is indicated on the fuel pressure gauge. The output of each of the 4 main tank pumps is 15–24 psi, and from the aux or external or the dump pumps is 28–40 psi. One low pressure warning light per main tank will illuminate if its pump operating pressure falls below 8.5 psi. One "TANK EMPTY" warning light for each of the ext or aux tank will illuminate if its operating pressure falls below 23 psi or its tank is empty.

DRY BAYS. Most of the components such as the cross feed, by pass, crossfeed separation, dump, crossfeed primer, and firewall shut–off valves, low pressure warning pressure switches, off load valve and so on, are installed in the 5 dry bays.

This is how the fuel gets to the engine. When the fuel boost pump is switched "on" it delivers fuel at a pressure of 15–24 psi via the NRV, the firewall shut–off valve, fuel heater and strainer (to warm the fuel) pressure warning switch (illuminates if pressure is below 8.5 psi), engine driven mechanical pump, fuel control unit, TD valve, fuel flow meter and finally to the six 'duplex' burners in the combustion chambers. The fuel system is designed in such a way that in case of the boost pump failing, its engine can be fed by gravity in level flight. However, the fuel system has a centre fuel manifold, crossfeed valves, crossfeed separation valve, the dump manifold (both the manifolds are connected but the NRVs and ext dump pump switches prevent interacting). This allows any fuel from any tanks to be fed to any engine. Fuel balance is maintained on the ground and during the flight.

AIR TO AIR REFUELLING. Provision is made for the entire fleet of 60 Hercules to receive fuel in flight. Each aircraft can receive fuel through a probe mounted externally above the right side of the flight deck. A pipeline is routed aft of the mounting and runs parallel and through the starboard inner wing section to join the refuelling manifold. Two NRVs are fitted – one is to prevent fuel draining out should the probe nozzle break off during contacts with the tanker and the other is to prevent fuel entering the probe pipeline. The controls for the AAR are located in a panel above the Navigator's instrument panel.

AAR refuelling probe above flight deck

The CMk1K is the tanker version and is additionally cleared to dispense fuel in flight to other aircraft via the Hose Drum Unit (HDU).

Route of the AAR refuelling pipe

The Andover fuel tanks

HERCULES TANKER – CMK1K. Two Andover transit tanks are fitted to the forward and two at the rear section in the freight bay. Each tank is about 14ft long and 4 ft in diameter and enclosed onto a frame. This single unit piece of equipment is secured to the floor points. The content is read from a vertical sight glass which houses a "blob" that rises when fuel is pumped into the tank. The graduated scale at the side of the sight glass shows the amount of fuel in Imperial gallons. Not only has this got to be converted to pounds but an adjustment is made because of the attitude of the aircraft in flight or on the ground. The tank has a receptacle on the top which allows fuel to be brought in via a long hose. This orifice also doubles up to determine the fuel physically by inserting the end of a broom handle! At the lower point of the 4 tanks, hoses (from each tank via a fuel cock) connect to the collector box which has 3 electric fuel pumps. These pump the fuel to the aircraft fuel manifold and to the 8 main fuel tanks. The total fuel load is 62900 lbs (main tanks) and 28000 lbs (fuselage Andover tanks). The fuel can only be dispensed to other aircraft in flight from the main tanks through the Mk17B Hose Drum Unit (HDU). The HDU is fitted on a frame and mounted on the aircraft ramp. A drogue deployment box is located in the cargo compartment door. A secondary serving carriage is fitted aft of the HDU to feed the hose into the drogue deployment box, to enable the aircraft to be pressurised when not refuelling. A pressure door is fitted around the delivery hose where it passes into the drogue deployment box. The door is opened manually, after depressurising the aircraft, before operating the HDU.

To assist in initial deployment of the drogue, a retractable air scoop is fitted on the underside of the drogue deployment box. When the refuelling hose is fully trailed it measures 80ft. Refuelling signal lights are fitted on each side of the drogue deployment box and floodlights inside the box illuminate the serving carriage. Hose floodlamps are fitted externally.

All the controls for the HDU are fitted beside the Navigators instrument panel. The supply of fuel for transfer is managed from the engineer's fuel panel.

The 80 feet fuel hose trailed for AAR

SPECIFICATION
LEADING PARTICULARS

PRINCIPAL DIMENSIONS
Span ... ... 132 ft 7 in
Length . ... C Mk 1 – 99 ft 6 in
　　　　　　　　　　C Mk 3 – 114 ft 6 in
Tailplane Span . ... 52 ft 8 in
Height (in) ... ... 38 ft 5 in

CARGO COMPARTMENT DIMENSIONS
Length ... ... C Mk 1 – 41 ft 0 in
　　　　　　　　　　C Mk 3 – 56 ft 0 in
Width ... ... 9 ft 11 1/2 in
Height (minimum) ... 9 ft 0 in

FUEL SYSTEM

NATO Code No Standard Fuel	UK Joint Service Designation	US Delegation
F–34	AVTUR/FSII	JP–8
F–40	AVTAG/FSII	JP–4

Alternative Fuels

F–35	AVTUR	JET A–1
		JET A
F–43	AVCAT	
F–44	AVCAT/FSII	JP–5

TANK CAPACITIES

Tank	Capacity Imp Gall	lb	Usable Fuel Imp Gall	lb
No 1 & No 4 tanks (each)	1124	8992	1116	8928
No 2 & No 3 tanks (each)	1033	8624	1024	8192
Auxiliary tanks (each)	758	6064	758	6064
External tanks (each)	1166	9328	1133	9064

Total Useable Fuel Capacity 8062 64496

Note: From structural considerations, the maximum fuel load (including unusable fuel) permitted in the wing and external tanks is 63,700 lb. Total unusable fuel volume is 100 Imp gall (800 lb at 0–80 SG). Maximum allowable usable fuel load is 62,900 lb.

Utility System
Pumps ... ... No 1 & No 2 engine–driven pumps
Operating Pressure ... ... 2900 to 3200 PSI
Reservoir Capacity ... ... 3.2 US gall (2.6 Imp gall)

Booster System
Pumps ... ... No 3 & No 4 engine–driven pumps
Operating Pressure ... ... 2900 to 3200 PSI
Reservoir Capacity ... ... 2 US gall (1.6 Imp gall)

AUXILIARY SYSTEM
Pumps ... ... Electric pump or hand pump
Operating Pressure ... ... 2900 to 3300 PSI
Reservoir Capacity ... ... 3.4 US gall (2.8 Imp gall)

Hydraulic Fluid (all systems) ..OM 15

FLIGHT CONTROLS
Flying Control Operation ... ...Utility and/or Booster system (normal) Manual by both pilots (emergency)
Flying Control Trimming ... ...Electric actuators
Flap operation ... ...Utility system (normal) manual (emergency)

LANDING GEAR
Type .. .. Steerable twin nosewheels, tandem mainwheel units
Track .. .. 14 ft

OPERATION:
Main Gear ... ... Utility system (normal) Manual (emergency extension only)
Nose Gear ... ... Utility system (normal) Auxiliary system (emergency extension only) manual (emergency extension only)
Minimum Steerable Turning Radius
(outer wing tip) ... ... C Mk 1 – 85 ft
　　　　　　　　　　　　C Mk 3 – 90 ft
Tyre Pressures ... ... Nosewheel 60psi
　　　　　　　　　　　　Mainwheel 95 to 100psi
Brakes Operation ... ... Utility system (normal, anti–skid) Auxiliary system (emergency, no anti–sid)
Nosewheel Steering Operation Utility system only

ICE PROTECTION
Airframe & Engine ... ... Hot air from bleed air system
Propeller & Windshield .. .. Electrical

AIR CONDITIONING, PRESSURISATION AND OXYGEN
Air Conditioning Supply ... ... Conditioned bleed air system air (engine, GTC or external supplied) Cold ram air
Pressurisation ... ... Max diff, pressure controller, 14.0 to 15.0 in Hg
　　　　　　　　　　　Max diff, safety valve, 14.6 to 15.9 in Hg
　　　　　　　　　　　Max negative diff, safety valve, 0.76 in Hg
Oxygen ... ... 2.5 litre liquid oxygen 300 PSI, minimum duration 96 man–hours
Portable Oxygen ... ... Four type MA-4 bottles with masks and adjacent re–charging point. Fully charged operating pressure 450 PSI (duration 30 minutes at 25,000 feet). Aircraft charged operating pressure 300 PSI (duration 20 minutes) One Mk 9 unit at Stn 245 charged to 1800 to 1950 PSI

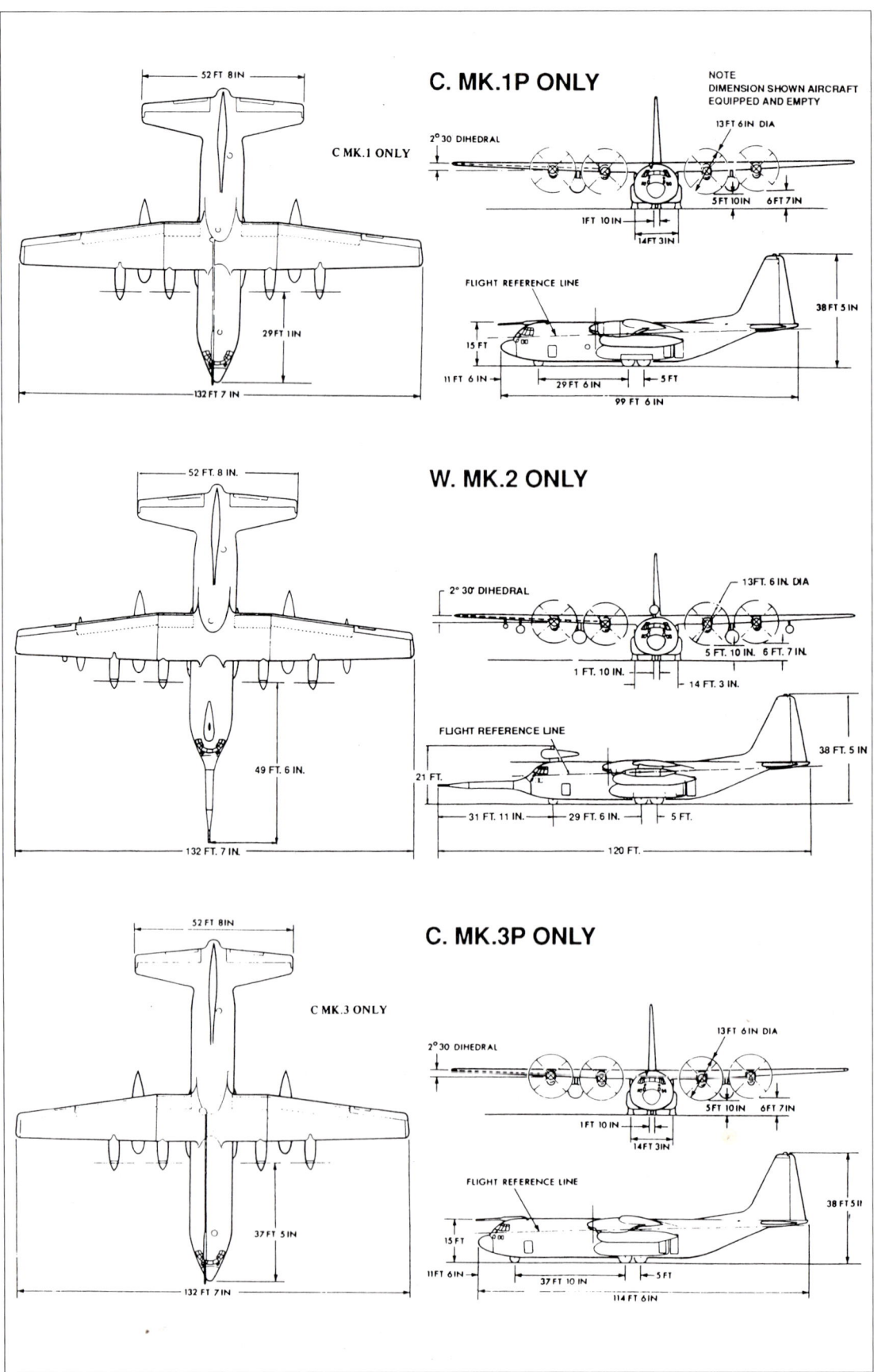

AIRFRAME SPECIFICATIONS CMk1 (C1P) and CMk3P (C3P)

	C1P	C3P
Powerplant:	4 x Allison T56A-15 turboprops giving 4910eshp	4 x Allison T56A-15 turboprops giving 4910eshp
Basic weight:	78,000lbs (approx)	83,000lbs (approx)
Max Take off Weight:	155,000lbs	160,000lbs
Max Fuel Capacity:	62,900lbs	62,900lbs
Max Payload:	44,000lbs	42,000lbs
Still Air Range with 3,000lbs payload:	2,950nm	3,000nm
Crusing TAS:	315kts	315 kts
Typical Max Loads:	92 Passengers	126 Passengers
or	64 Paratroops	90 Paratroops
or	74 Stretchers	97 Stretchers
or	5 Pallets	7 Pallets
or	1 Puma Helicopter	1 Puma Helicopter

Serial Range: XV176 - XV223 (48)   *C/ns:* 382-4169/4182/4188/4195/4196/4198-4201/4203-4207/4210-4214/4216-4220/4223/4224/4225-4228/4230-4233/4235-4238/4240-4247,4251-4253

XV290-XV307 (18)   *C/ns:* 382-4254/4256-4259/4261-4264/4266-4268/4270/4272-4275/4277

Conversions: CMk1K   XV192*, XV201, XV203, XV204, XV213, XV296
WMk2   XV208
CMk3 XV176, XV177, XV183, XV184, XV188, XV189, XV190, XV193, XV197, XV199, XV202, XV207, XV209, XV212, XV214, XV217, XV219/223, XV290, XV294, XV299, XV301/305, XV307

* XV192 re-converted to CMk1P

Number of C-130K built: 66

MAJOR AIRFRAME CHANGES OF THE RAF'S C130K MODEL.

1. **CMk1.** The standard first model following delivery from Lockheed and final fitting out by Marshall of Cambridge.

2. **CMk3.** The stretched version modified from the CMk1.

3. **WMk2.** The weather reconnaissance and research variant operated by the Meteorological Research Flight at Boscombe Down modified from a CMk1.

4. **CMk1LR2.** The standard Hercules with two Andover long range fuel tanks fitted in the Cargo Compartment.

5. **CMk1LR4.** Standard Hercules with four Andover long range fuel tanks fitted in the Cargo Compartment.

6. **CMk1PLR2.** Standard Hercules as CMk1LR2 but with a probe for Air-to-Air refuelling (AAR).

7. **CMk1PLR4.** Standard Hercules as CMk1LR4 but with a probe for AAR.

8. **CMk1P.** Standard Hercules as CMk1 but with a probe for AAR.

9. **CMk3P.** Stretched version with a probe for AAR.

10. **CMk1K.** Hercules tanker with a probe modified from a CMk1.

AXIAL-FLOW COMPRESSOR PURE JET/TYPICAL TURBOPROP

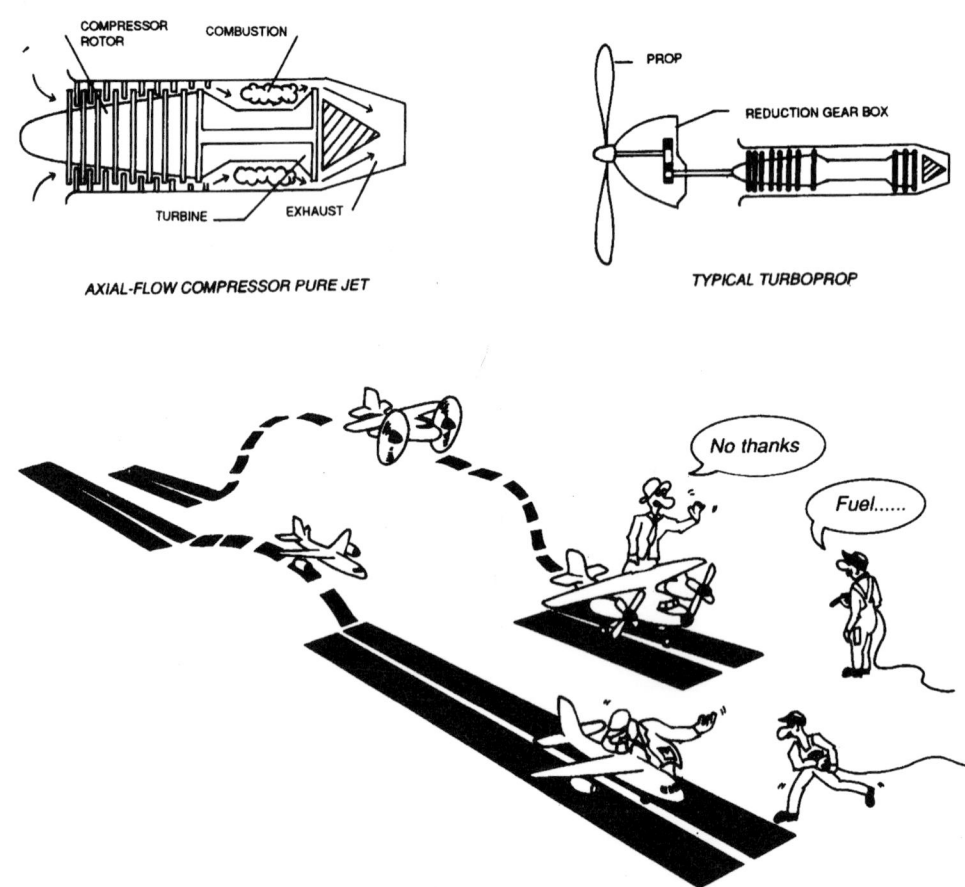

Why put a propeller on a jet engine?

At all subsonic speed the turboprop will produce more thrust than a pure jet engine of the same size, giving the following advantages:

1. The aircraft requires only a short runway for take off and landing.
2. The ability of the propeller to provide reverse thrust for braking efficiency.
3. The propulsive efficiency is greater at take off hence it gives a high initial take off thrust.
4. Econonmic at subsonic cruising speed.
5. Optimum range to payload relationship.

The pure jet engine of the same size as the turboprop with its large diameter propeller needs its turbine to accelerate the hot gas at a greater velocity. This causes a high 'energy loss' in the high velocity stream. However in the Hercules the propeller blades absorb the turbine energy, hence only a small amount of 'energy loss'.

CHAPTER TWO

PROPULSION

PRINCIPLES OF GAS TURBINE OPERATION

OPERATION OF A JET ENGINE. During operation, the jet engine draws air and compresses it. Air pressure is further increased within the engine by burning fuel. The burnt gases are directed through a nozzle at the rear of the engine. The compression and combustion processes are continuous within the engine; therefore the aircraft moves forward continuously.

As the work is accomplished within the engine, a great force is exerted in pushing the gases out of the rear of the engine, it is the reaction to this force that pushes the aeroplane forward.

CHARACTERISTICS OF JET ENGINE PERFORMANCE. In the turbo–jet the compressor and turbine wheel are on the same shaft at opposite ends of the combustion area. When combustion takes place the rapidly expanding gases flow through the turbine vanes and cause the turbine wheel to rotate, which in turn drives the compressor which packs air into the combustion area. The increased combustion pressure imparts additional force to the expanding gases. If there is some means of starting the rotation and combustion, the flow of power will be continuous.

The gas turbine has its limitations. Fuel consumption is very high, especially at low altitudes. Performance is relatively poor at low airspeeds resulting in long take–off runs and initial climb periods.

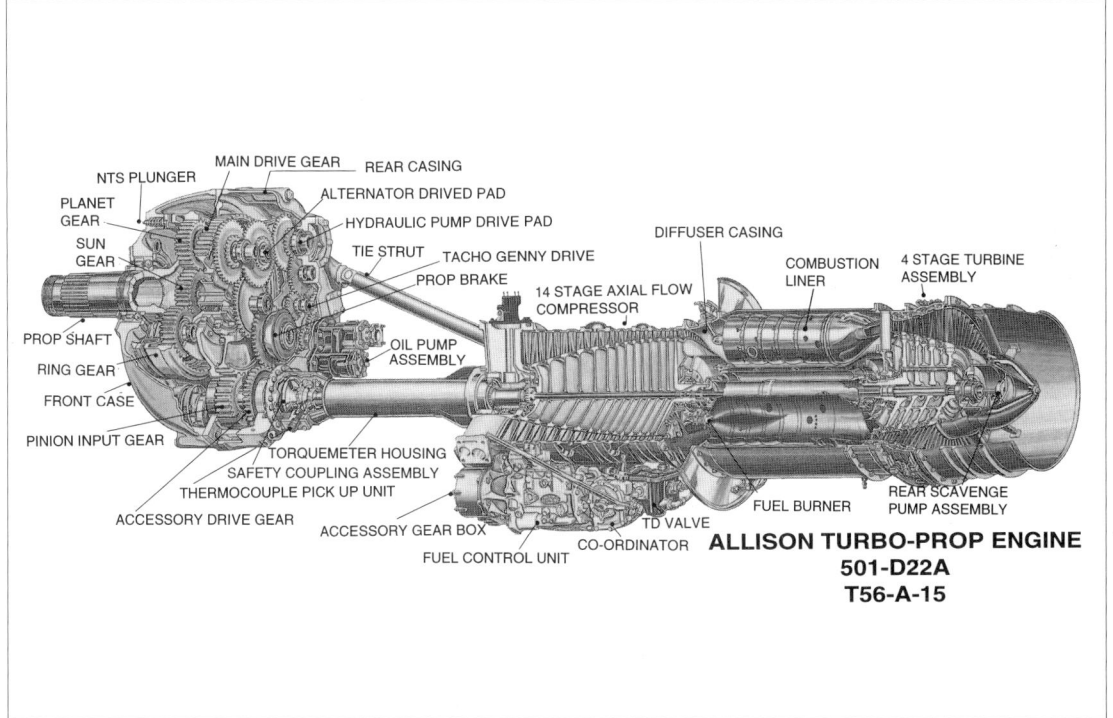

ALLISON T56–A–15 ENGINE

INTRODUCTION TO THE NON–TECHNICAL READER

INTRODUCTION. The Hercules CMk1 is powered by 4 Allison T56–A–15 engines which drive Hamilton Standard 54H60–91 propellers. Each engine is rated at 4910 ESHP, under ISA conditions at 100% engine RPM (13,820 rpm) a prop RPM of 1021, and a turbine inlet temperature (TIT) of 1077°C. The engine consists of an axial flow gas turbine power unit coupled to a torquemeter assembly, which drives a reduction gear box (RGB) assembly to which the 4 bladed propeller is attached. The power section, torquemeter assembly and reduction gear assembly, are installed in a nacelle to make up a "quick engine change (QEC) kit", attached by 4 large bolts to the wing spar. A QEC is interchangeable among engine positions and aircraft.

OPERATING PRINCIPLES

1. During engine operation air enters the power unit through the air inlet housing and is compressed as it passes through the 14 stage axial flow compressor. This compressed air flows through the diffuser, which directs the air to the 6 combustion liners where fuel is introduced and burned. The resultant hot gases pass through the aft end of the liners and through the turbine assembly, causing the turbine rotor to rotate. The turbine rotor drives the compressor, the engine accessories and the RGB assembly. From the turbine, the gases pass through an aperture formed by the turbine rear bearing support and the inner exhaust cone. Some thrust is created by the exhaust gases, which assists in driving the aircraft forward.

2. The RGB assembly, driven by the torquemeter assembly, converts the low torque and high speed of the turbine into high torque and low speed at the propeller shaft. This is necessary as efficient propeller operation requires a lower speed and higher torque than the turbine power unit alone can provide. Engine operation is controlled by co–ordinated operation of the fuel, electrical and propeller control systems.

3. A characteristic of this turboprop engine is that changes in power are not related to engine speed, but to changes in (TIT). During flight, the propeller maintains a constant engine speed known as the 100% rated speed of the engine. This is the design speed at which most power and best overall efficiency is obtained. Since engine speed remains constant, power changes are effected by changing the fuel flow. An increase in fuel flow causes an increase in TIT and thus an increase in energy available at the turbine. The turbine then absorbs more energy, which is transmitted to the propeller in the form of torque. The propeller then increases blade angle (coarsens) to absorb the extra torque and so maintain a constant engine speed.

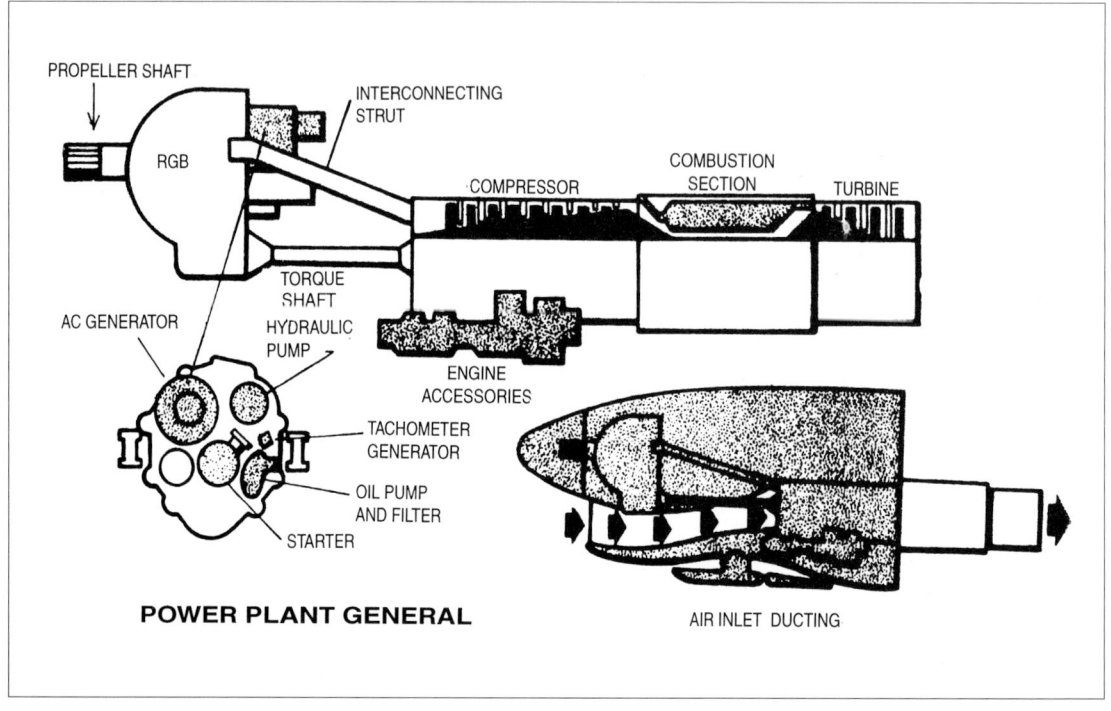

POWER PLANT GENERAL AIR INLET DUCTING

CONSTRUCTION. The T56–A–15 engine (power section) consists of 3 major units:

a. Compressor, Combustion Module (CCM). Made up of compressor combustion, turbine and accessory drive assemblies, it also includes fuel, oil, ignition and engine control systems.

L to R: Compressor, Combustion, and Turbine sections

b. Torquemeter Assembly. Composed of torque and reference shafts enclosed in a housing, it aligns the power section with the reduction gear assembly. Two tie struts assist in rigidly supporting the reduction gear assembly on the power section. The inner torque shaft transmits the torque from the power section to the reduction gearing.

c. Reduction Gear Assembly. The remote location of this assembly from the power section provides the following advantages: (1) Better air inlet ducting for increased engine efficiency. (2) Additional space for mounting accessories without increase of frontal area. (3) The ability to use an electronic torquemeter.

Rear of RGB showing long torquemeter assembly, starter motor and generator (top)

POWER SECTION CONSTRUCTION

1. Compressor Assembly. Consists of an air inlet housing, compressor rotor and casing and the diffuser assembly.

a. Air Inlet Housing. A structural part of the engine, it is a one piece magnesium alloy casting consisting of an inner and outer shell inter–connected by eight hollow struts which provide passageways for the engine accessories drive shaft, the anti–icing air, the engine breathing system and the pressure and scavenge oil systems. The outer shell provides the attachment points for the reduction gear tie struts and engine servicing stand bolts. It also carries the following components:

(1) Oil System Breather is mounted on the top of this unit.

(2) Engine Accessory Drive Housing. Mounted on the bottom of the air inlet housing, it serves as a sump for the oil system and houses the gears for driving:

SPEED SENSITIVE CONTROL)
SPEED SENSITIVE VALVE) FRONT FACE
OIL PRESSURE PUMP ASSEMBLY)

FUEL CONTROL)
FUEL PUMP) REAR FACE
EXTERNAL OIL SCAVENGE PUMPS)

These accessories are driven by a vertical shaft turned by a gear meshed with the compressor extension shaft which is positioned in the air inlet housing inner shell. Various "non–driven" components are mounted on the accessory drive housing and a magnetic drain plug is fitted at its lowest point.

(3) Two engine anti–icing valves are fitted on either side of the outer shell.

(4) Mounting for the torquemeter housing is situated at the forward end of the inner shell.

(5) Inlet guide vane assemblies are mounted on the rear of the air inlet housing. This assembly of

fixed hollow vanes directs the air flow into the first stage of the compressor rotor blades. Anti–icing air passes through them to prevent any build up of ice which could break off and damage the compressor.

b. Compressor Rotor. This consists of a series of fourteen wheels which are splined together at their outer rims and retained by a long central tie bolt extending through the wheel hubs. The rotor blades are held in place by retaining pins. A roller bearing is mounted on the No 1 rotor hub.

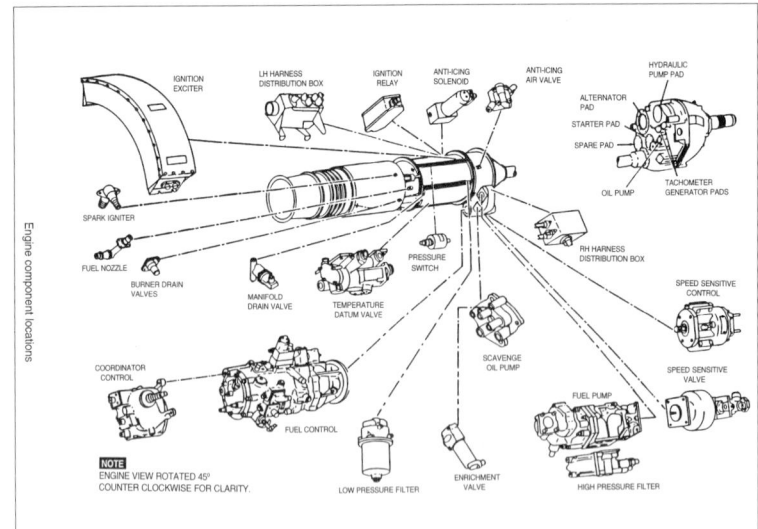

Engine component locations

c. Compressor Casing. A structural part of the engine, it is attached to the rear of the air inlet housing and surrounds the compressor rotor assembly. It is made of two sections being bolted together to form casing halves containing the thirteen rows of stator assemblies. The 2 casing halves are bolted together around the rotor assembly. Four acceleration bleed valves are mounted on the casing at both the 5th and 10th stages. Below 94% engine speed, the valves are open to "unload" the compressor and prevent compressor stall during starting and acceleration. Above 94% engine speed the speed sensitive valve directs 14th stage "bleed" air to close these eight valves. Studs on the outside of the casing provide for the mounting of electrical cables, necessary engine plumbing and the following non–driven components:

(1) Ignition exciter – upper right front.
(2) Fuel enrichment pressure switch– right centre.
(3) Low pressure fuel filter – lower right at front.
(4) Fuel flow transmitter – to rear of (3).
(5) Anti–icing solenoid valve – upper left front.
(6) Ignition relay – to rear of (5).
(7) Lift hand distribution box – left centre.
(8) Temperature datum valve – lower left.

d. Diffuser Assembly. The 14th stage compressor and outlet guide vanes are designed to direct the compressor outlet air into the diffuser at the proper angle. Therefore it contains the highest pressure developed in the engine. The assembly is made up of an inner cone carrying 6 hollow radial struts, which locate the outer shell. The compressor rear bearing is mounted on the forward end of the inner cone, whilst to its rear end is attached the front of the inner combustion casing. The outer shell is located between the compressor casing and the outer combustion casing, and carries the rear engine attachment plates. Three ports on the diffuser assembly struts provide passages for the supply of air to the bleed air manifold, such as for the operation of

10th stage acceleration bleed valve open (5th stage, forward of it)

Fuel nozzles and diffuser (below palm)

both 5th and 10th stage acceleration bleed valves, the 2 engine anti–icing air valves (located on the air inlet housing) and for air–conditioning and pressurisation. The engine fuel manifold encircles the diffuser casing and connects to 6 fuel nozzles located between the diffuser struts. Secured to the diffuser, these nozzles extend rearwards into the forward ends of the combustion liners, both locating and supporting them in the combustion section. A manifold drip valve is located at the bottom of the diffuser casing.

COMBUSTION SECTION. This is of "can–annular" design and consists of an outer casing, inner casing, inner casing liner, turbine coupling shaft and 6 cylindrical "through flow" combustion liners. Approximately 25% of the air entering the combustion section is required (at full power) to burn with the fuel in the combustion process – this being the "Primary Air". The "Secondary Air" surrounds the flame pattern, preventing it from impinging on the liner wall. This air then mixes with the primary air after combustion and reduces its high temperature to a desired level, known as the (TIT).

a.   Outer Combustion Casing. A fabricated steel assembly, attached to the rear of the compressor casing. A structural member used to support the entire weight of the turbine section, it forms the outer wall of the combustion section. Two spark igniters and 4 liner support (dummy plugs) assemblies are located at its forward end. These plugs extend into the combustion liners, thus axially positioning and retaining the liners within the casing. At the bottom of the casing, one at each end, are located 2 burner drain valves. These valves are lightly spring loaded open to drain fuel from the casing, but will be held closed whenever secondary air pressure exceeds 1 – 4 PSI.

b.   Inner Casing. This tubular steel assembly supports the 6 combustion liners and houses the inner casing sleeve to which it is bolted at its forward end.

c.   Inner Casing Liner. Again of tubular steel section, this fits into the diffuser inner cone. It is a "slip joint" to cater for expansion and contraction of the combustion section during engine operation. Pressure and scavenge oil lines are routed through the liner which houses the turbine coupling shaft.

d.   Turbine Coupling Shaft. Splined to the compressor 14th stage wheel, this shaft extends rearwards through the combustion inner casing liner to meet the forward end of the turbine. It is thus the means of transmitting the torque, developed in the turbine, forward through the compressor to the RGB via the torquemeter assembly.

e.   Combustion Liners (Cans). Six identical liners are housed between the outer and inner combustion casings. Positioned by spark igniters in Nos 2 and 5 and by liner supports in the other 4, these liners are designed to control flame length and position and to provide a rapid fuel/air mixing chamber. They are supported at their forward ends by the fuel nozzles and at the rear by the turbine inlet casing. "Cross over" tubes interconnect the liners to equalize internal pressures and provide paths for flame propagation during starting. Each combustion liner is divided into a primary (mixing) section, a secondary (dilution) section and a transition section.

L to R: Oil lines, inner casing liner 6 'cans', and turbine section

f.   Turbine Section. A 4 stage turbine assembly converts the heat energy of the expanded gases produced by the combustion section into mechanical energy in the form of torque.

g.   Turbine Inlet Casing. Consists of inner and outer shells connected by 6 hollow struts. The outer shell is bolted to the outer combustion casing whilst the inner shell bolts to both the inner combustion casing and its liner. It supports the front turbine bearing and first stage stator vane assembly, and locates the 18 dual thermocouples which indicate TIT, both to the indicator gauges and to the Temperature Datum (TD) control.

h.   Turbine Rotor Assembly. This assembly, together with the turbine vane assemblies extracts energy from the hot exhausting gases to develop the

Fitting and testing the 18 dual thermocouples

Rear turbine scavenge oil pump

torque which drives the compressor and eventually the propeller. The 4 stage turbine has spacers interposed between the turbine wheels which are splined together (curvic splines) and then clamped by 8 bolts. The first and fourth wheels have stub shafts which support the front and rear turbine bearings. The complete assembly is located in the engine by a tie bolt which extends forwards from the turbine rear support through the turbine rotor, through the inner combustion casing liner and screws into the compressor 14th stage wheel hub. Cooling air is ducted to the 4 stage rotor blades assembly.

i. **Turbine Vane Casing.** Secured to the rear of the turbine inlet casing outer shell, this section encloses the turbine rotor and provides the mountings for the turbine stator vanes. A structural member of the engine, it carries the turbine rear bearing support. Composed of an inner shell carrying 7 tangential struts to locate the outer shell which is bolted to the rear of the turbine vane casing. The inner shell, located by the turbine tie bolt, provides the turbine rear bearing support, houses the turbine rear oil scavenge pump, and forms the inner cone of the exhaust nozzle. A 12 degree down thrust tail pipe connected to the rear of the outer shell completes the exhaust section of the engine.

Turbine coupling shaft, the 8 bolts and the turbine section

TORQUEMETER AND REDUCTION GEAR ASSEMBLY

TORQUEMETER ASSEMBLY. This assembly is designed to provide a means of transmitting and measuring both positive and negative torque. Together with the 2 tie struts it also provides alignment and rigidity of mounting between the power section and the reduction gear assy. It consists of an inner and outer shaft, a "pick up" assembly, and a housing. The indicator which registers the torque is mounted on the engine instrument panel.

R to L: RGB, torquemeter assembly (above, the 2 tie struts), and the CCM

a. **Inner Shaft.** This solid steel "torque" shaft is splined into the compressor extension shaft at its rear end and is bolted to the outer member of the safety coupling at the RGB end. This shaft transmits the power from the engine to the propeller via the RGB.

b. **Outer Shaft.** This is hollow and fits over the inner shaft. The outer shaft is connected to the inner shaft at the power section end only. Concentricity of the 2 shafts is maintained by the torquemeter bearings.

c. **Pickup Assembly.** At the forward end of both inner and outer shafts is fitted a wheel, each with 40 rectangular teeth spaced at 90° intervals. Since no torque is transmitted by the outer shaft, the inner "torque" shaft wheel will move relative to the outer reference shaft, the direction being determined by whether the torque is positive or negative. Thus, during positive torque conditions the torque shaft will "lag" the reference shaft, whilst during negative torque the torque shaft will "lead". These are detected by the assembly's "magnetic pickups" which transmit an AC voltage when the engine is turning. The amount of voltage produced is measured in the torquemeter indicator and presented as a positive or negative reading. Power supply for the indicator is 115 volts 400 Hz single phase AC. The torquemeter thus provides the alignment of the power section to the reduction gear, the rigidity being provided by the 2 tie struts. As the torquemeter assembly passes through the air inlet housing, it is kept free of ice by enclosing the housing in a 3 piece cowling assembly through which air is ducted from the engine anti–icing system.

d.   Reduction Gear Box (RGB) Assembly. The prime function of the assembly is to convert the high speed, low torque output of the power section into low speed and high torque acceptable to the propeller. It also provides drives and mounting "pads" for various accessories, and houses 3 safety devices, namely – Propeller Brake, the NTS (Negative Torque System) and the Safety Coupling. An independent lubrication system is supplied with oil from the nacelle mounted oil tank

e.   Reduction Gearing. As the power section's speed is 13,820 rpm it would be impracticable to drive a large diameter propeller at this speed without running into blade tip speed problems. A reduction gear is used to reduce the propeller shaft speed to 1021 rpm. The overall reduction gear ratio of 13.54:1 is accomplished in 2 stages.

(1)   First Stage Reduction. This employs spur gears to give the initial speed reduction and also a drive for use of the accessories mounted on the rear of assembly.

(2)   Reduction Gear Driven Accessories. These consist of an AC generator, hydraulic pump, starter motor, tachometer generator and oil pressure and scavenge pumps for the reduction gear oil system.

(3)   Second Stage Reduction. The large main drive output gear of the first stage has a "sun" gear attached to its forward end around which rotate 5 "planet" gears. The final propeller drive shaft is attached to these planet gears and rotates at 1021 rpm when the engine is turning at 13,820 rpm (100%). The Direction of Rotation (DOR) of the engine (anticlockwise) is reversed at the propeller which has a clockwise DOR when looking from the front of the aircraft.

Large main drive gear, 5 planet gears, and the propeller control assembly (extreme left)

f.   Safety Devices

(1)   Propeller Brake. Completely automatic in its operation, this assembly provides a rapid "rundown" after an engine is shut down on the ground. it has 3 positions: Released, Applied and Locked. An apply spring mounted on the starter shaft tends to keep the brake applied when there is no starter torque or the engine speed is less than 21%. On start up, the brake is initially released by starter shaft torque. When the engine speed exceeds 21%, reduction gear oil pressure, ducted to a chamber created in the brake assembly, keeps the brake released. If the propeller is feathered in flight the brake is first applied by the "Applied" spring when engine speed drops below 21%. As the propeller feathered angle is 92.5° it will tend to rotate "backwards". This causes the inner cone to move forward on its helical splines and so the brake will "lock".

(2)   Negative Torque System (NTS). This system is designed to protect the aircraft from an excessive drag condition due to engine power loss. It will also prevent excessive overspeeding of the propeller by limiting the negative torque to a pre–determined value of 1260 in lbs, plus or minus 600 in lbs. This is accomplished by actuating a plunger which causes the propeller control system to increase blade angle giving a resultant decrease in propeller speed. Located on the front of the

reduction gear assembly, the system is completely automatic in operation. The stationary ring gear, locating the reduction gear train planet gears, mates by means of straight splines, with a ring gear coupling which is rigidly attached to a helical spline coupling. Against the coupling by spring pressure are the 14 NTS plungers. Only one of these, the upper, is used in the NTS system. With positive torque applied, ie the engine is driving, the coupling assembly is held in its rear most position by the anticlockwise force on the ring gear tightening the helical splines. The plungers also move to the rear, withdrawing the actuator rods under the follow up action of the springs. When the propeller is driving, the clockwise negative torque applied to the ring gear is transmitted to the helical splines, causing the coupling to move forwards. This movement causes the plunger to compress the springs and force the actuator rod into contact with the propeller mechanism in order to increase blade angle. This will cause the negative torque to be removed and the plunger to be withdrawn. If the "windmilling" persists, the cycle will be repeated and the propeller will be said to be "NTSing". This can be observed by placing the FEATHER VALVE AND NTS switch to VALVE and observing the green NTS light (on the co–pilot's side shelf) flashing.

SAFETY COUPLING (SC). The SC assembly is located between the forward inner shaft of the torquemeter and the reduction gearbox input shaft.

Partly stripped safety coupling

The outer member of the SC is connected to the former and the inner member to the latter. The intermediate member located between these two contains the "cone shaped springs and the helical splines". When the engine is driving the propeller (positive torque) the intermediate member moves forward, tightening the coupling. However, if due to fuel starvation or for any reason the engine stops producing power, the propeller will drive the engine (negative torque). This will cause the intermediate member to move rearwards against spring pressure to cause a "decouple" at 6000in lbs negative torque. This action disconnects the windmilling propeller from the engine to reduce the vast amount of drag induced.

ENGINE LUBRICATION. The stainless steel oil tank with all its ancillaries, such as the pressurising valve (maintains positive pressure of 3.5 psi at any height), dipstick, drain valve and so on are mounted on the nacelle above the engine. Many other components make up the oil system and some of them are as follows: shut–off valve, temperature transmitter bulb, spur gear pressure and scavenge pumps, fuel heater and strainer (warms the fuel), oil cooler, thermostat (for automatic cooling – maintains 78°–82°C), pressure transmitters, filters, pressure regulating valves, and all the plumbing.

POWER SECTION. Oil flows under gravity to the drain and shut–off valve, to the combined pressure/scavenge pump (spur gear type) located on the forward face of the accessory drive housing. Using a combination of internal drillings, internal and external pipes and jet sprays, oil under a pressure of 50–60 psi (normal operating pressure) lubricates the following: accessory drive gears and bearings, torque shaft mid–bearing extension shaft, compressor front and rear bearings, then to the front and rear turbine bearing. The return oil is scavenged via the rear turbine scavenge and the combined pressure/scavenge pumps.

REDUCTION GEARBOX (RGB) SYSTEM. The RGB system uses the same oil supply (via another route) but its pressure and scavenge systems are independent. Under gravity it flows to the spur gear pressure and filter assembly. Oil under pressure passes through an NRV, the pressure adjusting valve and pressure relief valve to all parts of the assembly for lubrication and cooling, and also to the propeller brake assembly. The return oil is scavenged by the main scavenge pump (during level or nose up flight) and the nose scavenge pump (nose down attitude). This oil joins the main scavenge pump flow and is then piped to the outlet from the power section oil pumps. Before returning to the tank, the oil passes through the fuel heater and strainer, and oil cooler.

ENGINE BREATHER SYSTEM (EBS). A breather mounted on the top of the Air Inlet Housing (AIH) provides the means of venting for the

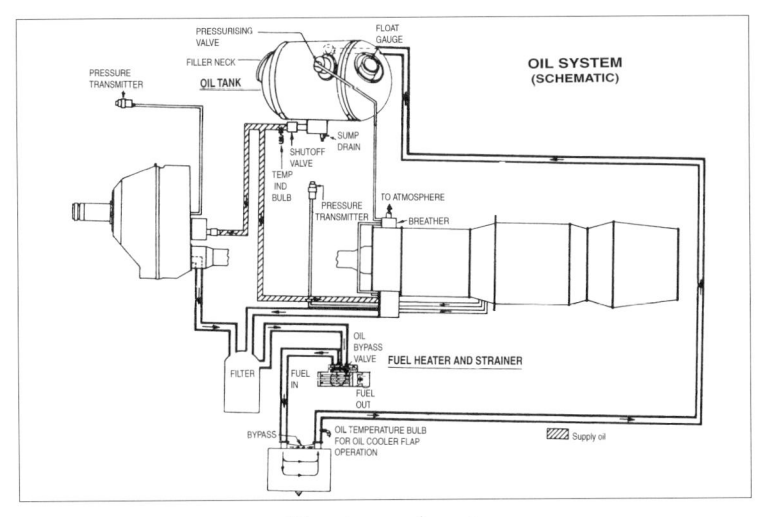

Oil system – schematic

accessory drive housing, AIH cavity, RGB assembly and the oil tank. The "lighthouse" cavity and the rear turbine bearing support cavity are vented via different systems. Hence, the tank contains 12 US gallons of OX 27 oil and an air space of 7.5 US gallons.

ENGINE STARTING SYSTEMS AND COMPONENTS. The engine is started by an air operated "automatic" system with AC and DC electrics. Numerous components are installed for this purpose, some of which are as follows:

a. SPEED SENSITIVE SWITCH (SSS) – located on and driven by the accessory drive housing. It has 3 micro switches actuated by a set of flyweights. The first switch is actuated at 16% RPM which opens the fuel enrichment and the fuel cut off valves, energises the ignition relay and closes the paralleling valve and the manifold "drip" valve. The second switch is activated at 65% RPM, which de-energises the ignition relay, the manifold drip valve (held closed by fuel pressure) and opens the paralleling valve. The third switch is actuated at 94% RPM. This action allows the fuel TD system to change from 50% to 20% "take" (if start temperatures increase rapidly the fuel flow is reduced) and also to change from start limiting (830°C) to normal limiting (1077°C) on its potentiometers.

SPEED SENSITIVE VALVE (SSV). The SSV is also located on and driven by the accessory drive housing and operates at 94% RPM. Below this figure, (to prevent compressor stall) the 4 acceleration bleed air valves on the 5th stage and 4 on the 10th stage are kept open, this being ducted overboard. Above 94% RPM the 8 valves are closed.

The pneumatic starter mounted on the reduction gearbox assembly consist of a turbine wheel assembly, gear assembly, engagement mechanism, governor assembly, cut–off switch, splined output shaft, and an integral splash type oil system. As the engine is self–sustaining, the ignition system is operative between 16–65% RPM. When 28V DC is routed to the condenser discharge type ignition exciter, a high tension continuous discharge of 2–8 Hz is given. As only the number 2 and 5 combustion chambers are fitted with igniter plugs, crossover tubes carry the flame generated.

POWER PLANT CONTROL SYSTEMS

CO–ORDINATOR CONTROL. This unit acts as the "middle man" between the throttle (engine power system) and the propeller. The co–ordinator control combines the operation of the propeller, "hydro–mechanical" FUEL CONTROL and electronic fuel trimming systems. It is controlled by the mechanical linkages operated by the throttle, and the other by the CONDITION LEVER. The co–ordinator itself controls the FUEL CONTROL SCHEDULING, and the PROPELLER and FUEL CUT–OFF VALVE linkages. There are 3 controls in the co–ordinator. The DISCRIMINATOR allows the condition lever to override the throttle control of the propeller whenever the former is moved to the

L to R: accessory drive housing, FCU and co-ordinator showing protractor

FEATHER position. The PROTRACTOR and POINTER are marked off from 0°–90°. When the throttle lever on the flight deck is at the flight idle gate, the pointer should read 34°. The last control is the 66° SWITCH. Above 66° the potentiometer will indicate the throttle position to the TEMPERATURE DATUM (TD) system for fuel trimming purposes.

THROTTLE CONTROL AND OPERATION. The 4 throttles and the 4 condition levers are located on the centre pedestal (between the 2 pilots). Each throttle cable is connected to a "quick disconnect" unit (mounted on the nacelle) as one continuous loop via a selection of linkages, such as pulleys (to change direction) and cable tensioners. Likewise, the condition lever cable is also connected to the same "quick disconnect" from where another set of cables connect these to the controlling unit on the co–ordinator control. From here, using short and long rods and linkages, the propeller system is controlled. The co–ordinator control is bolted to the rear of the fuel control unit. Hence movement of the throttle actuates the propeller system (valve housing) and the fuel control unit (via the co–ordinator). This action selects the fuel and the correct blade angle to absorb the power. This is available on the ground TAXI range (Beta), the throttle position being 0°–34°. In the flight range (Alpha) 34°–90°, only the fuel control is activated, and the propeller blade coarsens to absorb the extra power to maintain 100% RPM ± 2%. Regardless of the position of the throttle, the condition lever's movement to FEATHER position will close the fuel cock (shut–off valve) electrically and mechanically. Also, the propeller system is actuated to feather the propeller.

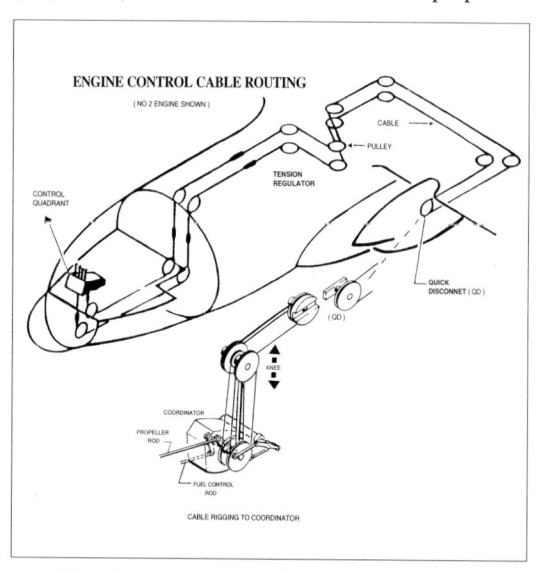

Throttle cable routing and the 'quick disconnect'

OPERATION. The engine is started with the throttle in the GROUND IDLE detent (18°). The LOW SPEED GROUND IDLE (LSGI) button (also near the throttle) is depressed which gives an RPM of 69–75.5% RPM. Therefore, this is the minimum power setting which also provides a minimum blade angle setting (Zero thrust). When reverse thrust is selected during reversing or landing or during taxying, moving the throttles rearwards towards 0° position, 65% of the maximum power of the engine is available. The blade angle changes to "negative" to a maximum of –7° and the RPM to 96–106% to absorb this power. The LSGI is available from 9° – 30° throttle position for starting, low speed taxying, reducing the noise levels and to conserve fuel. The throttle must always be at 18° when LSGI is selected. During operation the button will pop and the GROUND IDLE RPM of 94–102% will be established, if the throttle is moved outside this range inadvertantly. The correct action is to return the throttle to the 18° position. Throughout this "Beta" range, every single degree of movement of the throttle results in the correct fuel with the correct blade angle setting.

The flight (Alpha) range is from 34° – 90° throttle movement whereby, the throttle selects only the fuel, and the propeller system (governor action) maintains 98–102% RPM by coarsening the propeller. However, at 66° position the TD electronic system will "trim" the fuel to maintain a Turbine Inlet Temperature of 820 ± 20°C. Therefore, all the throttles are aligned to achieve this figure (nearly always!). From 66°–90° the TD system receives the exact position of the throttle from the potentiometer in the co–ordinator. The TD system then schedules the correct fuel to achieve the desired TIT for every throttle position.

CONDITION LEVER. The 4 condition levers which are located to the right side of the throttles have 4 marked positions. FEATHER is at the extreme rear position, which will feather the propeller and shuts off the fuel at the fuel control unit.

GROUND STOP is the next position (moving forward) which shuts off the fuel electrically and disarms the engine starting, fuel and ignition systems. Through the touchdown relay, should the lever be moved to GROUND STOP in flight there will be no system reaction.

RUN (moving further forward) arms the auto ice detection system and the speed sensitive control which energises the starting, fuel and ignition circuits for starting.

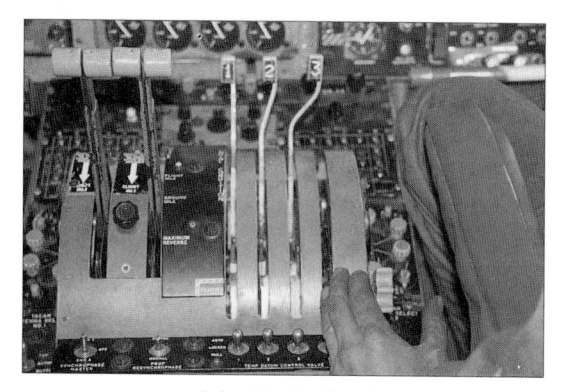

*4 throttles (left) and
4 condition levers (no 4 is at Feather)*

AIR START is at the extreme forward position and must be held against spring pressure. This position allows unfeathering of the propeller whilst keeping energised all the events of the RUN position. When released, the lever moves to the RUN position.

TEMPERATURE DATUM (TD) SYSTEM. This is an additional refinement to the fuel system. The FUEL CONTROL UNIT schedules 20% more fuel ie 100% plus 20%. The TD valve has 3 ranges of operation – NULL (100%), PUT and TAKE. Using the following components: TD valve, TD control and switches (AUTO, LOCKED and NULL), Co–ordinator, speed sensitive control, electronic fuel correction lights, and thermocouples the system has the ability to limit the fuel by bypassing 50% (TAKE) (out of the 100% NULL setting) during starting should the START LIMITING exceed 830°C and RPM is less than 94%. After starting, taxying and up to throttle position 66° a maximum of 20% (TAKE) is bypassed, should the TIT exceed the NORMAL LIMITING TIT of 1077°C. Above 66° throttle position the system can TAKE a maximum of 20% ie only 80% to the engine or PUT of 15% ie 115%. All these are with the control switches in the "AUTO" position. In the "LOCKED" position the valve is locked for a more balanced power for formation flying, and AAR. In the "NULL" position the system is switched off and the system will bypass 20% of the fuel ie 100% goes to the engine.

FUEL PUMP (FP). This engine driven pump assembly is bolted to the rear of the accessory drive housing and driven by it. It has a centrifugal pump which provides a head of pressure through a filter to the 2 spur gear pumps. These are termed primary and secondary. The former has an output capacity of 10% larger than the latter. Fuel then flows to an NRV, high pressure filter and to the FUEL CONTROL UNIT. During normal operation the 2 pumps operate in series but they are inefficient at low speeds. Hence a paralleling valve operates to allow these to operate in parallel (provides a large volume of fuel) up to 65% RPM.

Accessory drive housing. Technician pointing at the fuel pump. Note the 2 spur gear pumps (between thumb and forefinger)

FUEL CONTROL UNIT (FCU). This unit is the "heart" of the fuel system and is installed on the aft of the accessory drive housing and driven by it. It uses a combination of fuel "servo" pressure (hydro) and mechanical devices such as a "metering" valve whose spool is operated by 2 sets of fly weights and other shafts, cam assemblies and linkages. All these control and vary the orifice of the "metering" valve. Fuel from the FP enters the FCU during operation and provides the following:

1. Supplies fuel under control for starting and smooth acceleration to LSGI or NGI. It provides overspeed protection and limits maximum possible fuel flow.

2. Varies the fuel flow with changes in air pressure and temperature (density).

3. Provides 20% more fuel than the engine requires for the TD system to trim accordingly. A "cut off valve" is installed which can be closed electrically or mechanically to shut down the engine.

4. Permits to control the fuel flow by the throttle and a device to select LSGI (by depressing the LSGI button on the centre pedestal).

5. Controls the power available during maximum reverse. This fuel enters through the fuel shut–off valve to the fuel nozzles (via the TD valve, fuel flowmeter, and fuel manifold).

6. The **FUEL ENRICHMENT** valve gives an additional fuel and is selected from the NORMAL/OFF switch on the fuel enrichment sub–panel of the pilots starting panel. Fuel enrichment is always selected for an air start, after maintenance work on the fuel components and if the first start is unsuccessful. At 16% RPM, during the enrichment start, the fuel quantity increases (noticed on the fuel flow gauge) and lasts for 2–3 seconds. A pressure switch senses the fuel manifold pressure and at 50 psi de–energises the solenoid and the valve closes under its spring pressure.

The TD valve sits on the "NULL" position (by passing the 20% extra fuel) in "AUTO" or "OFF" position. In AUTO position it moves to restrict the flow, should an overtemperature occurs. This protection is not available in the "OFF" position.

The FUEL FLOWMETER measures the flow in pounds and its transmitter sends the signal to the gauge on the flight deck engine instrument panel. A pressure switch after this unit activates its associated fuel low pressure warning light at 8.5 psi (on the engineers overhead panel).

The FUEL MANIFOLD has a pressure switch activated by the enrichment system at 50 psi. It also has a manifold drip valve which is open when the engine is static but closes at 16% RPM when the engine is running. The manifold distributes the fuel to the 6 duplex FUEL NOZZLES. The fuel nozzle is of the dual orifice type. The first orifice opens at about 20% RPM (70 psi fuel pressure) to provide the atomized spray fuel at the correct angle for optimum burning. The second orifice's opening will vary with fuel pressure. At 90° throttle position the pressure will be about 400 psi (and still not fully open!). Two burner drain valves are installed at the bottom of the combustion outer casing. These open when the engines are shut down.

GAS TURBINE COMPRESSOR (GTC). The GTC requires fuel and DC power to operate and provide the bleed air necessary for starting the engines, air conditioning, anti–icing and for the ATM. The GTC is basically a jet engine located forward of the port landing blister. It consists of a two stage centrifugal compressor connected to a single stage turbine. It delivers 126 lbs/min of air at 35-45 psi to the aircraft bleed air manifold. The GTC accessory sections consist of the starter motor, centrifugal switch assembly, oil cluster, fuel cluster, acceleration limiter, and the load control valve.

The centrifugal switch has 3 micro switches which actuate at 35%, 95% and 110% RPM. At 35% it de–energises the starter, ignition and acceleration limiter (opens). At 95% it energises the air bleed valve switch circuit. On the GTC control (overhead panel) the amber start light is extinguished at 35% and the green light is illuminated at 95% RPM. At 110% (overspeed), its micro switch closes the fuel shut–off valve.

A sectioned GTC

PROPELLER

The Hercules propulsion system uses a turbojet engine and a propeller which are designed to operate as co–ordinated units. The engine provides a source of power and the propeller converts this power to thrust.

The propeller used on the power package is a Hamilton Standard, Model 54H60–91. It is a four–bladed propeller which has the following features: controllable pitch in the ground operating range (beta), constant speed in the flight range (alpha), de–iced and anti–iced spinner and blade assembly, reverse pitch, and full feathering. The propeller is hydraulically operated and includes a mechanical low pitch stop, pitch lock, and negative torque system. Electronic governing of the propeller is accomplished by using a speed derivative, throttle anticipation and a synchrophasing system.

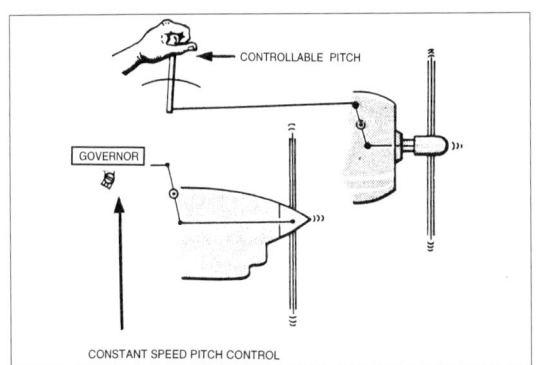

The propeller is a self–contained unit consisting of a rotating section and a stationary section. The rotating section includes the blades, dome, barrel and spinner. A pitch changing mechanism and pitch limit safety devices are located in the dome. The control assembly is stationary and contains the hydraulic fluid reservoirs, pumps, control valves and associated components required to provide normal and emergency control for the rotating portion of the propeller.

Movement of the power lever (throttle) through the flight idle gate will change the propeller from one operation to the other. Forward of the gate s the FLIGHT range and aft (rear) of the gate is the TAXI range.

HAMILTON STANDARD PROPELLER MODEL 54H 60–91

The propeller is sub–divided into the following:

BARREL ASSEMBLY. Consisting of two barrel halves which are matched and kept together for the life of the propeller, the function of this assembly is to retain the blades, transmit engine torque to the blades and to provide a positive method of attaching the propeller to the reduction gearbox propeller shaft.

BLADE ASSEMBLY. Each blade is machined from solid aluminium alloy, the shank being hollowed out to accommodate a balancing plug, and also to lighten the blade. Blade segment gears are splined on to Nos2, 3 and 4 blade butts to mesh with the gears on the rotating cam in the dome assembly. These gears are replaced on No 1 blade by a "beta gear" segment which is used to transmit blade angle signals to the propeller control assembly.

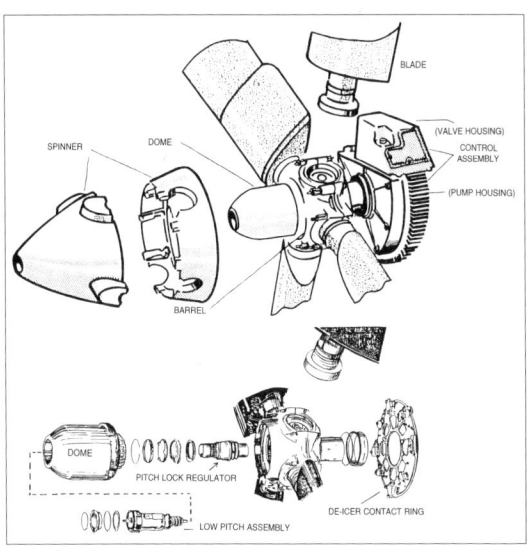

Propeller assembly sketch

DOME ASSEMBLY. Mounted on a shelf on the forward end of the front barrel half, a conventional blade angle change mechanism, together with low pitch stop assembly, is contained within the dome assembly. When the piston moves forward, the inner cam rotates and blade angle is decreased, the reverse happening when the piston moves rearwards. In the feather position, the stop ring lugs are locked by spring loaded latches which are "cammed out" when the propeller unfeathers. The low pitch stop assembly is contained within this assembly.

SPINNER AND ANTI–ICING ASSEMBLY. This assembly encloses the dome, barrel and control assemblies in a streamlined housing, with faired openings to accommodate the propeller blades. It consists of a spinner front section, rear section,

Propeller assembly. Below left arm valve housing (top) and pump housing (below)

together with an after body assembly which is stationary and encloses the propeller control assembly. An air inlet in the nose of the spinner front section allows cooling air to flow over the dome, barrel and control assembly and out through the engine nacelle vents.

DE–ICER CONTACT RING HOLDER ASSEMBLY. This assembly is bolted to the rear barrel half and is made up of four slip rings, four contact brush housings, a magnet and magnet counterweights. AC power is transmitted from brushes mounted on the propeller control assembly through the slip rings to the contact brush housings, which mate with contact rings on the propeller blades. The magnet is part of the pulse generating device used in the propeller synchrophasing system.

PROPELLER CONTROL ASSEMBLY. Made up of a pump housing and valve housing, this non–rotating assembly is mounted on the rear barrel half extension.

a. PUMP HOUSING. The lower part of the control assembly, it is divided into atmospheric and pressurised sumps, the atmospheric sump holds one quart of oil (OM15) and contains the gear driven main scavenge pump, the electrically driven auxiliary scavenge pump and the sump relief valve. For normal operations a main and a standby pump are used, driven by propeller rotation through a gear train, whilst the auxiliary is electrically driven. The main and auxiliary scavenge pumps are used to return oil from the atmospheric to the pressurised sump. The electrically driven pump is used only in the feathering and unfeathering operations.

The standby mechanical pressure pump has double the capacity of the main pump: to take over the main pump's function if it fails and to increase the output when large blade angle selections are made.

b. VALVE HOUSING ASSEMBLY (MECHANICAL BRAIN). This housing contains the various cams, valves and switches which control the flow of fluid to the propeller blade angle change mechanism.

Valve housing (top) and pump housing (below)

ALPHA SHAFT. A propeller control input shaft (Alpha Shaft) mounted on the valve housing, is positioned by the co–ordinator which is itself positioned by either the throttle or the condition lever in order to control the propeller operation. This shaft has four cams:

MANUAL FEATHER CAM. Disarms the NTS linkage in the Taxi range, arms it in the Flight range and operates the mechanical feather control when the condition lever is put to FEATHER.

SPEED SET CAM. Resets the speeder spring tension on the CSU pilot valve between 110–113% in the Taxi range, from its normal 100% in the Flight range.

BETA SET CAM. Schedules blade angle in the Taxi (Beta) range through the governor pilot valve. In the Flight (Alpha) range, the mechanical low pitch stops prevent the blade angle decreasing below 23°.

BACK UP VALVE CAM. Opens the backup valve in the Taxi range and closes it when out of this range.

BETA SHAFT. In the beta (Taxi) range, the beta shaft is a follow up for blade angle selection, which will stop blade movement when the selected angle is reached. The shaft is rotated through a feed back from the differential cam assembly.

Located on the beta shaft are a beta follow up cam, used to back off blade change signals in the beta range, a pressure switch back up cam, and a beta shaft back up cam. The pressure cutout back up cam opens the contacts of an 86° blade angle switch which prevents the pressure cutout switch from stopping the auxiliary pump motor before the blades have passed 86°.

The beta shaft back up cam unseats the back up valve above a blade angle of 36°. Since the alpha shaft is controlled by the throttle and the beta shaft by the beta feed back system, the two cams operate separately and at different times.

Dome (top), barrel, and blade assembly

PROPELLER OPERATION. All primary functions are accomplished through two fundamental actions, increasing or decreasing blade angle. Increase of blade angle is accomplished by directing high pressure oil to the forward side of the propeller dome piston, while oil from the inboard side is returned to the pressurised sump. Conversely, the decrease of blade angle requires high pressure oil at the rear of the dome piston.

Thus, all propeller functions are concerned with positioning the pilot valve as required, to produce the desired operation, with the exception of FEATHERING. For feathering, the control utilises a separate feather valve which is actuated to route pressure oil directly to the increase blade angle. This action overrides all other functions.

PROPELLER HYDRAULIC PRESSURE SYSTEMS. The propeller oil system contains 26 US quarts of OM15 hydraulic oil, and is divided into three parts.

a. **Main System.** Fluid for all pressure pumps is drawn from the pressurised sump, which is kept full of oil by the main scavenge pump transferring oil from the atmospheric sump.

The main pressure pump is used for all normal system operation, its output being ported through an NRV. The oil is next filtered before being directed as required by the pilot valve.

b. **Standby System.** In the event of main pump failure, when the standby pressure exceeds main pressure by 10–15 PSI, the standby pump NRV will open and allow the standby pump to take over. Both systems use a combination of relief valves, selector valve, relief valve spring pressures, a standby valve and a back up valve.

c. **Auxiliary System.** Both auxiliary pressure and scavenge pumps are electrically driven. The pressure pump uses the same pressurised sump as the main pump, and its output is used in Feathering/unfeathering and during static ground operation of the propeller.

CONTROL SYSTEM OPERATION

a. **Taxi Range (Beta).** Throttle position 0–34° movement in this range is used to select propeller blade angle – a "controllable fixed pitch propeller". This is arranged by increasing the speeder spring tension, so that it is ineffective in this RPM range, and using cams and mechanical linkages to control the pilot valve position.

When the throttle is moved in the Taxi range, below 34°, rotation of the alpha shaft turns the speed set cam to increase governor spring tension so that the flyweights will only be able to move the pilot valve should an RPM overspeed in excess of 110% occur. Additionally, the beta set cam rotates to a "low spot" which causes a linkage to move the pilot valve to decrease blade angle. When the desired blade angle is reached, the beta feed back shaft will re-centre the pilot valve and blade movement will cease.

Whilst the throttle is in the Taxi range, the back up valve will be open to allow increased pressure whenever a decrease in blade angle is selected. A higher pressure is required to release the low pitch stops at 23° blade angle and for reverse pitch operations.

b. **Alpha Range** (Constant Speed Operations). Above 34° throttle movement, the alpha shaft's movement will cause the speed set cam to set the speeder spring tension to control the engine speed at 100%.

The governor flyweights are driven by propeller rotation and will be balanced by speeder spring tension at 100%, thus centring the pilot valve. A stabilised "on speed" condition now exists.

Overspeed. When engine speed rises above 100%, the governor flyweights move the pilot valve against speeder spring tension. Oil is ported to the forward side of the dome piston to increase blade angle and thus decrease RPM. The flyweights return the pilot valve to the centre position and RPM is now stabilised at 100% and vice-versa during underspeed condition.

c. **Feathering.** The propeller may be feathered by either the condition lever or by pulling of the Fire Emergency control Handle. When the condition lever is moved towards FEATHER, the alpha shaft in the propeller control is rotated causing the manual feather cam to open the feather valve. At the same time, DC voltage is supplied to the feather override switch, the feather relay, feather solenoid valve and the auxiliary pumpmotor. As the blade angle increases, the RPM will decrease and so main pump pressure will fall. The electrically driven auxiliary pump will take over and supply fluid pressure to both feather and pilot valves to position them hydraulically (via the opened feather actuating valve and the feather solenoid valve). A metered flow of fluid passes through the barrel passages and will position a shuttle valve in the propeller hub assembly. Fluid flows via a surge valve to ensure smooth propeller action, to the forward side of the dome piston.

The blades move towards the feather position of 92.5°. Once above 86° (as soon as the pressure rises to approximately 1000 PSI) the cut out switch operates and the auxiliary pump stops. The propeller will now be feathered, the blade travel being limited at 92.5° by a stop ring. Two feather latches engage mechanically and hold the blades at 92.5°, the propeller will now be held stationary by the "locked" propeller brake.

d.   Unfeathering. To unfeather, the condition lever must be placed to AIR START. This movement, through the co–ordinator, rotates the alpha shaft. The beta set cam will reposition the pilot valve by setting spring tension, in order to port fluid to the rear of the dome piston. When the pressure reaches 175 PSI the feather latches release and the dome piston moves. The pressure is also applied to the pitch lock mechanism which disengages and allows the blades to decrease angle.

As soon as the propeller starts to windmill, the main and standby pumps begin to deliver pressure when then aids the auxiliary pump to complete the feather cycle. The auxiliary pump is only used until the propeller starts to windmill, and as soon as "light off" (ignition) occurs, the condition lever is returned to the RUN position and the pump will stop.

PITCH LOCK OPERATION. This system operates in the Flight range at any time the blade angle is between 25 – 55° and either oil pressure is lost or the propeller overspeeds to 103%. Located in the barrel, this Pitch Lock Regulator consists of a stationary pitch lock ratchet ring, a rotating ratchet, a pitch lock valve and flyweight assembly, and a pressure regulating valve. This safety feature prevents the loss of the propeller control. During normal operation, the two sets of teeth are kept apart by oil pressure. The teeth are undercut which allows an increase (allows feathering) in blade angle but prohibits a decrease. Above 103% the two sets of teeth mate – a fixed prop, but this condition is relieved when the RPM drops below 103%. Also, if the oil pressure is lost, the teeth mate. This pitch locked propeller can still be used, but limited. The RPM can now be varied by using the throttle. More fuel allows an increase in RPM and vice versa with less fuel. However, it is always shut down prior to landing or before.

Assembling the pitch lock regulator in PRF

LOW PITCH STOP ASSEMBLY. Located in the dome, this is a safety device to prevent an overspeed by limiting the minimum blade angle in the flight range to 23°. The assembly consists of three low pitch stop arms, a moveable wedge, serve valve pistons and springs, and an oil transfer tube. As the dome piston moves forward to decrease blade angle, it slides over the low pitch arms until the lips of the arms engage, when piston movement will cease. Blade angle will now be set at 23°. To further decrease the blade angle, the wedge must be retracted to allow the arms to "drop in". Retracting the throttle to the Taxi range for instance after landing causes the alpha shaft to rotate. At 28° throttle position the backup valve will be opened by its cam. Pressure will now be increased across the governor pilot valve and the low pressure relief valve will be biased to allow pressure to rise to approximately 250 PSI when the servo valve will crack and the piston will move to allow the arms to drop in. The blades can now move towards the reverse range.

Components – L to R; dome, low pitch stop, and pitch lock regulator

NEGATIVE TORQUE SYSTEM (NTS). Whenever the NTS plunger moves out of the reduction gearbox assembly, it contacts the linkage which operates the feather actuating valve and the feather valve. These valves will be positioned so that the feather valve will port fluid to the dome in order to drive the blades towards the feather position. When the negative torque is removed, the plunger will retract and normal propeller governor action will be restored. Below Flight Idle the NTS is inhibited by the action of the manual feather can on the alpha shaft.

Feather Valve and NTS Check Lights. Positioned on the co–pilot's side shelf, these four green lights are controlled by a three position switch labelled FEATHER – NORMAL – NTS. The lights enable a check of the mechanical NTS and Feather linkages to be carried out.

PROPELLER AND SPINNER ANTI–ICING AND DE–ICING. Blade De–icing is accomplished by RH AC busbar power applied to heater blankets bonded to the blade leading edges. The blankets, protected by steel strips, are made of heater wires embedded in synthetic rubber.

Spinner Anti–icing and De–icing. The spinner, afterbody, and plateaus are moulded from fibreglass, with the heater element wires embedded in it.

PROPELLER LOW OIL LEVEL WARNING SYSTEM. This system will illuminate a master warning light on the engine instrument panel, and an individual low oil warning light on the co–pilot's side shelf, whenever the oil in the pressurised sump falls by 2 US quarts. (The atmospheric sump contains one, the pressurised sump 6, and the whole system contains 26 US quarts).

PROPELLER SYNCHROPHASING

Introduction. All multi–engined, propeller driven aircraft are affected by propeller beat noise, which is produced when the propellers are turning at different speeds or their blades are not in the proper angular relationship. On the Hercules, this problem has been reduced to an acceptable level by a SYNCHROPHASER.

Synchronising the propellers will cause them to turn at the same speed, thus removing the rise and fall component of the noise and vibration. If the blade angle relationship is also corrected, the noise level, will be at a minimum. This is the function of the synchrophaser.

Additionally, the system provides a throttle anticipation circuit which ensures that there is no "lag" between positioning of the throttle and development of the required power. Also a speed stabilisation circuit is employed to electronically prevent "hunting" of the RPM during power changes.

GOVERNOR CONTROL SWITCHES. Three sets of switches control the propellers, the propeller governor control switches, the synchrophaser master and re–synchrophaser switches, and the fuel governor check switches.

Four propeller governor control switches are mounted on the co–pilot's side shelf. They have two positions, NORMAL and Mech Gov, a spring loaded guard holding each switch in the NORMAL position. Should MECH GOV be selected, the electronic control systems are all disconnected and the propellers will be governed mechanically by the pilot valve and speeder spring.

The synchrophaser master switches located behind the throttles have three positions, ENG 2– OFF – ENG 3, and are used to switch on the synchrophasing systems by selecting a master engine. Alongside these switches is the Propeller Resynchrophaser switch labelled RESYNC – NORMAL.

The fuel governor control switches are located at the rear of the overhead panel. Each switch has two positions, CHECK – NORMAL. Spring loaded to NORMAL, these switches are protected by a guard and are only used on the ground. Their purpose is to enable the propeller governor speeder spring to be tensioned in order to produce 106% RPM in the flight range. This increased speed allows the pitch lock and fuel "overspeed" governing mechanisms to be checked.

(1) Throttle Beta Switch. Located in the throttle quadrant, this switch is operated by the throttle so that, below flight idle, the synchrophasing system is inoperative.

(2) Throttle Anticipation. This circuit is employed to prevent the RPM "overrunning" when fast throttle movements are made. It functions only in the flight range providing NORMAL governing of the propellers is selected.

An anticipation potentiometer is in each valve housing. Movement of the throttle will rotate the potentiometer which will send a signal to the synchrophaser unit. This signal is amplified and passed to the speed bias servo motor, also in the valve housing. As this motor turns, it will alter the tension of the governing pilot valve speeder spring. For example, throttle movement towards the Take Off position will signal the servo motor to decrease speeder spring tension. This will allow the governor flyweights to position the pilot valve to increase blade angle, so that the propeller will be at its correct angle when the engine reaches its new power setting. A decrease in throttle setting will result in the reverse happening.

(3) Speed Stabilisation. When MECH GOV is selected and if the speed is disturbed by power changes or turbulent air, for instance, the "mechanical governor" will tend to "hunt" while re-establishing the set speed.

When the propellers are operating in NORMAL the speed stabilisation circuit will prevent this happening. The system uses the engine speed RPM indicators as a reference, an output from this instrument being fed to the synchrophaser unit. Should the speed wander outside the accepted "cyclic variation" of plus or minus 0.5%, a signal will be sent to operate the speed servo motor to change speeder spring tension and stabilise the RPM.

(4) Synchrophaser. The main components of this system are the main synchrophaser unit, four speed bias servo assemblies (one for each propeller), four pulse generators (one for each propeller), a manual phase and master control and Governor Control switches. Each speed bias servo assembly is contained in the valve housing and consists of an AC motor, a magnetic clutch and brake unit, and a feedback potentiometer. The motor is used to drive a gear train which will position a lever to alter speeder spring tension on the pilot valve.

Each pulse generator unit consists of a pickup coil mounted on the propeller control assembly and a magnet mounted on the de-icer contact ring holder, close to the No 1 blade, which rotates with the propeller. Every time the propeller completes one revolution, the magnet passing the coil will induce into it a voltage pulse. The time between pulses is the time the propeller takes to complete one revolution, and will therefore vary if propeller speed varies. These voltages pulses are applied to the synchrophaser.

In the synchropaser unit, the output pulse of the selected master propeller is used as a reference signal against which the three slave propellers are compared in time difference between pulses. A DC voltage is produced due to this time difference, the amplitude of it being proportional to the desired angular relationship of the propellers. Any alteration from the calibrated "master versus slave" voltage results in operation of the slave servo system to either increase or decrease propeller speed until the phasing is again correct, when the error signal will cease.

(5) Manual Phase Control and Master Trim Unit. Located on the co-pilot's side shelf, this system is only operated on the ground and the control panel is normally covered with a wire locked panel. It is used to initially set the phase angle of each propeller in relation to the master. Two sets of potentiometers in the phase control units are provided with screwdriver slots and lock nuts for individual adjustments. One set is used when No 2 engine is selected as master, the other set when No 3 is selected. The output of these potentiometers provides the calibrated "slave versus master" voltage mentioned earlier.

The master trim knob in the centre of the control panel is used to alter the speed of the selected master propeller. It will do this to a maximum of plus or minus 1%.

(6) Re-synchrophasing. During normal synchrophasing operations it is possible that the AC motor could be driven to the end of its travel, which means that a slave can only follow a master propeller for a maximum of plus or minus 2%. In order to provide further correction so that the slave will be able to phase correctly with the master, the motor must be "re-centred". To "re-centre" the motor the RESYNCHROPHASE switch is pushed to RESYNC. Releasing the switch to NORMAL restores the system to normal and the motor may now run an equal distance in either direction in order to remove any out of phase signal.

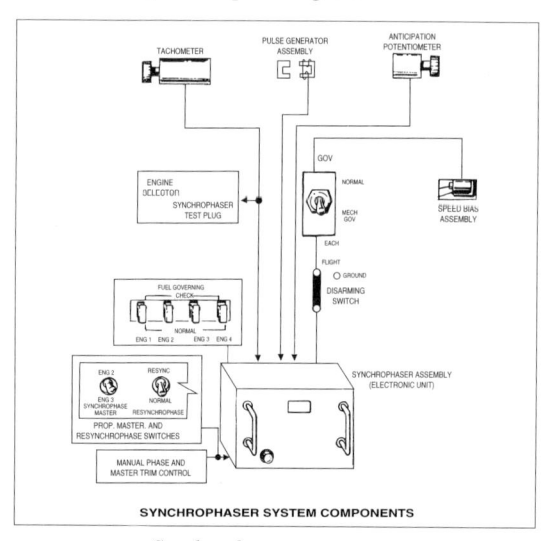

Synchrophaser components

(7) Fuel Governor Check Switches. Each engine has a fuel governor check switch located at the rear of the overhead panel. These switches are usually wire locked in the NORMAL position and are only used to check the pitch lock and fuel governor systems on the ground.

Placing the switch to CHECK against spring pressure supplies a voltage to the speed bias servo motor to cause it to increase speeder spring tension. This results in a decrease in blade angle and the RPM increases until speeder spring tension is again balanced by the flyweight force at 106%. When pitch lock occurs at 103%, it will be indicated by an increase in torque, fuel governor operation by a reduction in fuel flow (fuel topping action by the FUEL CONTROL UNIT at 105%).

SPECIFICATIONS

Power Plant

Engine. *Allison T–56–A–15, constant–speed, turboprop. Air starter*

Engine Oil System. *Separate tank per engine. 12 US gall (10 Imp gall) oil. 7.5 US gall 6.2 Imp gall) air*

Oil Type. *OX–27*

Propeller. *Hamilton Standard Hydromatic Constant–speed, fully feathering, 4–blade reversible pitch. 13 ft 6 in diameter*

Propeller Oil System. *Integral, 6.25 US gall (5.2 Imp gall) Oil OM15*

Gas Turbine Compressor (GTC). *Gas turbine with 2–stage compressor, supplying bleed air system. Electric starter, GTC oil specification as for engine*

QEC complete with propeller awaiting call!

Trainee fitting the tacho generator

QEC in PRF

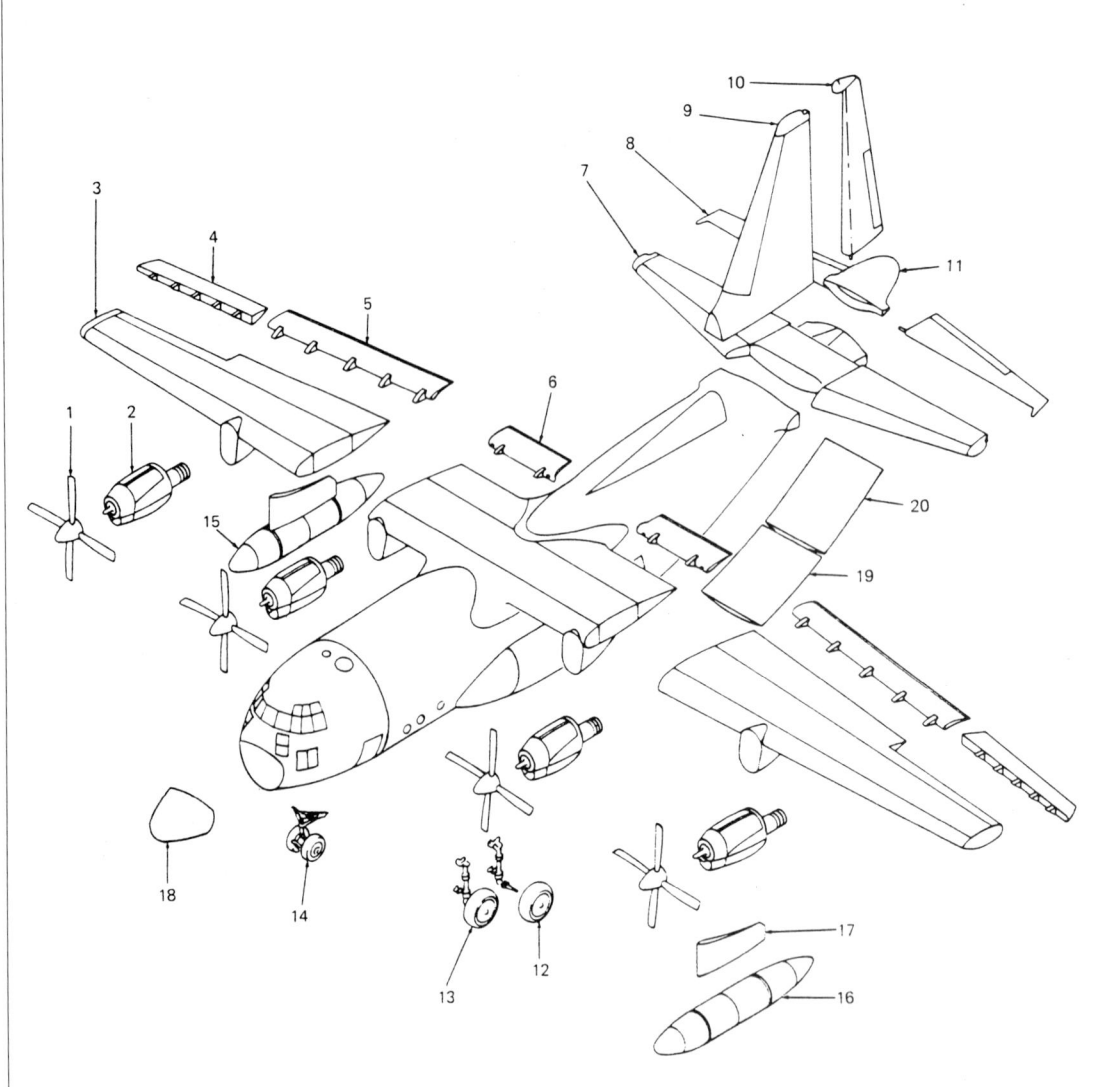

#	Component	Weight
1.	PROPELLER (WITH SPINNER)	1,046 LB
2.	POWER PACKAGE (DRY ENGINE)	2,946 LB
3.	OUTER WING (DRY)	3,962 LB
4.	AILERON	200 LB
5.	OUTER WING FLAP AND CARRIAGES	273 LB
6.	CENTRE SECTION FLAP AND CARRIAGES	160 LB
7.	HORIZONTAL STABILIZER ASSEMBLY	2,196 LB
8.	ELEVATOR (INBOARD COUNTERWEIGHT REMOVED)	281 LB
9.	VERTICAL STABILIZER	869 LB
10.	RUDDER (NOT INCLUDING BALANCE WEIGHT)	200 LB
11.	TAIL CONE	43 LB
12.	MAIN GEAR WHEEL (COMPLETE WITH TYRE AND TUBE)	402 LB
13.	MAIN LANDING GEAR (ONE GEAR COMPLETE WITH WHEEL, TYRE, AND BRAKE)	1,006 LB
14.	NOSE LANDING GEAR	573 LB
15.	WING PYLON TANK INSTALLATION	791 LB
16.	WING PYLON TANK (DRY AND LESS PYLON ATTACHMENT BOLTS)	639 LB
17.	WING PYLON SUPPORT (LESS WING ATTACHMENT BOLTS)	140 LB
18.	RADOME	218 LB
19.	CARGO RAMP	1,084 LB
20.	AFT CARGO DOOR	753 LB

Major component weights

CHAPTER THREE

ELECTRICS AND INSTRUMENTS

ELECTRICS

AC MAIN GENERATOR The AC Generator is a self excited, 3 phase, brushless, air cooled, constant speed machine designed to be driven via the reduction gearbox on the aircraft engine. The generator supplies 115/208 volts, 400Hz at a continuous rating of 40 KVA within a speed range of 5700–6300 rev/min. Primarily, the generator comprises of three individual generators in one. A permanent magnet generator (PMG), an AC excitor generator and a main AC generator.

AC generator

OPERATION Initial excitation of the generator is provided by the AC output of the PMG. The PMG is a 32–pole permanent magnet which is positioned on the end of the rotor. The rotor is driven at 6000 rpm via the gearbox. The magnetic field created by the magnets will induce an AC voltage in the PMG stator windings. This output is fed to an external system regulator, rectified and fed to the excitor stator field winding as direct current. The excitor stator field develops a 3 phase AC voltage in the excitor windings on the rotor.

The 3 phase AC output of the excitor windings is rectified to DC by rectifiers mounted on the rotor. The DC output from the rectifiers is then fed to the main rotor windings which causes the main 3 phase stator output winding to generate the AC 'working' voltage of the generator. The output is maintained at a constant voltage by increasing or decreasing the second stage field winding current via the external regulator system.

The generator also contains two contact devices, which are connected to an external warning circuit. In the event of a bearing failure the rotor will rotate out of true. The rotor will make contact with one or both of the devices to complete the warning circuit. The generator disconnect unit allows the generator drive to be disconnected when selected.

AIR TURBINE MOTOR GENERATOR (ATM GENNY!) The ATM generator is used on the ground to supply the aircraft's electrical requirements, eg lighting, instrument power, LOX systems, fuel systems, without the necessity of running the engines. It is driven by bleed air from the gas turbine compressor (GTC) or engine at 8000 rpm. The ATM genny is designed to supply 115/208 volts, 3 phase AC at 400 Hz and is rated at 20 KVA.

ATM Genny!
foreground – actuator from other system

OPERATION. DC is fed to the ATM by the regulator. This DC is fed to the rotor and causes excitation in the excitor stator windings. This is fed back to the voltage regulator. This AC is then rectified to DC and fed back to the main field winding on the rotor. This then causes excitation in the main output stator windings, which gives the 115/208 volts, 400 Hz AC output. The output is regulated by the amount of DC fed back to the field winding. The generator has to be cooled and this is done by blast air via an adaptor fitted to the anti–drive end.

AC ELECTRICAL POWER. The Hercules requires a combination of AC and DC electrical power to operate the engines and many of the aircraft systems. To simplify the system, it is divided into 4 main sections namely:

a. Primary AC system.

b. Secondary AC system.

c. DC system.

d. External power system.

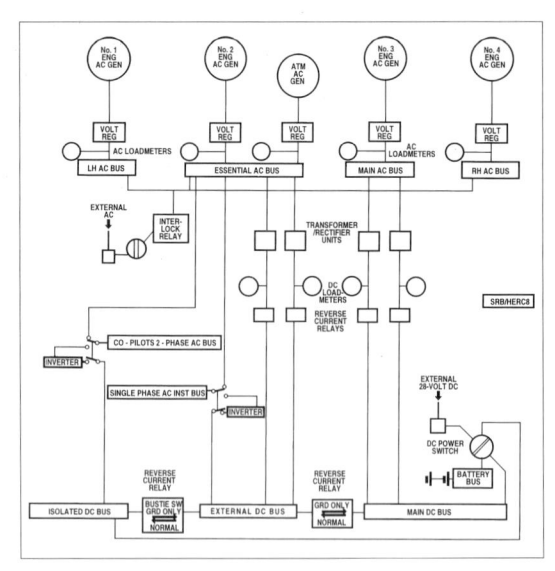

AC and DC electrical system flow chart

The primary AC system has a transfer facility. There are 4 AC bus–bars namely LEFT HAND (LH), ESSENTIAL (ESS), MAIN and RIGHT HAND (RH). The number one engine's generator feeds the LH bus, 2 the ESS, 3 the MAIN and 4 the RH. Any one generator from any engine feeds the ESS and MAIN bus bars and any 2 can feed all the

AC bus bars and other systems at FS 245, front main distribution panel (flight deck)

1. Primary AC System is provided by the 4 engine driven generators and an Air Turbine Motor (ATM) driven generator. The output of the generator is controlled by a Generator Control Panel (GCP), a voltage regulator (VR) and a frequency relay which forms a method for the automatic control and protection of a generator. The GCP and the VR are located under the flight deck floor. The GCP controls the operation of its associated generator, detects faults and provides protection.

Heavy duty contacts (top right), electrical rack (bottom), and the forward urinal

4 bus bars. The ATM generator will always feed the ESS bus bar. The transfer to the bus bars is made by 9 heavy duty contacts located on the Upper Main distribution panel at FS 245. If a generator fails in flight or on the ground, due to an earth fault or over voltage, its output is automatically removed from the bus–bar and field tripped and another generator assumes the load on that bus–bar. The aircraft generator's output is removed from its bus–bar when LSGI is selected on the ground (RPM 69–75.5%) by the frequency sensing relay and is restored when normal ground idle is established. There is a time delay of 5 seconds on the ATM generator should its frequency fall below the normal level, before its output is removed from the ESS bus–bar. Each generator has a control switch marked ON, OFF, FIELD–TRIPPED or RESET.

Pilot's side circuit breaker panels

The aircraft must be earthed at all times when it is on the ground and there are 4 earthing points on the aircraft.

There are numerous electrical equipment and components for the generators, TRUs, bus–bars and invertors, fitted to the front and rear of the Main distribution panel at FS 245, under the flight deck floor and on the flight deck. Numerous circuit breakers, fuses, current limiters and other protective circuit devices to protect all electrical equipment (the black boxes), gauges, primary and navigational equipment and so on are located on the flight deck.

All the controlling switches for the generators, invertors, battery, external AC and DC, voltmeters (AC and DC), frequency meter, loadmeters (AC and DC) warning lights, generator disconnect switches and the bus–tie switch are located on the engineer's overhead panel.

SECONDARY AC SYSTEM. This system is divided into 3 separate parts, each with a different output. These are:

a. Co–pilot's AC instrument bus–bar, with 115 volts, 3 phase, 400 Hz from the Essential AC bus–bar.

b. AC instrument and engine fuel control bus–bar with 115 volts, single phase, 400 Hz from the Essential bus–bar.

c. Two instrument bus–bars with 26 volts, single phase, 400 Hz.

1. Co–pilot's AC Instrument Bus–bar. This bus–bar is used solely to power the gyro units of the No 1 and No 2 ADIs (Attitude Direction Indicators) of the Flight Director Systems. The bus–bar is controlled by means of a 3 position switch on the electrical control panel labelled NORMAL – OFF – STANDBY. Placing the switch to the NORMAL position enables the bus–bar to be powered from the Essential AC bus–bar through a stabilising transformer. STANDBY position connects the bus–bar to the output of a 250 VA inverter which is driven by 28 volts DC from the Isolated DC bus. A power off indicator light labelled "SEL PWR OUT" is positioned near the switch and will illuminate on failure of the selected power to the bus–bar.

2. AC Instrument and Fuel Control Bus–bar. Supplies 115 volt single phase, 400 Hz from one of the following sources:

a. "A" phase of the Essential AC bus–bar.

b. An inverter driven by 28 volts Essential DC to produce 115 volts, single phase, 400 2500 VA.

From this bus–bar all AC operated instruments and the engine fuel control system are powered. It is also controlled by a 3 position switch on the electrical panel. In the NORMAL position the bus–bar is powered by "A" phase of the Essential AC bus–bar. When selected to the STANDBY position, it connects the bus–bar to the output of the invertor. A power failure warning light labelled "SEL PWR OUT" will illuminate when the selected power source fails. If, whilst the inverter is the selected power source it fails, automatic transference of the bus–bar to the Essential AC bus–bar will take place, but not vice versa. When this happens, the SEL PWR OUT light will glow until the switch is placed in the NORMAL position. Both invertors are located under the flight deck floor.

3. **Instrument Transformers.** Two transformers are mounted behind the left hand distribution panel. The primary winding of the transformer is connected to the 115 volt AC Instrument and Engine Fuel Control bus–bar. The output of the secondary windings is 26 V AC which is used to power all the pressure indicating instruments. There is no individual control of this system. When the AC Inst and Eng Fuel control bus–bar is energised, so are the inst transformers.

A variety of instrument, compass, and auto pilot transformers and other components (pilot's side)

4. **C12 Compasses Supply.** Two tappings are taken directly from the Essential AC bus–bar to provide the power source for the No 1 and No 2 C12 compass systems. Transformers reduce the 115 volts to 26 volts AC and this is fed through two further circuit breakers to the compass systems. There is no individual control over the power supply to the compasses. If the Essential AC bus–bar is powered, the power to the compass systems is available.

The DC Supply System is provided by 4 transformer rectifier units (TRUs). Each unit changes 3 phase AC to 28 volts DC up to a maximum of 200 amps. A 24 volt 36 amp/hr lead acid battery is installed in the port side of the nose section as an emergency source of power, its main use being to start the GTC, or operate refuelling valves when external power is not available.

Transformer Rectifier Units. The 2 TRUs supplying the DC bus–bar located under the flight deck floor are supplied from the Essential AC bus–bar. Power for the other 2 TRUs supplying the Main DC bus–bar is from the Main AC bus–bar. The only controls for the TRUs are the 12 input circuit breakers, 6 on the Essential AC, and 6 on the Main AC bus–bar. In addition, there is one circuit breaker for each TRU, controlling a "bleeder" resistance.

DC Loadmeters are positioned on the overhead panel, one for each TRU. The scale is calibrated from –1 to + 1.25, being the percentage of the unit current rating, 200 amps being equivalent to 100%

Reverse Current Relays. One reverse current relay is provided in the circuit between each TRU and its associated DC bus–bar. Should a fault occur or the DC bus–bar voltage exceed the TRU output, the relay will open and disconnect the DC bus–bar from low output TRU.

The Battery system provides a means of operating certain essential DC equipment when external power or power from the TRUs is not available. The system is controlled by a DC external power and battery switch located on the overhead control panel. The battery is connected directly to the battery bus–bar, it being permanently "live" whilst a battery is connected. Several items are connected to this bus–bar and these can be operated independently of any other power source. Some of these are the alarm bells, jump lights and the emergency depressurisation switch.

DC DISTRIBUTION. There are 4 DC bus–bars in the aircraft, these being the:

a. Battery bus–bar.
b. Isolated DC bus–bar.
c. Essential DC bus–bar.
d. Main DC bus–bar.

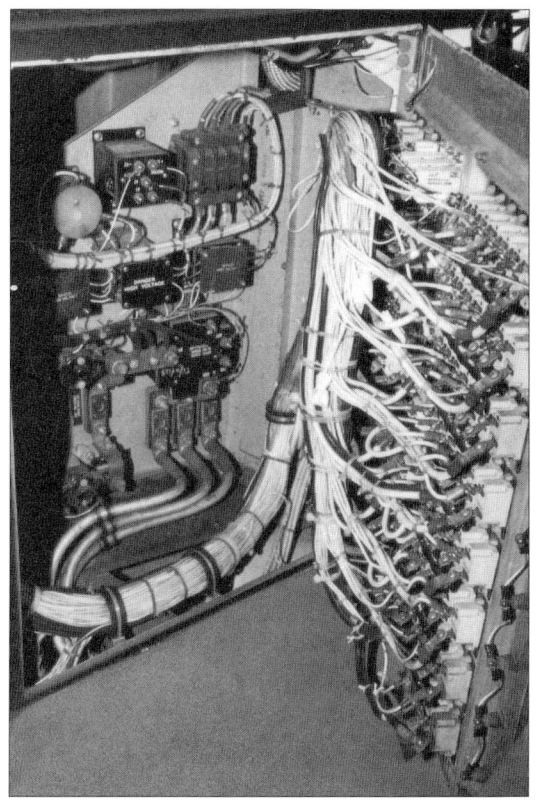

Battery bus and relay, isolated bus and other components (rear of forward pilot's cct bkr panel)

The battery bus–bar is connected to the Isolated DC by the battery relay. The Isolated to the Essential DC bus–bar is via a manually operated reverse current relay (bus tie switch). On the ground a further relay (actuated by the touchdown auxiliary relay) allows battery power to flow from Battery bus–bar to the Essential bus–bar. A further automatic reverse current relay allows current to flow from Essential to the Main DC bus–bar. In flight the current flow is from the main DC to the battery bus–bar. On the ground, with DC power connected, current flow is from Main DC to the battery bus–bar.

EXTERNAL AC POWER. A NATO 6 pin socket is situated under a flap close to the battery compartment. The large 4 pins carry the 3 phases and an earth. The controlling 28V DC current is carried by the 2 small pins. The AC External Power Ready Light on the Engineer's overhead panel illuminates to indicate that the AC power is of the correct phase rotation. To connect this power to the aircraft, the AC External Power switch must be operated.

EXTERNAL DC POWER SOCKET. This socket has 3 pins. Two long pins carry the power, the short one carries the controlling power for indication and switching purposes. DC External power ready light is situated next to the control switch. When illuminated it indicates that DC power is available and is of the correct polarity.

Battery and external AC and DC power receptacle

RADIO/NAVIGATIONAL AIDS (NAVAIDS)

COMMUNICATION CONTROL SYSTEM
The communication control system (CCS) provides for communication between five crew member positions on the flight deck, two positions in the cargo compartment and a ground crew jack box. The station boxes on the flight deck also provide for selection of communication and navigation audio signals and for selection of a radio transmitter. This requires a complete intercom system to give communication facilities for both aircrew in flight or ground crew during servicing.

VHF/UHF COMMUNICATION RADIO The Hercules aircraft has three independent systems providing 2–way voice communications in the VHF and UHF bands.

VHF – 118 to 135.975 MHz 720 channels at 25 KHz spacing.

UHF – 225 to 399.95 MHz 7,000 channels at 25 KHz spacing.

The systems are labelled as follows:

Box 1 (UHF/VHF) – where the control unit is convenient for the captain.

Box 2 (UHF only) – where the control unit is convenient for the co–pilot.

Box 3 (VHF only) – where the control unit is convenient for both the captain and co–pilot Radio

Under flight deck floor – U/VHF Box 1 and 2 (centre), engine and airframe control cables (top)

transmissions are of a relatively low power, using a line of sight propagation method. Antennas utilized for transmission and reception of signals are situated on the upper and lower fuselage.

HF COMMUNICATION RADIO Two separate, identical HF radio installations provide single side–band and AM operation, giving 2 way

HF 2 box – bottom of electrical control rack

communication in the 2 to 30 MHz frequency range. Long range radio communication is achieved by refraction of HF signals in the inosophere and returning them to earth to reach their intended reception areas 1,000 Km or more away. Maximum RF power transfer is achieved at the fixed–wire antenna by matching the output of the transmitter/receiver via an aerial tuning unit.

The selective calling (Selcal) signalling system provides a method of calling an aircraft from a ground transmitting station, when the aircraft is not continuously monitoring the airwaves. It is used in conjunction with the HF system and provides the pilot with a visual indication that the aircraft is being called.

INSTRUMENT LANDING SYSTEM (ILS) ILS is a precision runway approach aid which consists of fixed ground transmitters and airborne receivers and indicator equipment.

The ground transmitters emit localizer and glidepath signals which define the approach path to the runway. The airborne receivers provide signals of aircraft displacement from the ILS centre line and glide path, giving the pilot an indication of his line of approach.

The glideslope gives an indication of fly up/down while the localiser gives left/right indication of the centre of the runway. In addition, a marker system operates giving the crew a visual and audible warning of distance to go to the runway.

RADIO COMPASS – AUTOMATIC DIRECTION FINDER (ADF) An ADF system is installed operating in the medium frequency band, providing direction finding and homing facilities and reception of communication signals. It uses the directional properties of a loop antenna to locate the bearing of a ground transmitter. It gives an indication of the relative bearing of any suitable selected transmitter, with additional audio reception of the signal for station identification, or reception of weather broadcasts and other information.

OMEGA NAVIGATION SYSTEM (ONS) The Litton LTN–211 Omega/VLF navigation system (ONS) is a long range navigation aid operating in the very low frequency (VLF) band of 10–14 KHz. The system provides accurate position, navigation and guidance data necessary for long range navigation. It displays the present position in latitude and longitude co–ordinates, track angle, ground speed, heading, drift angle, cross–track and track angle error, desired track angle, way point positions, distance and time to way points, wind direction and velocity.

In addition to the primary Omega/VLF derived mode of operation, the system is configured with a back–up dead reckoning (DR) mode based on the available aircraft velocity and heading. The DR mode is automatically selected when the number and quality of received Omega/VLF signals is below that required for position determination and navigation.

LONG RANGE NAVIGATION–LORAN The Loran is a low frequency hyperbolic navigation system and provides position information. The Loran–C system consists of fixed land based transmitters that are organized into groups called "chains" that provide signal coverage for a certain geographical area. Each Loran–C chain is comprised of one Master station and up to four Secondary stations.

The ground stations transmit with a carrier frequency of 100 KHz which is within the Low Frequency (LF) radio band. Propagation is by ground waves which allow for a high degree of accuracy and long range coverage.

The following is a brief description of the Radio Aid to Direction Azimuth and Range (RADAR) equipment, as fitted to the Hercules aircraft.

Identification Friend or Foe/Secondary Surveillance Radar (IFF/SSR) is designed to identify as friendly or enemy those targets detected by the interrogating radar. The system employs a ground based transmitter which interrogates the target. If the target is fitted with the appropriate transponder a coded reply is sent back to the interrogator/receiver, identifying the target as friendly. If no reply or the wrong reply is received then the target is assumed to be the enemy.

The Station Keeping Equipment (SKE) installation "forms" an airborne all weather facility, which enables up to 36 aircraft with identical installations to fly in close formation, by electronically locating and identifying each other.

The Tactical Airborne Navigation (TACAN) system provides the pilot with distance and bearing information, indicating the position of his aircraft with respect to the surface beacon that he has selected. He can also receive a continuous reading of his distance from another aircraft. This facility is used when air to air refuelling, and is known as air to air distance measurement. A surface beacon is not required as each aircraft transmitter/receiver will reply to the other ones interrogation. A surface beacon can provide distance information for up to 100 aircraft and bearing information for an unlimited number. In the air to air mode, a number of aircraft up to a maximum of five, may simultaneously receive distance replies from a single aircraft, however, no bearing information is available. There is an updated version of this system known as the TACAN 118 variant. The 118v is a digital system which is basically the same as the old TACAN but has an increased range and is more reliable.

The Radar Altimeter (RADALT) is an airborne altitude sensing radar system that provides a continuous indication of aircraft altitude up to 5000 ft. There is an audio visual warning whose level of operation is set by using a separate control. If set to 100 ft, then if the aircraft went below 100 ft the audio visual warning would be activated.

The Decca Doppler Radar System is a navigation aid that works independent of ground stations and measures ground speed and drift using the Doppler principle. It also receives aircraft heading from the gyro compass. Using this information the Doppler system continuously displays ground speed drift angle and distance gone along the track of the aircraft. With the use of additional computers the system also digitally displays present position, how far left or right of track you are, and distance to go along the track to a pre–set point.

Radome removed to expose CCWR

The function of the **Cloud Collision Warning Radar (CCWR)** is to provide the aircrew with a radar picture showing a scaled down plan view of the terrain ahead, and clouds within a wide sector ahead of the aircraft. This system is also able to discriminate between potentially dangerous and less turbulent areas of cloud, and show the difference on the relevant displays.

ADI (top) and HSI (below)

Auto pilot system and components (near crew entrance door)

HORIZONTAL SITUATION INDICATOR HSI.

The HSI is fitted directly below the Pilot's and Co-pilot's ADI. Each indicator gives a plan view display of the aircraft heading and aircraft position relative to a selected radio beacon, ie Tacan VOR/ILS.

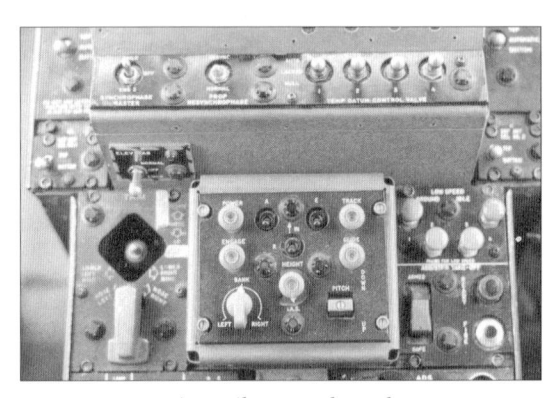

Auto pilot control panel

FLIGHT SYSTEMS

FLIGHT DIRECTOR The American Flight Director System (FDS) on the Hercules aircraft, consists of a twin information display system. The two identical systems consist of a multi–axis gyro (MD1), which supplies pitch and roll information to the Attitude Director Indicator (ADI). Also feeding the ADI are the Rate Transmitting Gyro, which supplies a rate of turn indication and various radio aids eg ILS, TACAN and DOPPLER, which supply steering information.

C12 COMPASS The C12 compass system is another twin system. The first unit in the system is the C12 compass, a single axis gyro which supplies an azimuth output. This output is fed with the errors created by the earth's magnetic field, detected by the Magnetic Azimuth Detector (MAD) and the hard and soft magnetism created by the aircraft, corrected by the Remote Magnetic Compensator (RMC) to the Amp Power Supply (APS) the brain of the system. To allow the Navigator to set in latitudes and manually synchronize the system, he is provided with a control unit called the Digital Controller. The information from No 1 compass for instance can be fed to the Captain's HSI compass card, BDHI compass card, Co-pilot's RMI compass card, Navigator's left BDHI card, Doppler, Tacan 1, VHF nav 1, and the Flight Director computer (autopilot unit).

MK10 AUTOPILOT. Unfortunately, the Smith's MK10 auto–pilot is not directly compatible with the American FDS, on which it relies for most of its information. Therefore, the first and most important unit is the Adaptor Unit, which converts the American analogue AC to analogue DC. This analogue DC is passed to the Locking Unit where switching selects which information is switched through the system. Also fed into the Locking Unit at this point is "Barometric" height and airspeed from the Pressure Unit. All information from the Locking Unit is passed through the Platform Control Unit (PCU) where it is used to level or offset the Gyro Unit. The Gyro Unit consists of three rate transmitting gyros set to detect movements in all three axis, and two monitors to detect slip and pitch. Any movement of the aircraft or of the gyro frame (manually selected by the Pilot via a control unit), the Flight Control Panel (FCP) results in an output being sent to the Servo Control Unit (SCU), where magnetic amplifiers boost the signals to drive the control surfaces via servo motors.

FIRE WARNING SYSTEMS

Fire and overheat warning and protection on the Hercules is divided into the following systems:

a. Nacelle Overheat Warning, which actuates warning lights at the top of the co–pilot's instrument panel. A test circuit is provided for pre–flight checks.

b. Engine Fire Warning, will, when activated, produce a steady light in the Fire Emergency handles ("T" handles) and the Master Fire Warning Panel (MFWP). A test circuit is provided for pre–flt checks.

c. Turbine Overheat Warning, which actuates flashing lights in the "T" handle and the MFWP. Operation of the test circuit will check lights and flasher unit.

d. Fire Extinguisher System, consisting of 2 fire extinguisher agent bottles, agent routing valves and a 2 position bottle discharge switch.

e. Hand Fire Extinguishers. There are 3 of these positioned in the flight deck and 9 in the cargo compartment. These are intended for fighting internal fuselage fires.

Nacelle Overheat Warning System. The Nacelle encloses an area around the engine whose temperature will increase with radiated engine heat. Normal venting of this area will provide adequate heat dissipation during normal engine operating conditions. However, should local overheating occur through a bleed air leak, warning will be given to the crew before damage can occur. The system consists of 6 detectors in each engine Nacelle. Four warning lights, 2 panel lights, a test switch, 4 blocking rectifiers and 5 circuit breakers are located on the flight deck. The detectors are of the thermal switch type and are automatically reset. As the outer shell is heated it will expand lengthwise at a greater rate than the spring struts, causing them to straighten until at approximately 300°F (149°C) the contacts touch and the warning light circuit is made.

Four numbered, square, warning lights and one master warning are mounted at the top left corner of the co–pilots instrument panel next to the Nacelle overheat control panel. The panel lights illuminate the placard "CAUTION NACELLE OVERHEAT" on the control panel, when a warning light is activated by the system or when the test switch is placed to "TEST".

When a detector senses a temperature of 149°C its contacts will close. The associated warning light will be illuminated by 28V Essential DC through its own NACELLE OVERHEAT DETECTOR circuit breaker. The other 3 warning lights will be prevented from illuminating by the blocking rectifiers.

ENGINE FIRE DETECTION SYSTEM

The fire detection and warning system indicates the presence of fire in the engine Nacelles or the GTC compartment. It consists of a separate visual warning system for each engine, and one for the GTC, with a common test circuit. An audible warning system, with a speaker located in the flight deck roof, is provided with a separate test circuit.

The sensing element consists of an "Inconel" alloy tube that encloses twin wires embedded in a special ceramic core. The electrical resistance of the ceramic core decreases with a temperature increase, permitting a small current flow between the wires and the outer earthed section of the Inconel tube. When the temperature in the engine Nacelle or GTC compartment reaches a certain value, the flow of current is sufficient to trigger the "control unit" which energises a relay to supply 28V DC to the warning system. When the warning system is energised, the 2 bottom bulbs of the associated "T" handle will illuminate with a steady glow, as will those in the MFWP. The MFWP relay is also used to activate the audible warning system. Situated above the engine start panel, this panel contains the turbine overheat test switch, the audible warning test switch and the engine fire test switch. A break in the sensing element would not prevent an actual fire activating the system. In this way, the continuity and operation of the complete fire detection and warning system is checked on the Engine Fire Test Switch.

Turbine Overheat Warning System is provided for each engine and consists of 4 thermal switch detector units mounted in the "hot section" of the engine aft of the firewall. When an overheat condition of approximately 370°C occurs, any one of the detectors will activate the keyer unit for the warning lights on the flight deck. The warning is given as "flashing" lights on the "T" handle (top 2 bulbs) and on the MFWP. When this happens, its associated "T" handle is pulled which automatically isolates many systems operated by the Fire Isolation Circuit described on the aircraft fire extinguisher system.

The 2 BCF fire bottles

AIRCRAFT FIRE EXTINGUISHER SYSTEM
A "two shot" bromochlorodiflouromethane (BCF) fire extinguisher system is connected through a series of directional flow valves to each of 4 engine Nacelles and to the GTC compartment. Each bottle contains approximately 19 pounds of BCF agent and is discharged each time the system is actuated. Each bottle is charged with 600 psi of nitrogen as a propellant for the BCF. The 2 bottles are located in the same compartment as the ATM above the port wheel well.

Fire Isolation Circuit. The purpose of this system is to confine a fire to the area in which it starts until it can be extinguished. Five "T" handles on the fire emergency control panel are the controls for the isolation circuits. One push pull handle for each engine and the GTC are located on the panel. Each handle actuates many switches by the pulling of the "T" handle. The switches control circuits to accomplish many functions automatically, some of which are the closing of the fuel, hydraulic, oil and bleed air valves. Simultaneously the propeller is feathered, the starting control circuit is de–energised and the fire extinguisher valve is positioned to the affected engine.

A 3 position agent discharge switch labelled No 1 – OFF – No 2, is located in the centre of the fire emergency control panel. Once a fire emergency control handle has been pulled, holding the switch in the "No 1" position will cause the "No 1" agent bottle to be discharged. There are 4 directional control valves which route the BCF agent to the correct engine or the GTC.

System Operation. Assuming a fire warning is activated on No 2 engine, the operation of the system is as follows:

a. No 2 Condition lever pulled.

b. No 2 "T" handle pulled.

c. Agent discharge switch held to No 1 position.

d. The fire isolation circuits are actuated to isolate No 2 engine, shut it down and feather the propeller.

e. A rotary switch in the fire extinguisher control assembly rotates until electrical contact is made between the battery bus–bar and the proper control valve. (In No 2 dry bay).

f. The control valve solenoid is energised to position it to No 2 engine.

g. At the same time, a connection is made completing the circuit from the battery bus–bar, through the rotary switch to the discharge switch (in the No 1 position) causing the bottle to discharge.

h. The BCF agent flows through stainless steel tubing to the No 2 engine Nacelle where it is forced through small holes to vaporise and smother the fire.

ANCILLARY SYSTEMS

AIRCRAFT LIGHTING includes exterior and interior systems, and 7 portable emergency lights. The "exterior lighting" provides lighting for take–off and landing (one retractable type under each wing), taxying (one inside of each MLG door), formation flying (numerous) and 2 wing leading edge illumination. For recognition purposes, 2 anti–collision lights (one under fuselage and one on top of the fin) and navigational lights (on the wing tips, fuselage and rear of the empennage – duck's bill!) are fitted.

INTERNAL LIGHTING (Flight Deck). The pilot's and co–pilot's instrument panels are lit by 115 AC 400 Hz single phase. The rest by 28V DC. These include the engineer's overhead and front engine instrument panels and the navigator's station. Edge lighting is provided for the centre pedestal, each side shelf and the fuse and circuit breaker panels. Overall overhead illumination is provided by 4 white home lights. Extra lighting (floodlight) is provided for all the instrument panels. The floodlights and the dome lights can also be switched on by the "Thunderstorm lights" switch. All the lights can be dimmed to any intensity. A "wander light" is located overhead at each crew position.

UNDER THE FLIGHT DECK one light illuminates the electrical rack area. Another light is fitted outside the pressure bulkhead in the nose wheel area.

CARGO COMPARTMENT LIGHTING. On the roof, dome lights each containing a red and a white bulb, are spaced throughout from the front to the rear. Floor lights are mounted along the edge of the cargo floor. At the ramp area, further lighting is provided by 2 swivel mounted clear spot lights for night loading of equipment and general use. For air–to–air refuelling there is lighting for the probe. Additional lighting is fitted for the CMK1K (tanker). Where the hose exits through the ramp scoop door, general lighting is provided. Two sets of control lights are fitted externally on either side of the aperture (drogue housing) where the hose comes out. These are coloured red, amber and green – similar to traffic lights but smaller. Around the refuelling basket radiation Beta lights are fitted, which light up in the dark.

Battery operated emergency light

EMERGENCY LIGHTS. Battery operated, these portable lights provide illumination for normal and emergency use. They are located adjacent to the 7 emergency escape exits. Operation of this light is by a 3 position switch – OFF, ON, ARMED. When set to ARMED, it illuminates automatically if the aircraft decelerates by $2^1/_2$g, or a failure of the Essential DC bus, or when it is removed from its location.

POWER OUTLETS. There are numerous AC and DC power outlets throughout the aircraft (sockets located on the port and starboard walls) for the use by such items as the Aldis lamp and power for test equipment. The ones in the cargo compartment are utilised for the cargo winch (loading), iron lung equipment (medical), missile support and portable galley (hot drinks for the passengers).

WINDSCREEN WIPER. There are 2 windscreen wipers. One is fitted for the pilot's front window and the other for the co–pilot. Both wipers are controlled by a single, 6 position switch located on the forward of the co–pilot's side shelf.

JUMP LIGHTS. Each set contains a red and a green light. There are 2 sets on the flight deck and 5 in the cargo compartment. They are all controlled by 2 switches, one from the pilot's side shelf and the other one from the co–pilot's. These lights are utilised for airdrops – paratroopers, stores and during emergencies.

ALARM BELLS. Powered by the Battery bus–bar, the 4 alarm bells located in the cargo compartment are controlled by either of the 2 switches from the flight deck.

DOOR WARNING SYSTEM is installed at each door and at the ramp with a warning light and a switch adjacent to it. A master door warning light

Port air deflector door open

will illuminate on the pilot's coaming when a door is not closed (so will the individual door warning light).

AIR DEFLECTOR DOORS. These deflect the airflow from the port and starboard para doors useful when stores and paratroopers are despatched. One is fitted forward of the port para door, and the other the starboard side. Operated by a 3 position switch from the pilot's or co–pilot's side shelf they open outwards by an actuator. The door is hinged at the front.

ICE DETECTION AND PROTECTION SYSTEM

BLEED AIR. The engines, airframe and radome are heated by hot air. The windshields and propellers are heated electrically.

ICE DETECTION SYSTEM. Each engine is equipped with a probe but only those in Nos 2 and 3 engines are used. The amber (ice warning) and green (no ice) lights, the test switch and the cancel button are located on the engine starting panel and the reset switch at the top of the overhead panel. The relays are on the forward roof rack (hogg's trough!) near FS 245. When the airspeed is over 40 knots the probe system starts functioning. When the airflow over the probes is restricted, for example, in icy conditions, its pressure switch is de–actuated. This puts on the amber ice warning light and starts the heating system automatically, provided the master (reset) switch is in the "AUTO" position. Obviously the engines and propellers anti and de–icing switches must be in the 'on' position. The "NO ICE" green light comes on when the probe is free of ice for 90 seconds. The heating continues until the reset switch is held momentarily to "RESET" then "AUTO". The system can be operated manually by moving the reset switch to "manual".

WINDSHIELD ANTI–ICING. Nine out of the 23 windows are heated by the NON ELECTRO STATIC ACTIVATION (NESA) system. The power transformers, temperature control boxes and relays are located behind the co–pilot's lower C/B panel. Sandwiched between the glass panel luminations of each of these windows is a resistance material. The AC current is applied to it and is controlled by 2 switches from the overhead panel. One switch is for the front panels, whilst the other is for the side and lower panels.

PITOT HEAD HEATING. The ram air provided by the 2 pitot heads (port and starboard) behind the radome, must be free of icing at all times. Hence these are heated by 28V DC.

Prior to take–off, the flight engineer places the 4 engine anti–icing and the 4 propeller anti and de–icing switches to "ON" and the reset switch to auto. Pitot head and NESA switches to "ON".

PROPELLER ICE PROTECTION. The rotating spinner front section and the non–rotating afterbody (houses the propeller control unit) is anti–iced by the "A" phase of the RH AC. The spinner centre section and the spinner fairing are de–iced by the "B" phase. The 4 blades' heating element (the rubber boots) are de–iced by the "C" phase. The system is on when their switches are in the "ON" position and the "RESET" switch is in the "AUTO" or "MANUAL" position.

SIMULATOR

The 6 axis motion system in action!

The Technical aspect of the AST Simulators is something that is always on the move technologically, as new systems are superseded and new equipment is installed.

One of the 4 monitors

Hydraulic and Pneumatic Equipment. The hydraulic equipment drives a 6 axis motion system giving movement in roll, pitch, heave, yaw, sway and surge. The flying controls are driven by a hydraulic control loading system to give feel to the pilot and his number two's yoke. The toe brakes are given feel by tapping pressurised air off of the breathing air system.

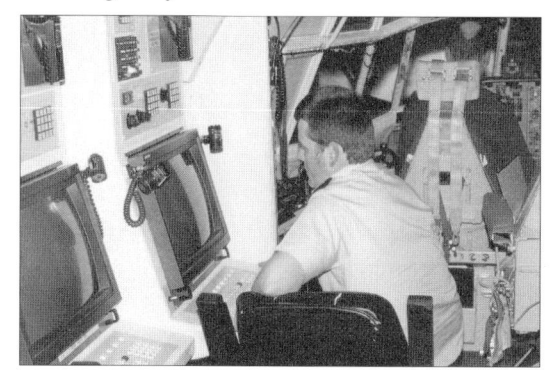

Graphic display systems

Visual System. Image generation using pipeline processing techniques to drive display equipment to give a dusk, twilight or night visual display at 4 monitors that are placed on top of the flight deck to produce a display in front of the aircrew on a large collimating mirror.

The "Link Miles" Hercules simulator (graphic display systems at bottom left)

Graphic Display Systems. Generation of graphics and alpha numerics at various monitors within the Instructor console areas giving the instructors access to numerous malfunctions, data pages, display pages and control of the aforesaid.

Computer Equipment. The system as a whole is controlled by CCC 8/32 mainframe computers, the visual system is controlled by an INTEL computer, and the graphics by a PDP11/04. Associated operational software being Coral, Fortran and CAL.

Aircraft Systems. All the aircraft systems are simulated as close to the real thing as possible, so that alot of the actual equipment on the flight deck is as on an aircraft with a few items of equipment on board being modified so that they can be driven by electrical signals.

Digital to Analogue Conversion Equipment. Converts digital information from the computers into analogue signals to drive all the onboard aircraft system equipment.

Diagnostic Equipment. Various systems have built in diagnostic systems, but there is also equipment available within the Workshops for diagnostic work, such as various oscilloscopes, digital analysers, automatic test equipment for servicing instruments, the ABI boardmaster a piece of equipment for fault finding down to chip level on Pcb's, and various other test equipment.

In the near future they will be undergoing a refurbishment program when most of the hydraulic and mechanical equipment is going to be either changed, upgraded or given a thorough servicing.

AIRCRAFT INSTRUMENTS

ENGINE INSTRUMENTS. Located between the pilot's and co–pilot's panel, the various engine instruments associated with the Hercules deal with engine speed, fuel flow, oil temperature, oil pressure and quantity, engine torque, turbine inlet temperature and oil cooler flap position. When everything is satisfactory with the aircraft in flight, the indicating pointer of each of the eight groups of gauges are aligned with each other to provide the flight crew with an at–a–glance indication of aircraft engine unserviceability.

PITOT STATIC INSTRUMENTS. The Pitot Static System supplies ram air pressure and atmospheric pressure to operate the altimeters, airspeed indicators and vertical velocity indicators.

ALTIMETERS There are three altimeters fitted to the flight deck. They indicate aircraft height by means of an aneroid capsule, which expands or contracts, with the various air pressures, driving a pointer or counter.

AIRSPEED INDICATORS. There are two airspeed gauges, which provide indicated aircraft speed (IAS) information, and are fitted to the pilot's and co–pilot's main instrument panel. One other is known as the true airspeed indicator as it uses air temperature to obtain a more accurate reading and is positioned on the navigator's panel.

VERTICAL VELOCITY INDICATOR. There are two vertical velocity or rate of climb indicators fitted to the main instrument panel, one for the pilot and one for the co–pilot. These indicate the rate at which the aircraft is climbing or descending.

ENGINE INSTRUMENTS

The engine instruments are used to monitor the performance of the engine under various operating conditions. Each of the four engines is monitored by the following instruments:

a. Tachometer Indicator.

b. Torquemeter Indicator. 115 VAC 400 Hz single phase.

c. Turbine Inlet Temperature Indicator. 115 VAC 400 Hz single phase.

Engine instrument panel

d. Fuel Flow Meter. 115 VAC 400 Hz single phase and 28 VDC.

e. Fuel Pressure Indicator. 26 VAC 400 Hz single phase.

f. Fuel Quantity Indicator. 115 VAC 400 Hz single phase.

g. Oil Temperature Indicator. 28 VDC.

h. Oil Quantity Indicator. 28 VDC.

i. Oil Pressure Indicator. 26 VAC Inst Trns single phase.

j. Oil cooler flap position indicator. 28 VDC.

Tachometer Indicator System. A tachometer system is provided to measure the engine speed. Each system consists of a three phase generator, mounted on the inboard pad of the reduction gearbox of the engine and a synchronous rotor indicator. The indicator registers the percentage of normal rated engine RPM. The generator is driven at 4200 RPM when the engine RPM is at 100%. A gear train provides a main dial pointer indication of 0 to 100 percent. The small pointer, provides readings of 0 to 10 percent.

Torquemeter Indicating System. The engine torquemeter system consists of a transmitter which is part of the engine torquemeter circuit breakers and electrical wiring. The system measures the torsional deflection (twist) of the extension shaft as it transmits power from the engine power section to the reduction gear section. This deflection is detected by magnetic pickups, the signal is supplied to an amplifier where it is amplified and drives the servo motor in the indicator. The indicator reads in inch pounds of torque and has two pointers.

Turbine Inlet Temperature. Each system consists of eighteen dual junction thermocouples mounted around the turbine section of each engine. One junction of each thermocouple is connected to the turbine inlet temperature indicating system and the other to the temperature datum system. During engine operation, the thermocouples are heated by gas entering the turbine. This causes the thermocouples to generate a small voltage which is proportional to the temperature of the incoming air. The thermocouples are connected in parallel by the harness assembly which averages the electrical signals and transmits the resulting signal to the indicator in the cockpit. The indicator has a main dial reading degrees centigrade in hundreds and a sub–dial reading in ten degree increments.

Fuel Flow Meter. The fuel flow system indicates the rate of fuel consumption of each engine. The fuel flow indicating system includes a transmitter and indicator for each engine and a fuel flow power pack. The transmitter receives 15V, 3 phase, 4 cycle AC power from the fuel flow power pack. The power pack operates on 28V power from the Essential DC bus and AC power for the indicators. The transmitter on each engine is located on the right side of the compressor.

Fuel Pressure Indicator. The fuel pressure indicating system measures the output pressure of the booster pumps. The system is composed of an indicator and transmitter (Bourdon tube pressure sensor) and electrical circuits. The indicator is located on the fuel control panel of the overhead control panel. The indicators are of the synchronous type (auto syn).

Fuel Quantity Indicator. The system consists of eight individual capacitor type systems and a totalising system. Each of the systems includes several tank units, one compensator and two indicators. The individual systems are connected to the totaliser system through a relay totaliser group. One indicator for each tank is on the flight station fuel control panel and the other is on the refuelling control panel. The total fuel indicator is on the flight station fuel control panel. The totaliser relay group is located on a rack overhead in the cargo compartment. The selector switch on the refuelling panel must be in the "OFF" position for the totaliser indicator to operate, and a RED warning light on the overhead panel indicates that the fuel selector switch is not in the "OFF" position.

Oil Temperature Indicators. The bulb for each engine is in the oil supply line above the engine. The indicating system for each engine is an electrical resistance type. The resistance of the temperature bulb is in one arm of a wheatstone bridge. The other resistors of the bridge are in the indicator. A galvanometer in the indicator measures current flow through the bridge and the pointer of the galvanometer indicates temperature in degrees centigrade.

Oil Quantity Indicators. Four separate indicating systems are provided. Each system consists of a float type tank unit and an indicator. A tank unit is on the oil tank for each engine. A low–level warning light is installed on the pilot's instrument panel. Low level limit switches in the four tank units are connected in parallel with the warning light, so operation of any one of the switches illuminates the light.

Oil Cooler Flap Position Indicators. The system comprises of a transmitter in the oil cooler flap actuator and an indicator on the engine instrument panel.

Other Pressure Indicators

a. Engine and Reduction Gearbox Oil pressures – 26 VAC 400 Hz single phase.
b. Hydraulic Oil Pressure (co–pilot's panel) – 26 VAC 400 Hz single phase.

They are 'synchro' type instruments, which consist of a transmitter and receiver. The transmitter uses a bourden tube as a pressure sensor, which positions a rotor in relation to a star wound stator. The rotor induces a magnetic field into the stator, which is transmitted to the receiver. The receiver is similarly star wound, and its rotor is free to align with the transmitted field. A pointer is geared to the rotor. Pressure gauges have twin pointers. One reads Reduction Gear Oil Pressure and the other reads Power Section Oil Pressure.

CIK (Tanker) Navigator's panel

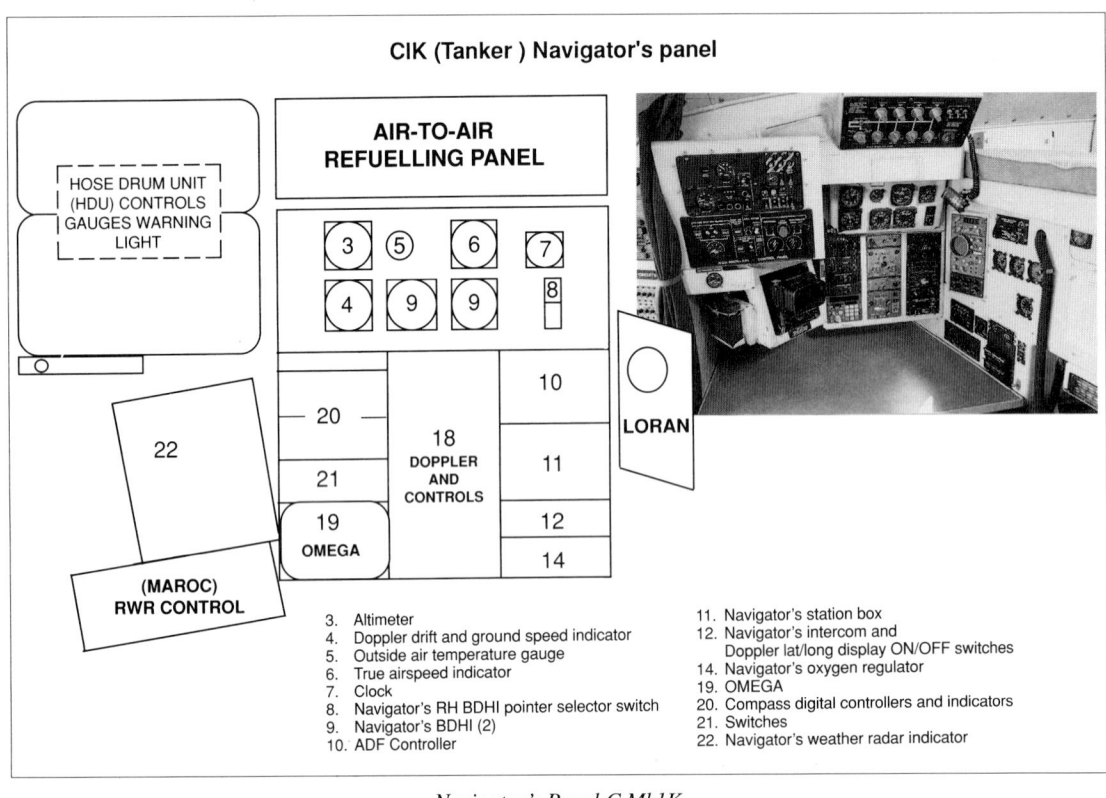

AIR-TO-AIR REFUELLING PANEL

HOSE DRUM UNIT (HDU) CONTROLS GAUGES WARNING LIGHT

3, 5, 6, 7
4, 9, 9, 8
10
20
18 DOPPLER AND CONTROLS
21
11
19 OMEGA
12
14
LORAN
22
(MAROC) RWR CONTROL

3. Altimeter
4. Doppler drift and ground speed indicator
5. Outside air temperature gauge
6. True airspeed indicator
7. Clock
8. Navigator's RH BDHI pointer selector switch
9. Navigator's BDHI (2)
10. ADF Controller
11. Navigator's station box
12. Navigator's intercom and Doppler lat/long display ON/OFF switches
14. Navigator's oxygen regulator
19. OMEGA
20. Compass digital controllers and indicators
21. Switches
22. Navigator's weather radar indicator

Navigator's Panel C.Mk1K

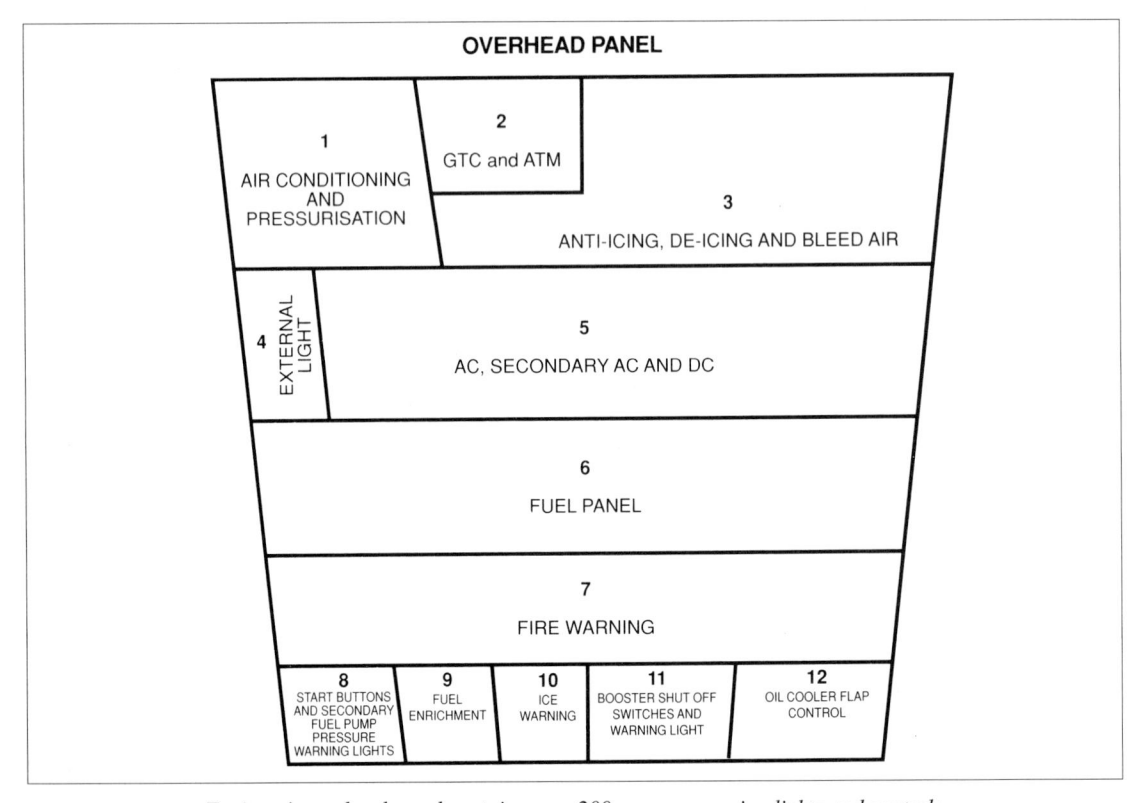

OVERHEAD PANEL

1. AIR CONDITIONING AND PRESSURISATION
2. GTC and ATM
3. ANTI-ICING, DE-ICING AND BLEED AIR
4. EXTERNAL LIGHT
5. AC, SECONDARY AC AND DC
6. FUEL PANEL
7. FIRE WARNING
8. START BUTTONS AND SECONDARY FUEL PUMP PRESSURE WARNING LIGHTS
9. FUEL ENRICHMENT
10. ICE WARNING
11. BOOSTER SHUT OFF SWITCHES AND WARNING LIGHT
12. OIL COOLER FLAP CONTROL

Engineer's overhead panel contains over 200 gauges, warning lights and controls.

Top half of overhead panel

Lower half of overhead panel

FRONT INSTRUMENT PANEL

(PILOT)

3. Accelerometer
5. Selcal light
6. Bearing, distance, heading indicator
7. Radial magnetic indicator
8. Radal meter
9. Standby attitude indicator
11. Master door warning light
12. Clock
13. Airspeed indicator
14. Horizontal situation indicator
15. Autopilot engage and trim indicator
16. Attitude director indicator
17. Altimeter
18. Master fire warning light
19. Flight director selector switch
20. Mode selector switch
21. Vertical speed indicator
22. Marker beacon light (3)
23. Marker sensitivity switch
24. Compass selector switch (HSI)
25. Selector compass failure indicator
26. IFF failure warning light
27. Engine low oil quantity warning light
28. Weather radar indicator
29. Autopilot auto trim warning light
30. Elevator tab position indicator
31. Electronic fuel correction light (4)
32. Rudder tab position indicator
33. Aileron tab position indicator
 . On some aircraft items 32 and 33 are transposed

(GAUGES)

A. Torquemeter
B. RPM
C. Turbine inlet temperature
D. Engine fuel flow
E. Oil temperature
F. Oil pressure
G. Engine oil quantity
H. Oil cooler flap position

(CO-PILOT)

1. Propeller low quantity warning light
2. ULLA release light
3. Landing taxi lamps panel
4. Landing gear control panel
5. Radial magnetic indicator
6. Airspeed indicator
7. Flap position indicator
8. Cabin altimeter
9. Outside air temperature indicator
10. Nacelle overheat light (4) and test panel
11. Selected navigation system off indicator
12. Attitude director indicator
13. Horizontal situation indicator
14. ADI repeat indicator
15. ADI comparator light
16. Altimeter
17. Vertical speed indicator
18. Flight director selector switch
19. Mode selector switch
20. ADI repeat switch
23. Bearing, distance, heading
24. Clock
25. Oxygen quantity warning light
28. Oxygen content gauge

Pilot's instrument panel

Co-pilot's panel and engineer's panel (left)

SPECIFICATIONS

Electrical System

Generators .. .. Four, engine–driven 200/115V, 400 Hz, 3–phase 40 kVA (Air), 25 kVA (Ground)
One, ATM–driven, 200/115V, 400 Hz, 3–phase 30 kVA (with fan), 20 kVA (no fan)
Inverters ... ... One, 115V, 400 Hz; 2–phase, 250 VA
One, 115V, 400 Hz, single–phase, 2.5 kVA
Instrument Transformers ... ... Two, 26V, 400 Hz single–phase (C–12 compasses)
Two, 26V, 400 Hz, single–phase (instruments)
External AC . ... 200/115V, 400 Hz, 3–phase, 40 kVA capacity, phase rotation A–B–C
DC TRU .. .. Four, 28V, 200 ampere (nominal)
Battery . ... One, lead–acid, 24V, 36 ampere–hour
External DC . ... 28V, 400 ampere capacity

Autopilot and Flight System

Autopilot ... ... Smiths Mk 10A
Flight System ... . CPU – 65 (twin)

Communications Radio

Cabin Address ... ... UA 578 + AN/AIC – 13
Havequick V/UHF ..PTR 1751 WWH
HF (Twin) ... ... HF 103 (ARI 23090)
Intercommunication UA 60 (ASRI 23111)
Privacy Communication ... ... MA 4227
Selcal (Twin) ... ... AD 900 (ARI 23197)
SATCOM .. .. SOO
UHF (Single, Box 2) .... . ARI 23301
VHF (Single – Centre Box) . ... AD 120 (ARI 23288)
VHF/UHF (Single, Box 1) ... ... ARI 23300

Navigation Radio

ADF . ... AD 360 (ARI 231190)
Doppler . ... Decca 62M (ARI 23122)
IFF/SSR . ... Cossor 1520 (ARI 23134)
Loran ... ... Decca ADL21 (ARI 23180)
Omega ... ... Litton LTN–211/08 (ARI 23314)
Radar Altimeter . ... AN/APN–171 (V)(ARI 23219)
SAR Homer ... ... BE 373
Tacan (Twin) ... . AN/ARN – 72
Tacan 2 (Post Mod 5381) ... . AN/ARN–118 (ARI 23368/1)
UHF DF AN/ARA–50
VHF NAV (Twin) & Marker ... ... AD 260 (ARI 23118)
Weather Radar ... ... E 290 (ARI 23175)

Additional Equipment

Flare/Chaff Dispenser . AN/ALE 40
Loral (IRCM) ... ... AN/ALQ–157(V)
Maroc (Orange Crop) .. ARI 18233
Station Keeping Equipment (SKE C) AN/APN–169C

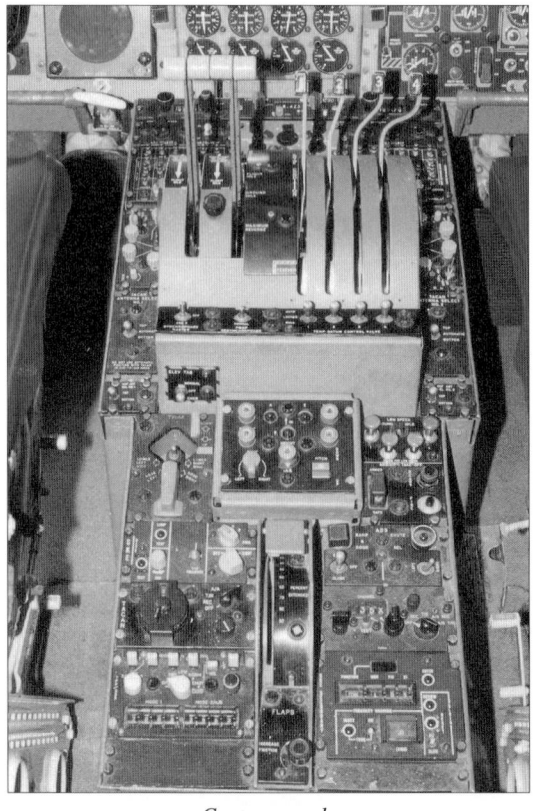

Centre console

CHAPTER FOUR

A AND B LINE SERVICING SQUADRONS (ALSS AND BLSS)

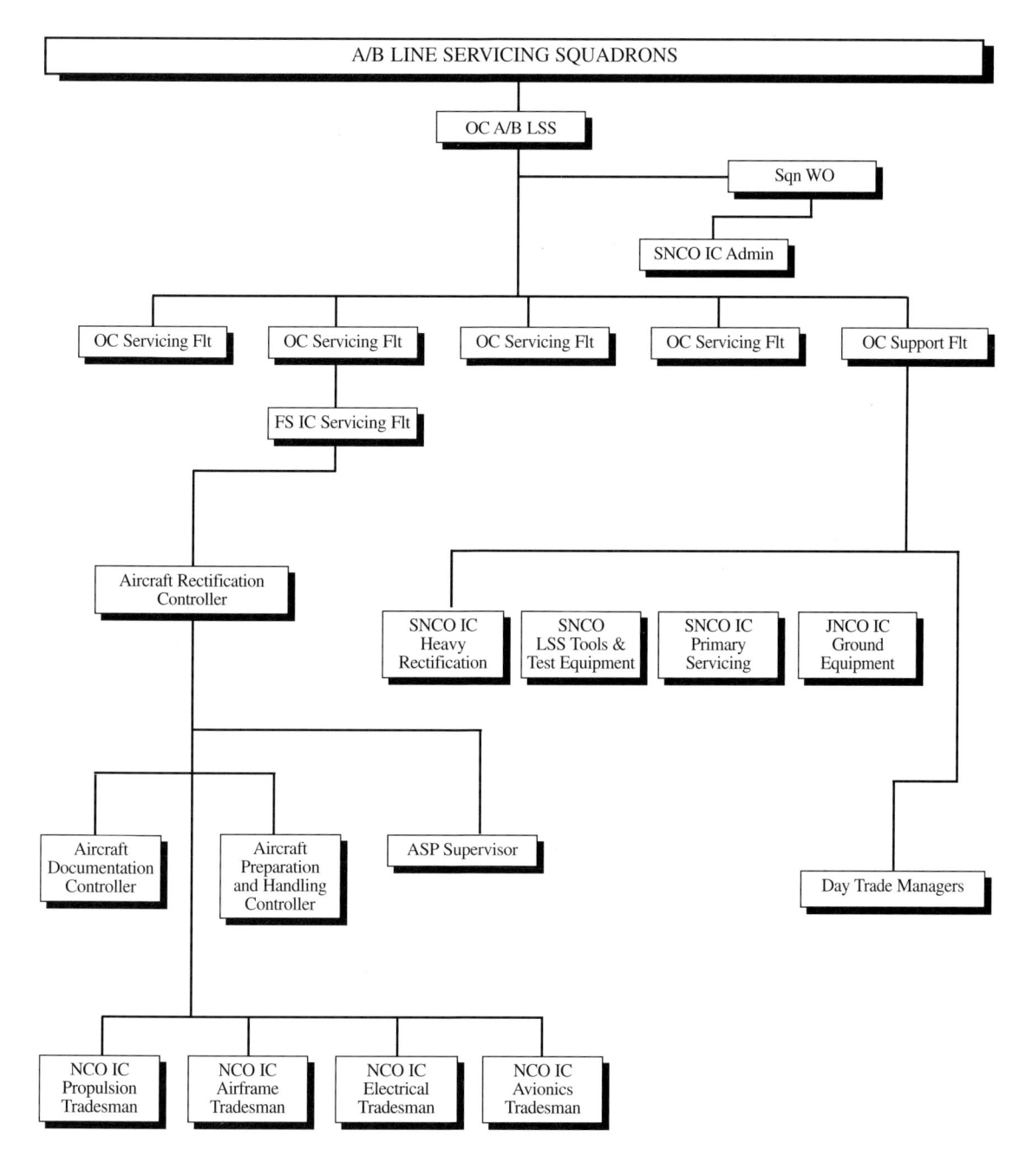

```
A/B LINE SERVICING SQUADRONS
            │
        OC A/B LSS
         │      │
         │      └── Sqn WO
         │              │
         │           SNCO IC Admin
         │
   ┌─────┬──────┬──────┬──────┬──────┐
   │     │      │      │      │
OC Svc OC Svc OC Svc OC Svc  OC Support Flt
 Flt    Flt    Flt    Flt
        │
   FS IC Servicing Flt
        │
   Aircraft Rectification Controller
```

Under OC Support Flt:
- SNCO IC Heavy Rectification
- SNCO LSS Tools & Test Equipment
- SNCO IC Primary Servicing
- JNCO IC Ground Equipment
- Day Trade Managers

Under Aircraft Rectification Controller:
- Aircraft Documentation Controller
- Aircraft Preparation and Handling Controller
- ASP Supervisor

- NCO IC Propulsion Tradesman
- NCO IC Airframe Tradesman
- NCO IC Electrical Tradesman
- NCO IC Avionics Tradesman

A AND B LINE SERVICING SQUADRONS (LSS 'A' AND LSS 'B'). The Line Servicing Squadrons (LSS) at RAF Lyneham consist of A and B Lines and are commanded by Squadron Leaders. Both A and B Lines comprise of 5 flights, each with a total of some 410 Officers, SNCOs and Airmen/Airwomen. The Line Squadrons are responsible for the 1st line maintenance of the fleet of 61 Hercules aircraft. Each Line maintains 30 aircraft each, and the unique WMK II aircraft (Snoopy) operates out of Boscombe Down (Meteorological duties). Each Line has specialist fit aircraft; whilst 'A' Line looks after the few CMK1s for SF flights, 'B' Line maintains the CMK1Ks (tanker). The maintenance involves handling, flight servicing, random rectifications, installations and removal of specialist Role Equipment and general cleanliness of the aircraft. Working to a shift pattern, 4 out of the 5 flights on each LSS provide engineering coverage 24 hours a day, 365 days of the year. The 5th flight, known as Support Flight, works a standard working week carrying out Primary and Primary Star Scheduled servicings.

OC ALSS AND OC BLSS SUPPORT FLT – JOB
The OCs of the 2 Support Flts are responsible for all aspects of engineering within A and B Line that are not immediately concerned with aircraft generation. To this end, they manage some 40 personnel including the Day Trade Managers, a dedicated Primary/Primary Star servicing team, a heavy rectification team and the Sqn Admin personnel. Due to the scope of their responsibilities, they are required to provide continuity across the Sqn for Quality Assurance, Health and Safety at Work, administrative staffing and security matters. In addition to planning and allocation of engineering tasks within their own remit, they have to co-ordinate with the 4 line shifts to ensure best use is made of the Sqn resources. They assist in coordinating the actions of the 4 junior engineering officers under the direction of OC A and B line, for whom they are the designated deputies.

Additionally, OC Support Flt for ALSS is required to liaison with 47(SF) Sqn on all matters covering the maintenance and associated problems to ensure the maximum utilization of the SF fleet. OC Support Flts liaise with OC HAEDIT to assist in engineering investigations and trails. He is also required to brief the relevant OC LSS on all long term problems likely to effect the Sqn.

OC Support Flight and Trade Managers

SERVICING FLIGHTS. Each of the 8 servicing flights established on A and B LSS are commanded by a Junior Engineering Officer. He is assisted by a FS and some 40 tradesmen. Working from the line servicing control, the flight control staff comprise as per the line diagram. In addition to the aircraft, the ground equipment (including tools and test equipment) has to be serviced and controlled from within the manpower resources of the servicing flights. Whilst support agencies at Lyneham provide the specialist assistance, the day to day control of this equipment remains largely with the flight personnel.

Whilst all tradesmen receive basic technical training, the art of specialisation on the Hercules aircraft is obtained via courses at the Hercules Maintenance Ground School and OJT (On the Job Training). Simply, familiarisation followed by examination and authorisation on each task required.

OC SERVICING FLIGHT. Each of the four servicing flights in 'A' Line Servicing Squadron (ALSS) and four in BLSS is commanded by a Junior Engineering Officer (JEngO) normally of Fg Off or Flt Lt rank. These JEngOs are mostly graduates. However, some come from the ranks of technical trades, either gaining degrees at RMCS Shrivenham or other universities or progressing with HNC. After selection they go through a six months Initial Officers Training (IOT) course at RAF College, Cranwell followed by a six months course in Engineering subjects, such as aerodynamics, weapons, avionics and engineering management, then after graduation they are posted out. Those who arrive at Lyneham can be posted to A or BLSS as OC Servicing Flight and work closely with the FS. Some of the responsibilities of the JEngO are the overall co-ordination and supervision of engineering operations of the Hercules for the daily tasking, whether it is for a local or an overseas route task.

He looks after the safety of men, equipment and building by issuing instructions when a meteorological warning is received. He co–ordinates through the flight trade SNCOs for correct procedures for the testing, rectification and preparation of the aircraft. Any aircraft incident like the delay of flight or an incident report, such as a lightning strike in flight, by the aircrew has to be actioned by him.

He ensures a smooth handover during shift change, and an adequate level of man management to generate serviceable aircraft and fulfil the Station disaster and crash plans. He reviews the Flight Servicing Schedules and SNCOs check lists and ten per cent quality checks on servicing performed by his shift. He presides over the administration, the welfare and morale of the flight personnel and investigating any aircraft insecurity. At the end of 18 months this inexperienced JENGO becomes a matured engineer to be posted to RAF College, Cranwell for further training for 6 months and then to be posted to a job not associated with aircraft directly, for instance OC Ground Equipment Flight.

JENGO and FS in the control office.

FS IC Servicing Flight. This experienced SNCO with many years experience is responsible to the JENGO on many matters laid down in his terms of reference, such as information on servicing and the state of the aircraft received from the flight. Working closely with the JENGO many of his duties have been described in the previous section with the exception of the welfare of the shift personnel. However, he does see that those NCOs who are detailed for secondary duties and daily servicing of the Squadron vehicle such as the Mini and Land Rover are carried out satisfactorily. He collects correspondence and mail from the squadron administration section and details personnel for detachment and route support servicing duties, as well as ensuring that personnel have signed all the relevant servicing columns on MOD Form F700.

Aircraft Rectification Controller (ARC). He is responsible for the allocation of aircraft for the flying programme and the delegation of priorities for rectification work to the 4 Trade managers who control the various trade elements established on each flight.

Aircraft Documentation Controller (ADC), ensures that the aircraft log books (F700) are correctly compiled, and meet all the requirements to allow the aircraft to carry out any intended tasking.

The Aircraft preparation and Handling Controller (APHC) is responsible for ensuring that all aircraft required for flight are serviced, replenished and all ground handling tasks (ie marshalling and parking) are carried out.

The ASP Supervisor (Ramp Tramp) is normally a SNCO who patrols the Flight Line ensuring the smooth running of all Ground Handling, correct procedures and priorities of men and equipment, and to provide liaison between the servicing control and the outgoing and incoming movements of aircraft.

Ramp Tramp always lends a hand

NCO IC Propulsion, Airframe, Electrical and Avionics. The 4 Trade Managers are responsible to the Flight Commander through the ARC for the rectification of any defects which may arise, following post Flight debriefs from the aircrew members or husbandry Servicing due to the periodic requirements of the schedule. Each Trade Manager heads a team of up to 10 JNCOs, airmen and airwomen.

Two of the four Trade Managers and Technicians

FORM 700 (F700)

The F700 is a register of the service history of the aircraft in the RAF. At Lyneham the F700 relates to the Hercules aircraft and consists of 2 books. The book one travels with the aircraft when it goes on a task. At the end of it the book is kept in the control office of A and BLSS, or the AES when it goes for the Minor and Minor Star servicing. The book has 7 sections, each showing the state of the aircraft. For example the LIMITATION LOG in section one, line one might say, "number 2 compass is 10 degrees out after turns. Rely on number 1". This brings attention to the air engineer who in turn will inform the crew prior to the flight. Section 4 (F725) amongst other information records the airframe hours and the fatigue life of the aircraft within its flight parameters. Also in the same section is the F705 (Flight Servicing Certificate). This records the daily servicing history, eg the A/F B/F, T/R and the fuel state. The signed signature block ensures the servicing has been done. There are also 2 further columns relating to the Captain of the aircraft as having handed the aircraft (after landing) or accepting (prior to the flight). Section 6 is the short forecast sheet and shows when critical components are checked, or replaced, and oils replenished. For example lines 1–4 states that after 65 ± 10 flying hours the propeller oils and the magnetic plugs are checked.

The book 2 is the Maintenance and Component Replacement Control Document. This book records all components life, both "flying hours" and "calendar based" that need changing. Also long term forecasts which are checked meticulously by the controller and transferred to Section 6 in book 1. This book does not travel with the aircraft.

AFTER FLIGHT SERVICING (AF) AND BEFORE FLIGHT SERVICING (BF). The flying programme for the daily tasks (route or local flights) arrives from Engineering Plans less than 24 hours before its scheduled departure. An AF lasts for 7 days at Lyneham and for 3 days if the aircraft is abroad. On average, within 6 hours of an aircraft's landing time an AF is carried out. A BF is needed within this period if the aircraft is to be scheduled for a sortie (technical ready) and this servicing lasts for 24 hours. However, as most of the checks in the AF are duplicated and to save time, a composite AF/BF is performed together. This is done by the Hercules composite trained tradesman. hence the electrical tradesmen will do the checks on the engine and airframe and vice–versa. Therefore only 2 composite tradesmen are required for a combined AF/BF. If replenishment of fuel, oil, hydraulic fluid or the Elsan (chemical portable toilet) is called for, a third tradesman is involved. Furthermore for ALSS if the IRCM navigational or any special fit is required by the 47(SF) flight or for BLSS the tanker (CMK1K) sortie, a further specialist tradesman is required.

The composite checks take about 4 hours. One person does the exterior checks and the Elsan, and the other, the interior (Flight deck and cargo compartment). The checks are laid out in the Flight Servicing Schedule AP101B. These consist of checks to be performed in an orderly walk round manner as they are grouped into work areas. As the servicing schedule itself is a book, only a brief description is given here. In all the checks he or she is looking for wear and tear abnormalities, cracks, damages, tyre and accumulator pressures, fluid levels, leaks and so on. Finally all the electrical and avionics equipment switches are positioned correctly.

External Checks with electrical AC power connected to the aircraft.

(1) Battery compartment – acid spillage, cables, sump jar (venting system) circuit breakers, current limiter.

(2) Inside nose wheel area – tyre pressures, steering jacks and cable, door security, left side emergency brake accumulator (1000 lbs psi $\pm$ 300) brake selector valve, brake pipes. Radome components, above nosewheel uplock. Right side LOX container, pipes, normal brake accumulator (1500 lbs psi $\pm$ 300).

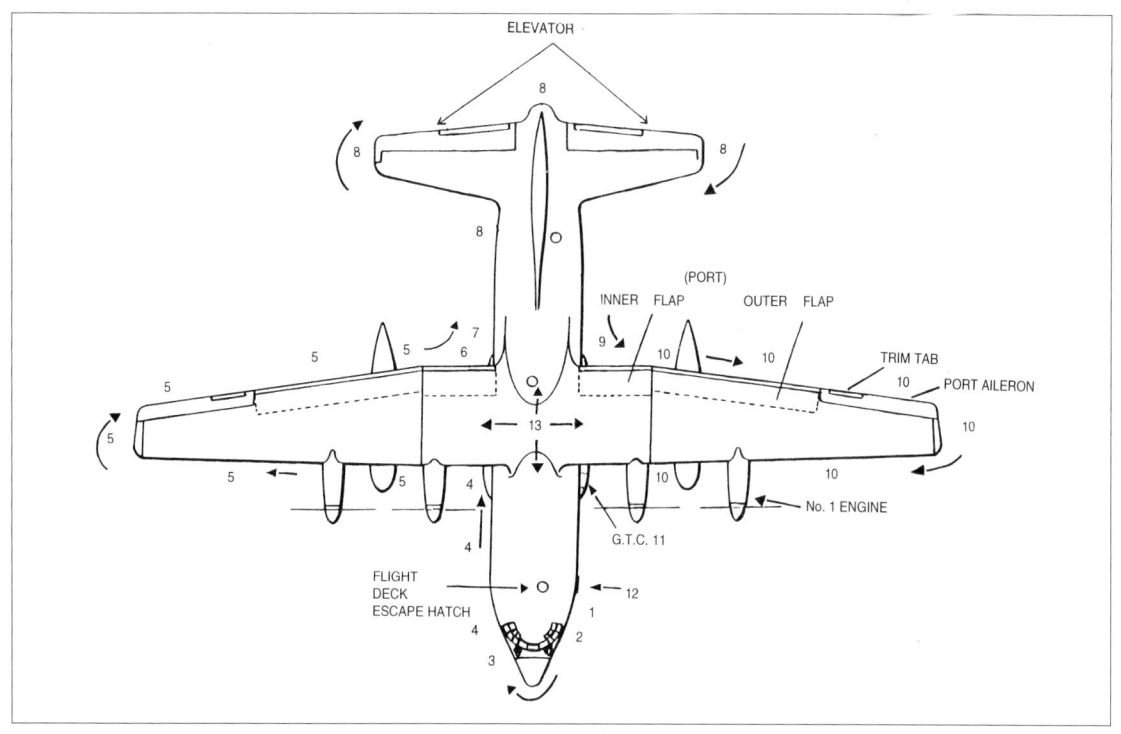

Numbers in illustration refer to External Checks paragraphs

(3) External forward fuselage – windows, radome and airframe area, pitot heads, lox filler compartment and vent orifice, outside air temperature sensors (2).

(4) Starboard (Stbd) fuselage to wing root area – airframe skin, cargo compartment air conditioner (intake and exhaust) and windows.

(5) Stbd underwing – flap area, underwing root to tip, numbers 3 and 4 engines, align propeller blades, oil cooler (intake and flap) engine front air intake and first stage compressor, fuel and oil drain outlet (sharks fin) rear turbine area, jet tail pipe, stbd external fuel tank and wing tip.

(6) Stbd Main Landing Gear (MLG) – the door assembly, brake units, normal and emergency brake pipes and hoses, tyre pressure within limits.

(7) Single Point Refuelling (SPR) panel – all selector switches 'OFF' and, beside the SPR panel the surge suppressor pressure is noted.

(8) Rear fuselage area and empennage section including the ramp and door area.

(9) Left main landing gear – same as right (MLG) plus the 2 main fire extinguishers agent pressures.

(10) Underwing – same as right wing plus the number 1 and 2 engines.

(11) Gas turbine Compressor (GTC) – inside GTC compartment and exhaust section, record hour meter.

(12) The crew entrance door – seal, hinges and the 2 door jettison hooks.

(13) **Overwing check** – fuselage, wings, empennage, all top aerials, the 4 dinghy container panels and the CO_2 discharge bottle indicators.

(14) Lights check – landing, taxy, navigation, formation and leading edge. All bottom aerials (under fuselage).

(15) Put blanks on the 4 engine air intakes (these are removed prior to the Air Engineers arrival at the aircraft).

Internal Checks – look for cracks, dents, lamination on windows, chaffed electrical cables, fluid leaks from hoses and pipes, check and stow intercom leads.

Flight Deck – 23 windows (clean and check for any delamination). Check tell–tale wires on the covers (guards) on fuel dump valves, fuel dump pumps, generator disconnect, emergency de–pressurisation and hydraulic booster valve switches. Fire extinguisher – 2 fuses, Mic, tele leads, signal pistol and mounting, spare fuse box (replenish if required). Daily use first aid kit (DUFAK), smoke goggles (4 off), Pilot's, Co–pilot's, Air Engineer's and Navigator's instruments (over 250) for loose mountings and any damage. Replace any unserviceable light filaments on these instruments. Check all CBs in, check CBs and current limiters on the main distribution panel. Place aerial selector switches correctly, clean the floor, and tidy seat belts and check the 3 passenger life saving jackets (LSJ) and the seal on the crews (LSJs) stowage box. All the emergency equipment, emergency light and all relevant Air Publication books. Record oil and fuel and lox contents.

At the crew entrance door, serviceability of the door release handle and the door. The galley area, water tank, oven, stowage of blanks (hydraulic pump, generator starter motor), spare magnetic plug box, signal pistol cartridges (6 red, 4 amber and 4 green), Air Publication books consisting of Dash 1A to 1M, the 2 tactical chocks and emergency light.

In the cargo compartment starting from Flight Station 245 (FS 245) to the ramp door area a systematic check:

Forward urinals, windows, nose landing gear valve emergency lever. The emergency equipment to lower or raise the MLG and flaps

Utility Hydraulic System – reservoir and level, accumulator pressure (1500 lbs psi ± 300) suction boost pump, main landing gear (MLG) valve switch and the maze of pipes. MLG windows and above, port wing isolation valve (lever down), then rear to the aileron booster pack assembly auto pilot servo motor and cables and flap control unit. The asymmetric flaps brake unit button and at the ramp area; the auxiliary hydraulic pump, hand pump, reservoir, and level indicator, accumulator (300 lbs psi ± 100), emergency water flasks, emergency survival pack type 'A', safety valve (pressurisation) rudder and elevator hydraulic booster packs assemblies and auto pilot servo motors and cables. All the hydraulic pressure relief and diverter valves. All the 10 ramp uplocks and 14 hooks on the cargo door and its uplock assembly. Stowage bins for the LSJs, chains. The rear top escape hatch assembly, forward on to rear of starboard rear wheel area, the MA4 emergency portable oxygen bottle and charging system, and the stbd MLG windows. Forward to the booster hydraulic system reservoir the level, accumulator, pipes. All the emergency equipment including the portable fire extinguisher and emergency lowering of the MLG (stowage near booster and utility system reservoirs). The starboard emergency escape hatch, and back to FS 245 to check the portable oxygen bottle and charging system and the emergency Mk9 Oxygen bottles. Also by now the flight control and throttle cables, lights and the 5 emergency lights left out of 7, and GTC oil level would have been checked.

THIRD PERSON
External and Internal for Refuel. The flight deck fuel figures are noted and the flow of fuel from the bowser is pumped in via the SPR panel.

If any engine oil replenishment is needed, a stand is utilised to reach the nacelle engine cowling and the neck filler cap. Contents are noted from the flight deck oil contents gauge and the filler dipstick. Internally, if any of the three hydraulic system needs replenishment the reservoir sight glass is used as the contents indication. Externally, if any of the 6 wheels tyre pressures are outside limits an air trolley is brought for this purpose.

TURNROUND (TR) SERVICING. When an aircraft lands and remains on the ground for more than 4 hours a T/R servicing is needed before the next flight provided the A/F servicing is within limits. In a T/R the checks to be done equal to about 80% of the A/F and B/F checks. Hence the T/R is avoided unless absolutely necessary as it takes about 3 hours.

CONTINUOUS OPERATIONS (CONT OPS) AND REFUEL. If an aircraft lands and the engines are shut down but is to take off again within 4 hours (and within the A/F servicings' limits) no checks are needed. The Flight Engineer notes any minor unserviceabilities on F707A and the off–going captain signs the F705. The ground crew who marshall the aircraft onto the parking bay do the refuel. No servicing is done provided the on–coming captain accepts the aircraft in its present state. If time permits the minor unserviceabilities are rectified provided it does not invalidate the servicing.

CONT OPS RUNNING CHANGE. Mostly on local sorties when only the crews change, a "running crew change" takes place without the need for engines shutdown.

Battery compartment and external power receptacle

Inspecting the air intake

Checking the tread for wear

Checking the GTC area and noting the hour meter

After inflation a final check of the pressure

Post flight inspection of the jet pipe

*Inspecting the urinal.
Note the Elsan honey bucket!*

*Testing the fire warning system.
No 1 engine 'T' handle beside thumb*

Securing the signal pistol

Cleaning the cupola

Cleaning the windows

*Noting the fatigue meter reading
(overhead roof forward of wing spar)*

Utility system reservoir and components

Inspecting the SATCOM aerial

Over wing fuel contents check

Supporting the tanker's fuel dispensing 'basket' for checks prior to an AAR sortie

The 'pull off' checks on the probe of the receiver aircraft

Crane hoisting a propeller

A chief tech and Cpl fitting a propeller at a civilian airfield. Note the unfamiliar stand and hoist!

Lubricating the tanker's 'basket' – refuelling receptacle

Replenishing No 1 engine oil tank

Marshaller in action. Note the taxy lights

Refuel bowser hose connected to the SPR

SPR panel (trainee under supervision)

Replenishing the LOX system

Below freezing point when the controls are ice locked the airframe is de-iced

RECTIFICATION. What happens when a snag is found during the A/F and B/F servicing? As an example the tradesman doing the external checks finds a leak on the number one engine cowling just aft of the propeller blades. He reports it to the aircraft rectification controller who confers with the NCO IC Propulsion team who will investigate in depth. This involves hooking on a stand to the Land Rover and placing it under the engine. After opening the cowling and investigating he will have the answer. If the leak is severe and warrants a propeller or an engine change the servicing stops. The NCO then does the paperwork and the ball rolls for the rectification. In this case a crane and a new propeller ordered which will take some time to arrive. The 2 tradesmen are now moved to a new aircraft allocated by Eng Ops and they will have to start from the beginning again on the A/F and B/F checks.

Throughout the A/F, B/F, T/R and when any rectification has to be done the safety of the personnel is paramount. Hence the mandatory regulations laid down in the Safety and Servicing schedule AP 101B... 5A2 is adhered to. For example, if the ignition igniters are to be replaced on the engine, its circuit breaker is tripped and flagged to prevent the discharge of high electrical energy – lethal to the tradesman.

Additional Checks on A/F, B/F, T/R and Cont Ops.

(1) On para or MSP sorties the Role Equipment personnel are involved and they will sign on the F700 after completion.

(2) On tanker sorties the BLSS technician has to perform additional checks.

(3) On SF flight sorties the ALSS technician has to fit and check some avionics/radar equipment.

(4) If a receiver aircraft is required for air to air refuelling sortie, BLSS perform extra checks, including the 'pull off' checks (exercising the fuel probe nozzle), to ensure the smooth withdrawal from the tanker's basket.

A AND BLSS DTMs

The Day Trade Managers (DTMs) office is manned by 4 Hercules experienced Chief Techs of the Airframe, Avionics, Electrical and Propulsion trades. Working a 5 day, 40 hour week they closely liaise with the shift working flights and Primary Trade Manager to provide continuity and other professional advice. The DTMs are busy people, especially as they are a focal point for on–Station and outside agencies who regularly have queries or who need information about the aircraft. Other facets of the job consist of maintaining the high standards of quality required to maintain these ageing machines. They keep a history of faults using a Kardex system or on computer and identify recent similar faults with a view to identifying trends. There are the occasional meetings to attend and a method of information feedback to the flights is used in the form of quarterly newsletters which highlight to them any general problems or things they should be aware of, but done so in a "semi light hearted manner". OC LSS, OC Supp Flt and the WO all regularly contribute towards the DTMs workload, which can (and does) often make their job a rather hectic and demanding one!! ALSS is responsible for the maintenance of the SF mini–fleet and the DTMs get heavily involved with the problems of the various add–on systems of which there are many in the Avionics and Electrical trades.

PRIMARY SERVICING SECTION

PRIMARY SERVICINGS. The Primary is due when the aircraft has flown for 250 hours or 5 months, and the Primary Star servicing at 500 hours or 10 months. Extensions can be granted by Strike Command on the timescale or the hours provided there is a valid reason. It takes 3 days for the servicing of the Primary and 4 days for the Primary Star.

Eng Plans have a forecast sheet and Eng records at EWSF will do the necessary paperwork. The F700 will also indicate when the servicing and other component changes are due. With the paperwork completed (nothing moves without authority) the aircraft (with the F700) is taken to the wash bay. After washing, it is then brought to the authorised bay and given an engine ground run which will show any problems on the engines and the ancillary equipment. The fuel load is adjusted for jacking later. The aircraft is towed into the hangar and chocks are placed on the front and rear of the wheels. The Primary servicings are as follows:

a. Out of Phase Servicing (OOPS). These are servicings due on certain systems such as propeller oil levels or the removable magnetic plugs, both due at 65 ± 10 hours or it could be the replacement of a major item such as the aircraft battery.

b. Rectification. Either those found during the servicing or as required in the F700.

c. Standard Servicings. Some of which are described below. After placing the staging and stands in place, servicing commences. As the schedules run to several volumes only a few are mentioned here.

d. Propulsion. The 4 engines are given a thorough inspection by the Eng Technicians and the filters on the oil, fuel and hydraulic systems are checked. If the hydraulic filter has popped it is not only replaced but the system is flushed, cleaned and replenished. The turbine section is checked for cracks using a boroscope, and the tail pipe area examined. On the reduction gear box the NTS gap is checked for clearance and adjusted if out of alignment.

After the post engines ground run the fluid contents are established and replenished. If during the run the efficiency is low in any engine, it is investigated for such things as bleed air leaks on the bleed air valve and the anti–icing valves and clamps. OOPS on the magnetic plugs, starter oil, propeller oil and the low pressure fuel filter takes place. Other ancillary equipment on the fuel, hydraulics and bleed air systems are checked. Water drain checks are done on the fuel tanks, the fuel system heater and strainer, and on the air conditioning vent valves.

On the GTC, the door hinges are lubricated and its oil level established. The ATM gearbox oil level is checked.

AIRFRAME. The 4 airframe technicians are each responsible for one of the 4 zones the aircraft airframe is divided into.

Man 'A'. He checks the maniplane for any loose rivets, cracks or other damages and lubricates the ailerons, aileron trim tab and the flap rollers.

Man 'B'. He is responsible for the internal checks – flight deck and cargo compartment. On the flight deck, the aircrews seat covers and the water in the galley are changed. In the cargo compartment the urinal unit is pressure tested. If it leaks, the floor panel is removed and the pipe repaired at FS 245. Walking rearwards the utility and booster hydraulic systems are checked for leaks, not only from the maze of pipes but also from the suction boost pumps, landing gear and flap selector valves (utility system, port site) but also from the anti–skid valves. The intercostal clips on the wing joints (stringers joining the box section) are inspected. At the ramp area the ramp hinge, hooks, locks are lubricated and a functional check on the ramp and door is carried out. The hydraulic fluid on the ramp actuator is bled and replenished. The sloping longerons at the elsan (toilet and urinal) area are checked for damage and corrosion. The elevator and rudder hydraulic booster packs and all the diverter and pressure reducing valve and so on are inspected for leaks and damage.

Man 'C'. Working in a sequence around the external fuselage and under, he pumps grease on the nose (NLG) and main landing gears (MLG) nipples, the NLG and MLG doors are then lubricated and all the aerials are checked.

Man 'D'. The empennage section calls for a cherry picker, and Man 'D' lubricates the rudder and disconnects the rudder trim tab which is checked for cracks/damage, lubricated and re–fitted.

The electrical and Avionics tradesmen are borrowed from one of the shifts in the flight line. They will isolate and remove electrical units like those under the flight deck floor to gain access (for example) by the airframe tradesman to remove and rectify the flight deck air conditioner. At the empennage the avionics tradesmen may be called if the HF aerial cable needs tensioning. All aerials are checked.

At the end of the servicing the aircraft is returned to the flight line. For a Primary Star an extra day is involved and some of the extra checks are as follows:

PRIMARY STAR

The primary star servicing is due every 500 flying hours or every 10 months. This involves all the primary servicing plus an extra day for additional checks, some of which are as follows:

a. PROPULSION. The engines and the GTC fire extinguisher system are checked for operation by disconnecting the pipe from the 2 BCF fire bottles. In its place an air hose is connected. Each of the 5 emergency "T" handles are pulled in turn. Thus, each time the compressed air is fed through the hose it will exit through the engine nacelle and the GTC compartment. Also, the integrity of components, such as the fire detection control unit and the fire control valve of each engine/GTC, are checked. On the reduction gear box, the generator is removed and its drive lubricated and re–fitted. The 4 generators are checked and tested during the post engine run.

PRIMARY AND PRIMARY STAR SERVICING

Adjusting the valve housing assembly

Nearly there, final servicing on the propeller

Draining the fuel heater and strainer of residual water

Greasing and adjusting the NTS gap on a new engine

Fitting a new filter on the aileron booster pack assembly

The CAU being checked and lubricated

The port aileron trim tab is re-fitted

Repairing the SPR panel (left), and servicing the Mk9 oxygen bottles (right)

Tightening the clamp on the cargo compartment CAU

Fitting a new fuel contents gauge

Checking the lower aerials

Applying grease on the MLG grease points

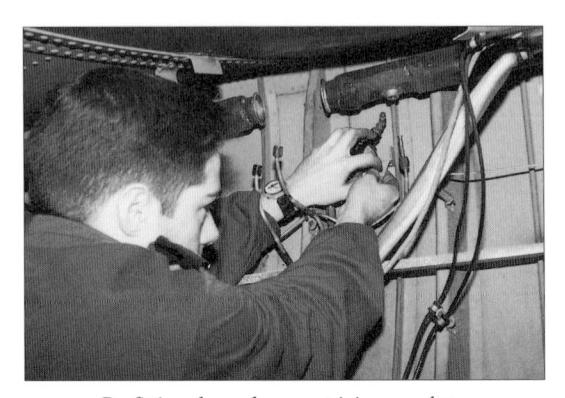

Re-fitting the radome ant-icing regulator

b. **ELECTRICS.** The 18 pairs of thermocouples are checked for corrosion and damage. A resistance and current flow check is then carried out by using a purpose built bonding tester.

AIRFRAME. Crawling under the flight deck floor (between the NLG inspection window and the electrical rack), the airframe tradesman removes the Cold Air Unit (CAU) from the flight deck air conditioning unit. This is taken outside the aircraft, checked, lubricated and then re–fitted. But this servicing on the cargo compartment's CAU is performed in situ (forward of the starboard main wheel well). Inside the nose wheel well, components of the radome anti–icing, such as the regulator and shut off valve, and filter are checked. On the flight deck galley, all wirings and plug points for the oven and hot water flasks. In the cargo compartment, the retrieval winch (used during paratroop sorties) mountings are inspected.

ENGINE GROUND RUN. After any major component replacement such as the hydraulic pump or the igniters an engine run is carried out. However, if the propeller assembly or the QEC or both are replaced, an engine test ground run is required and various functional checks are carried out in accordance with the AP schedule. Assume number one propeller has been replaced, the engine ground run is performed as per the test schedule.

Starting the Engines

1. One operator acts as the safety man outside the aircraft on intercom and with the fire–extinguisher. On the flight deck are two operators of the rank of corporal or above. One sits on the captain's seat and the second on the co–pilot's. The third technician sits on the Air Engineer's seat and acts as the safety man. He is in direct control on the radios with Ground (in ATC building) and with Station operations. During an engine start an external AC power sources is connected to the aircraft. When all the start checks have been completed by the two operators, the technician starts the GTC from the engineer's overhead panel. The bleed air manifold is then pressurised with the output from the GTC. The left hand operator moves the number 3 condition to the RUN position and pushes the starter button. Simultaneously the number 3 bleed air valve is opened by the technician. The starter button's integral filament lights up and the starter valve opens. This supplies a regulated amount of air to turn the starter motor which rotates the engine and propeller via the reduction gear.

2. Air now flows through the 14 stage axial compressor.

3. The compressed air (high temperature and pressure) enters the diffuser. Most of this air flows through the six combustion chambers and some around them for cooling. Finally this exits through the four stage turbine unit and the jet pipe.

The start is now controlled automatically by the micro–switches in the Speed Sensitive Control (SSC).

At 16% RPM the SSC actuates the following:

a. Fuel shut off valve opens and provides fuel to the burners.

b. The ignition relay is energised proving high voltage to the igniters.

c. The manifold drip valve is closed. It opens below 16% to drain away unburnt fuel.

d. The parallel valve is closed. The two mechanical fuel pumps run in parallel. At low RPM it is inefficient to run in series.

The operator calls fuel flow, ignition, oil pressures, hydraulic pressure and parallel. The combination of the starter motor, FCU and the combustion products allows the engine to accelerate smoothly.

At 60% RPM the starter button is released. Further acceleration of the engine disengages the starter clutch which allows the engine to increase rpm free of the starter.

At 65% RPM the SSC actuates the following:

a. The power to the igniter is switched off.

b. The manifold drip valve released. It is now held closed by fuel pressure.

c. The parallel valve opens. The two pumps now run in series and the operator calls "Series".

At approximately 72% RPM the engine stabilises. After a few seconds the operator pulls the LSGI button and the engine accelerates to about 96.5% and

ENGINE GROUND RUN

Preparing to tow the aircraft to an engine running bay

Cpl's left hand fingers on No 2 engine start button whilst the Sgt co-pilot monitors!

Nos 1 and 4 engines on nearly full power. Note the prop tip vortex

No 1 engine is pitch locked (note the 105% RPM on the 1st row, 2nd gauge)

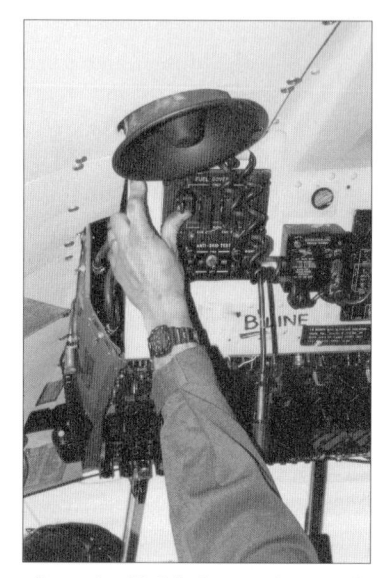

Operating No1 fuel governing switch

Phase angle check using the 'sophisticated' test kit during the air test at 15000ft

stabilises. The operator removes his hand from the condition lever.

Before 94% RPM the TD system limits the Turbine Inlet Temperature (TIT) to 830ºC by reducing the fuel by up to 50%. Above 94% the TD system limits the TIT to 1077ºC and also the compressor bleed valves close at the 5th and 10th stages.

The other engines are then started in the following sequence: number 4, 2 and 1. When the oil temperatures and pressures are within limits, the number 1 engine is shut down, using the emergency "T" handle. This ensures the operation of the feather valve "electrically" and that the propeller feathers. The "T" handle is reset and the engine started again. The numbers 4 and 1 engine throttles are moved towards the T/O position to achieve 19600 in lbs torque or 1077ºC TIT. The 2 throttles are retarded to a position which gives about 5000 in lbs torque. The RPM would be 98% and the number 1 engine TD system is set to LOCKED. The number 1 Fuel Governor Switch (FGS) above the engineer's overhead panel, is switched on, against spring pressure, and held. This action alters the tension of the spring "electrically" on the pilot valve (inside the valve housing). Both throttles are moved forward. The indications of the pitch–lock will be of the torque on number 1 engine rising slowly and its RPM increasing towards 103%. (If the throttles are then moved forward the RPM will not increase above 105% as the governor in the FCU will reduce the fuel flow – fuel topping). Both throttles are retarded to give 98% RPM (on number 1 engine) and a torque indication of about 7000 in lbs (2000 in lbs more than its previous non–pitch lock figures). The FGS is released and nothing happens because the pitch–lock teeth is constructed such that they allow the propeller blades to coarsen only. The TD switch is set to the AUTO position and both throttles are moved to achieve 19600 in lbs torque. The RPM, TIT, and torque of number 1 will be near or the same as number 4 engine. Both throttles are retarded towards the flight idle gate, their torque figures noted, and then to the NGI position. A reverse check is done on these two engines (the throttles of 2 and 3 engines will be moved to the Flight Idle position). All throttles are brought to the NGI position. The number 1 engine is now shut down by moving the condition lever to the FEATHER position. This ensures that the feather valve and its mechanical linkages have operated. Also, the FCU's fuel cock is closed mechanically. After starting number 1 again, further checks are carried out: to re–index the propellers, the NORMAL and MECHANICAL governing RPM, anti and de–icing checks and so on. It could take anything from 30 minutes to more than an hour for these checks. After the F700 paperwork is completed the aircraft needs an air test. Two electricians and their test kit will accompany the flight for "phase angle check" on the 4 propellers. This could again be completed within one hour or sometime more. To describe all these in this book is not possible as the "Engine Propulsion Power Plant Testing" section is in itself a large book"!

HEAVY RECTIFICATION (HEAVY WRECKS!) (HR)

Belonging to Support Flight, this section is run by a Sgt, 2 Cpls, one J/T and 2 SACs. They can be called to assist the flight line shift such as during the integrity and deep servicing on XV300 recently. Working only on day shift means this same crew has continuity on the task assigned to it. Their function is to look at the F700 for any heavy rectification due, such as fuel leaks, landing gear leg change, ramp and door change and so on.

An example is when the aircrew noticed a problem on the NLG after landing. They noted the problem on the F700 and debriefed the NCO IC airframe tradesman who found the axle to which the 2 wheels are mounted was misaligned. The necessary paperwork was raised and the HR took over. After jacking the aircraft, investigations began which showed that the symmetry of the NLG was misaligned with the uplock. The 2 wheels were removed, followed by the doors and the whole leg assembly, which exposed the trunnion. Checks proved that it was in fact the trunnions which were misaligned. This could have been caused by heavy shock loadings on landing or normal operation during a long period of time. The civilian company, Marshall aerospace replaced the trunnions. The HR team then re–assembled all the components and a functional check was carried out. The functional test, whilst on jacks, involved gear up and gear down, in normal and emergency selections and free fall (the speed of the forward airflow is replaced by a spring). The aircraft was then returned to the flight line where an air test proved the system was serviceable.

HEAVY WRECKS!

BLSS looks after 'SNOOPY'

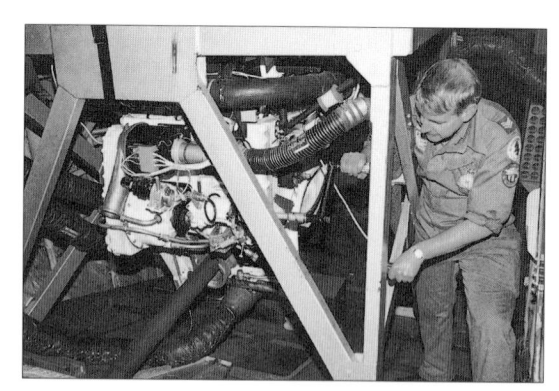

The Mk17 HDU's hand wind mechanism is being checked (after heavy servicing) on the CMk1K

Aircraft fully trestled for rectification work

Not a Singapore sling! A propeller sling being positioned

Port MLG wheel being re-fitted

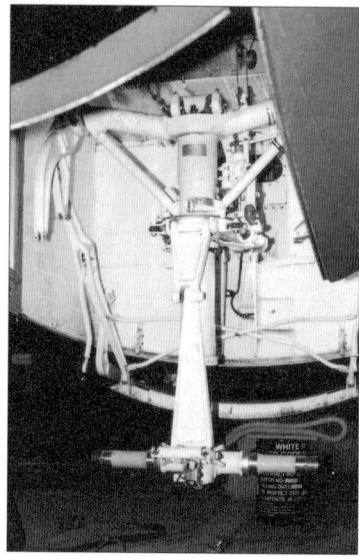

Nose wheels removed to expose assembly

Carrying out leak check on port static vent

LYNEHAM GROUNDCREW IN THE GULF

The biggest recent deployment of engineers from the A and B LSS and AES was, of course, the Gulf conflict in 1991. Approximately 150 airmen and officers (including WRAF) deployed into the conflict area in support of the massive air transport effort. Many more personnel were detached for short durations around the fighter bases in Britain and Germany to help them to deploy their personnel and equipment by Hercules to the Gulf. To cope with the loss of manpower at home, engineers from throughout the RAF were detached to Lyneham.

These people were integrated into all elements of the LSS and Aircraft Engineering Squadron. This assistance enabled both the LSS to continue with the full range of daily and scheduled maintenance despite record flying hours which, in some months, were twice the normal rate. One major consequence of these high flying rates was that the Primary Teams had to work shifts and were completing their servicings in 24 hours instead of three days.

Out of the conflict area, massive demands were placed on the engineers who, like many others were using makeshift facilities and making the best use of any accommodation available in very crowded airfields. Accommodation for the Hercules aircraft themselves also caused problems as a great diversity of types and nationalities of aircraft were operating from the same bases. Despite these problems, the engineers from the LSS at Lyneham performed magnificently, undertaking everything that could be required of them and more.

They even took on extra tasks such as assisting with the handling of visiting aircraft that had no ground crew of their own. But things were not all bad for the personnel deployed to the Gulf. Those stationed in Riyadh agreed that the food prepared by the field kitchen in a tent was "better than you get at home".

The success of our Forces throughout Operation Granby was due, in no small measure, to the support provided by the Hercules. The adage "first in, last out" certainly applies to the Hercules and all her support personnel, of which operation Granby and Operation Haven were prime examples.

It is unfair to single out any single squadron or one achievement throughout the campaign. Suffice to say that their success story, as a result of professionalism, loyalty and dedication of the aircrew and groundcrew alike, both in the Middle East and at Lyneham, as well as the motivation and determination of those attached to Lyneham throughout the campaign, speaks for itself and should represent an achievement to which they can all be proud.

Lyneham ground crew at one of the landing zones in the Gulf in 1991

HERCULES DETACHMENT (HERCDET) MOUNT PLEASANT AIRFIELD (MPA), FALKLAND ISLANDS (A and B LSS and AES).

A new chapter in the history of the Royal Air Force opened on 17th October 1982 with the arrival at Stanley of Hercules tanker aircraft XV192 and XV201, flown by Sqn Ldr David Farquhar OC Hercules Detachment (HERCDET) from No 24 Sqn and Flt Lt David Turner from No 30 Sqn. At the time, these aircraft were to become the workhorses of Lyneham's latest and most operational detachment, HERCDET at Stanley.

As the motto of the detachment "Support, Search, Save, Supply" indicates, the role of the Hercules Tanker, or C1K, in the Falklands, is not only varied but also revolutionary. Never before had RAF Hercules been used to support Air Defence Operations. The primary role of C1k as to give the Stanley based Phantom aircraft the capability, by air–to–air refuelling, to remain on Combat Air Patrol for extended periods. This capability greatly strengthened the Air Defence of the Falklands Islands Protection Zone (FIPZ). During 1992 the Phantoms were retired and replaced by the Tornado F3.

The secondary roles of the C1Ks are threefold; to provide Maritime Surveillance in and around the FIPZ, to provide Tactical Support through airdropping vital supplies and mail to the Garrison on South Georgia, and finally, to provide long range Search and Rescue cover for all military operations in and around the FIPZ. In addition, and complimentary to the air–to–air refuelling role, a considerable amount of fighter affiliation was carried out with the Phantom. The affiliation provided attack training for the Phantom crews and vital attack evasion training for the C.1K crews.

The HERCDET then became No 1312 Flight in November 1983 and it continued to maintain the high standard set by the initial crews. By now Stanley began to take shape as an RAF station and the airfield was cleared of most debris except the damaged Argentinean Pucaras and other aircraft which were laid at the roadside between the coastell and the ATC.

At Lyneham the aircraft is serviced by two separate lines, namely "A" Line (ALSS) and "B" Line (BLSS) separately and the flying squadrons are allocated aircraft from both these lines for their daily tasks. At Mount Pleasant Airfield (MPA)the detachment is like a family: aircrew and groundcrew together form part of the squadron and as such there is no inter–line or inter–squadron squabbles. They worked as a team successfully.

When MPA was opened in May 85 the Tristars of No 216 Sqn began to operate the schedules. No: 1312 Flight moved to MPA and was allocated their place of work on the north side of the airfield close to the Fire Section and the ATC. It had its own offices, accommodation for the QRA groundcrew and aircrew and a large storeroom in an area known as "Albert Square". The ISO containers outside provided a large storage room and portakabins provided a weekend recreational facility which was known as Queen Vic! For some reason the crew prefer to eat in the aircrew feeder a few yards. The Lyneham groundcrew at MPA spend their 4 months tour in a different environment. their shift duties are as follows:

a. 12 hours shift for 3 days.

b. 24 hours QRA standby duty on the 4th day.

c. 2 days off.

RAF MPA is the home for Sea King and Chinook HC.1 of No 78 Squadron, Tornado F.3s of No 1435 Flight and two Hercules C.1Ks with No 1312 Flight.

Technician assessing a minor snag

Hercules tanker refuelling a Phantom

Ground crew detachment at 1312 flight MPA (Jan '95)

CHAPTER FIVE

AIRCRAFT ENGINEERING SQUADRON (AES)
A AND B FLIGHTS

ORGANIZATION LINE DIAGRAM – AES

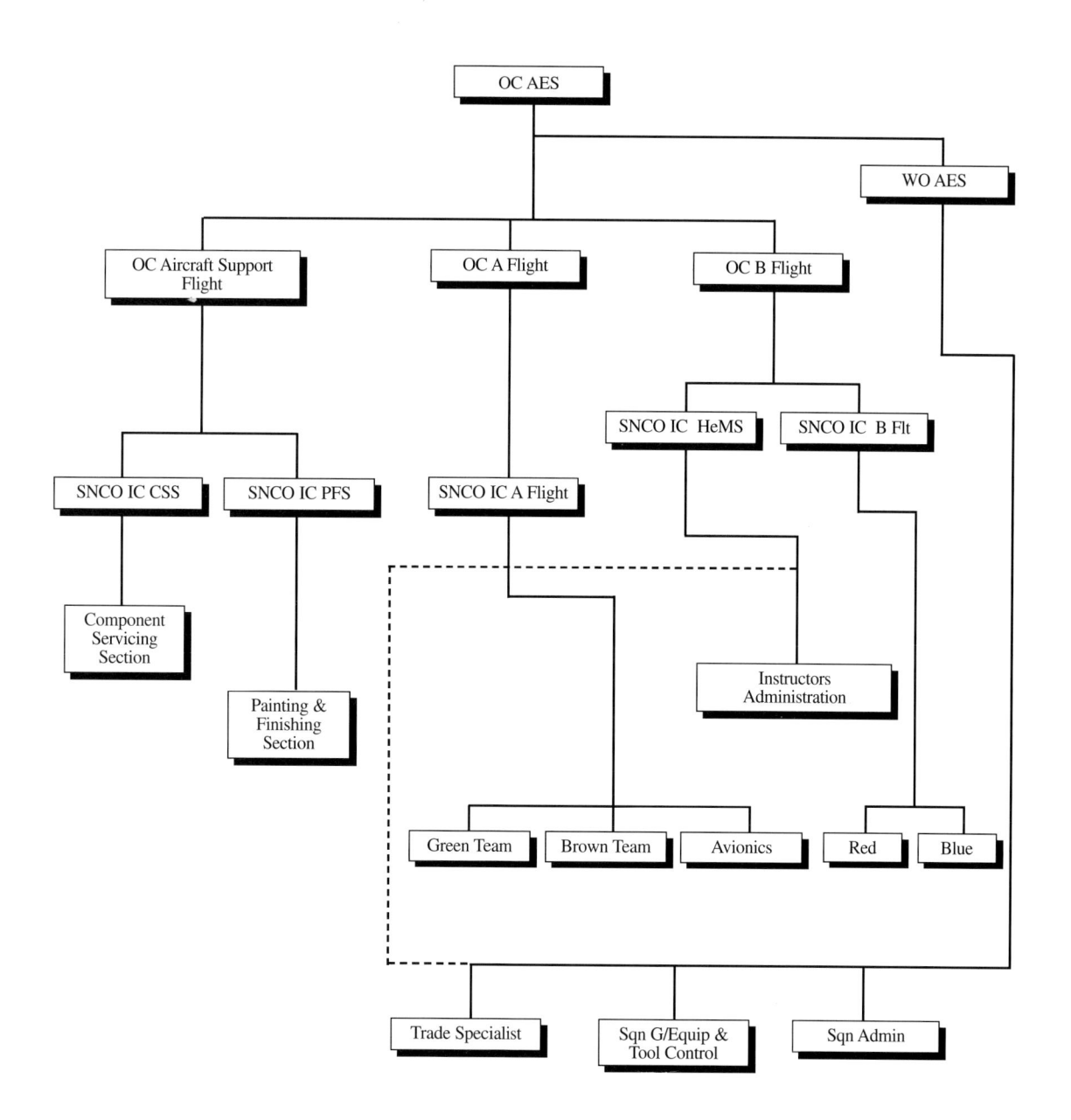

```
                              OC AES
                                │
        ┌───────────────────────┼───────────────────────┐
        │                       │                    WO AES
        │                       │
┌───────┴───────┐       ┌───────┼───────┐
OC Aircraft     │       │       │       │
Support Flight  │    OC A Flight │   OC B Flight
        │                       │       │
        │                       │   ┌───┴────┐
        │                       │ SNCO IC   SNCO IC
        │                       │  HeMS      B Flt
   ┌────┴────┐                  │
SNCO IC   SNCO IC          SNCO IC A Flight
 CSS       PFS
   │         │
Component  Painting &                    Instructors
Servicing  Finishing                    Administration
 Section   Section

        Green Team   Brown Team   Avionics   Red   Blue

           Trade Specialist   Sqn G/Equip &   Sqn Admin
                              Tool Control
```

AIRCRAFT ENGINEERING SQUADRON (AES). AES is based in C1 and C2 hangars and consists of maintenance element of 4 minor/minor star servicing teams, an avionics servicing team and the structural repair team.

Servicings take 24 days for a minor and 28 days for a minor star. A servicing team consists of 2 Chief Technicians, 5 Sergeants, 7 Corporals, 8 Junior Technicians and 10 Airmen. At the commencement of the servicing the aircraft is collected from the flight line and positioned in the hangar. It is then completely defuelled, raised on jacks and surrounded by a set of staging which is used to work on the upper surfaces of the aircraft. Once this is in place, works starts in earnest, with the non–destructive testing and the schedule maintenance running concurrently. Also any modifications and special engineering instructions are carried out, whilst any components that require replacement or servicing are removed and sent to the relevant bays. The Propulsion trade is kept busy at this time as they have all four engines to comprehensively overhaul along with their associated control runs.

When all these tasks are complete, the aircraft functional checks are carried out, including flying controls, hydraulics, undercarriages and any other systems that may have been disturbed. This may take between 2 to 3 days, depending on what problems arise. The aircraft staging is then removed and the aircraft is lowered to the ground and prepared for ground runs. The aircraft is taken out to the flight line where engine runs take place and the settings and performance of each engine is checked against laid down parameters. On completion of this phase the aircraft is taken back to the hangar where final quality checks are carried out and the preparation for air test is completed.

The final stage is the airtest, debrief and correcting any faults before returning the aircraft to the flight line to continue its daily flying task.

Also operating in C1 Hangar is the Avionics Servicing team, consisting of one Sergeant, 4 Corporals and one Junior Technician. This team is responsible for all Avionics servicing on the Squadron, as there are 4 aircraft servicing teams, they can at times be extremely busy. As aircraft approach their airtest date, they have to concentrate on that and this can mean them having to work shifts to fit in with all the other last minute things that are required.

The Structural Repair Team consisting of one Sergeant, 3 Corporals and 3 Junior Technicians maintains a supporting role for the servicing teams within AES, carrying out metal repairs and replacement of primary and secondary structure. The allocation of work is controlled by the Structure Liaison SNCO who is located in the squadron headquarters, also in C1 hangar. Anybody selected for this team has to demonstrate a good skill of hand at metal repairs and are required to complete a 3 week refresher course on the use of power tools and repair techniques.

Both hangars are very busy with a different challenge every week. Keeping these ageing aircraft serviceable is a major achievement and highlights the high professional standards of the many men employed in AES.

OC AES. The Officer Commanding AES is normally a Sqn Ldr and is responsible to OC Eng Wg for both Aircraft Servicing Flights and Aircraft Support Flights. He is there to provide airframe specialists advice, investigate and report defects during second line servicing and ultimately sign out a 'serviceable' Hercules aircraft at the end of second line servicing. Another aspect of his job is to liaise with OCs A and B Line Servicing Squadrons and OC EOPS on the flow of aircraft due for Minor and Minor Star servicing. Also working with OC EWSF for any embodiment of modifications. OC EES for electrical engineering and with OC MES on engine propeller and component support. He acts as OC Eng Wg's representative co–ordinating with civilian contractors and maintenance unit employees on aircraft repair work. He also oversees the training of personnel in the Station's Hercules Maintenance School.

WO IC AES. The Warrant Officer co–ordinates professional advice to OC AES from his trade Specialist SNCOs, who in turn co–ordinate this information from A and B Flights SNCOs. He maintains the standards and trade practices and allocates manpower to the flights. He controls and co ordinates the second line maintenance activities and reports to OC AES on any problems or delays that might occur. He has direct control of the Sqn Orderly Room. The Sqn Stores also comes under his wing. He maintains and distributes engineering documentation and makes sure that Marshall Aerospace of Cambridge civilian working party complies with their contract. He acts as the Quality Audit Controller for all AES Engineering. As with all Warrant Officers, he is seen as a "father figure" for the section and his door is always open should anyone need advice or help.

HERCULES AEDIT. The Hercules Aircraft Engineering Development and Investigation Team (H–AEDIT) was formed in Aug 87 to assist the aircraft Support Authority in resolving the problems associated with an ageing aircraft. Stationed at RAF Lyneham, this small team is tasked by HQLC. The H–AEDIT has been responsible for the introduction of many modifications and Special Trial Fits in support of Op Granby and Op Cheshire. These fits include chaff and flare, secure communications and protection for the main landing gear during rough strip operations.

The team of one officer, 9 SNCOs and an Adjutant is responsible for investigating engineering problems arising as a result of the aircraft's changing role, the constant need to reduce life cycle costs, the introduction of new equipment and an evolving maintenance policy. The work is technically demanding but highly rewarding and has given the members of the team the opportunity to travel overseas on trials programmes.

The think tank

HERCULES MAINTENANCE SCHOOL (HeMS). The HeMS is located within C2 hangar. It is a lodger unit and comes under direct control of Strike Command. The instructors here provide pre–employment training prior to working on the Hercules aircraft. About 50 courses are held annually in the 12 aircraft trades. Students are of all ranks including officers. Aircraft managers course for SNCOs and Officers are also held here. In addition, they provide training for civilians from aircraft companies, such as Marshall Aerospace and for Service personnel from Boscombe Down. Foreign Air Forces too, like Norway, come here for training. The RAF mechanics who are trained at Halton go to A or B Line for on the spot job training. For formal training they have to attend courses at HeMS. Sgts and Chief technicians who are selected to become Ground Engineers are given a 6 months full time course on all aircraft trades. The training methods and all training aids and kits used are the best. These are updated with changes in technology, modifications, SIs and so on. The instructors are all SNCOs with many years of experience on the Hercules.

Instructing instructors at HeMS

MINOR

MINOR servicing is due at every 1000 hours or 20 months and a MINOR STAR servicing at 2000 hours or 36 months.

MINOR. Some of the checks are as follows.

AIRFRAME. To facilitate a logical sequence the airframe is divided into four areas, namely:

a. Wings

b. Landing Gear

c. Flying Controls

d. Fuselage

Wings Team. The aircraft is prepared by the LSS prior to a washing at the wash bay. It is allowed to dry. Flaps are selected down and a fuel plot is done with the main tanks full. They look for fuel seeps and leaks and at the structure. With the aircraft on jacks the overwing refuel caps are removed for the laminar air duct to remove fuel vapour and fumes. Assuming a seep is found on the number 2 tank near its dry bay, a lengthy process is involved in locating and rectifying it.

Flying Controls. With AC electrical power on and the auxiliary hydraulic ground test valve open, this connects the aux system to the utility system) the control surfaces are checked for full and free range of movements, and the flaps are selected up and down. If, for example, as often happens the

Wash bay

hydraulic booster pack on the aileron is leaking beyond its acceptable limits it has to be replaced. The sequence of change is as follows:

a.   With electrical and hydraulic power off, the pipes to the pack are disconnected and blanked.

b.   The aileron control cable is disconnected at the input and output ends.

c.   The auto–pilot servomotor cable is disconnected.

d.   Two technicians (for Aileron pack) are needed to remove it from its mounting. The new one is fitted and after all the connections are made, a functional test is carried out.

e.   As the control cables have been disturbed a SNCO carries out a further independent inspection functional test. MAIN AND NOSE LANDING GEAR (MLG)(NLG). The 2 nose wheels are removed and the steering cable is disconnected from the steering collar. When the collar is lowered the bearing surface of the NLG shock strut will be exposed. The NDT team will inspect this for any damage or cracks using eddy current testing equipment. The assembly is then re–fitted and a functional test is carried out. On the MLG the wheels are removed. The electrical tradesman will remove the electronic anti–skid components and the NDT team will inspect the struts. The whole unit is then re–assembled and checked. The NLG and MLG doors are inspected and lubricated.

FUSELAGE – EXTERNAL.   A thorough inspection of the fuselage skin and the windows is carried out.

FUSELAGE – INTERNAL. The soundproofing is removed and the panels are checked. All the fire extinguishers are removed and sent to the structures bay. The 10 emergency water flasks are removed and sent to ASF. The signal pistol is removed from the navigator's station and sent with the 14 (6 red, 4 green, 4 yellow) cartridges to the armoury. The emergency first aid kit is sent to Medical Centre for safe keeping. The ramp and door are tested and the elsan and the urinal area inspected. Special attention is paid to the longeron in this area and any corrosion is removed. If after scraping the paint the corrosion is excessive, an NDT inspection is called for.

PROPULSION. An engine run is carried out, if possible, prior to the aircraft being towed into the hangar. One propulsion tradesman per engine, and one on the flight deck carries out the following checks simultaneously. On the QEC the air intake is inspected with the naked eye but for the turbine section a boroscope is used. On the propeller all the four blades are inspected for damage paying particular attention to the de–icing rubber boot (element) and for any delamination on the root area. The QEC is stripped of all the removable panels which will expose the maze of ancillary components such as cables, pipes, hoses, bleed air ducts, mechanical linkages and so on. Servicing on the RGB and the Compressor, Combustion Module (CCM) is performed in an orderly manner. A misplaced tool involves a lengthy 'loose article check'. On the RGB the NTS plunger is wound out, greased and re–adjusted. At the rear face of the RG the following components are removed: starter motor, generator, hydraulic pump and the tacho generator. The drive for each of these components is checked for wear and tear and is then lubricated. If, for example the generator drive is damaged or worn the QEC is removed. The propeller is removed and kept on a prop stand but the QEC is sent to PRF for deeper servicing. If, every drive is serviceable, the seals are inspected and all the components re–fitted. The engine control cables are removed and serviced on the work bench. They look for wear and any worn cables or pulleys replaced.

All the filters from the oil, hydraulics and fuel systems are replaced, contents drained and replenished. At the same time the OOPS are done. As the QEC is divided into zones, the tradesmen now inspect for cracked pipes, chafing (cables and pipes), corrosion, broken or missing 'P' clips (these secure and support the many loops of electrical cables and pipes). The two igniters are removed and swapped (if one is unserviceable it is replaced). On the propeller section's pump housing the hydraulic fluid is drained and replenished. The dome cap and transfer tube is removed to check that the teeth that mate with the root end of the blades are not damaged. When all the servicing is complete the engine controls are rigged and checked for correct movement. A further independent check of this is done by an SNCO. A 'BETA' schedule check is done on the propeller valve housing whilst the flight deck propulsion tradesman moves the throttle levers. The dry bay checks for the fuel and hydraulic valves would have been done by now. To test that the extinguishing agent can reach the engine, the emergency 'T' handle is disconnected by the electrical tradesman. The team then disconnect the pipe at the joint near the aircraft bottles. Pressurised air is introduced through the pipe and checked at the outlets on the engine. At the end of the servicing, two days are set aside to ground run the engines and test the pressurisation of the aircraft. This involves checking all throttle lever settings from take–off/max power to full reverse torque and also all condition lever positions including feathering the propellers. This can mean a lot of starting, checking and stopping. All systems associated with the engines are leak and functionally checked, adjustments are made and when complete the aircraft is prepared for a post minor air test.

ELECTRICS. The electrical tradesmen firstly assist the propulsion and airframe trades by the removal of electrical equipment which might otherwise hinder or obstruct them in removing or rectifying their trade based equipment and components. For example, as in the case of removing the undercarriage electrical conduits, terminal blocks and transducers for the airframe tradesmen to remove the MLG struts. The electrical servicing sequence is simplified by dividing the aircraft into zones ie from the nose to the tail and from wing to wing. On the flight deck the tradesmen check all the engine and engineer's overhead panel instruments and gauges, along with the hydraulics, lox and the flap gauges on the co–pilot's instrument panel and the rudder, aileron and elevator trim tab gauges on the Captain's panel. On the generators the terminal connections are checked. All the lights (flight deck and cargo compartment), micro switches, including those for the ramp and door and the air–conditioning thermostats. To check the flap asymmetric brake has applied, the terminal block near the flap control unit is shorted. The emergency Brake Selector Valve (BSV) is reset and further test selections are carried out, each time the BSV is reset. Any modification kits to be installed will be done at this stage and any life expired equipment will be replaced. Any unserviceabilities will be diagnosed, then rectified or replaced. For example, the F700 shows the following unserviceabilities:

1.   Number two engine fuel gauge inoperative ...

2.   During test the number one fire system indication on the emergency 'T' handle is intermittent.

For number one, the fault is probably not on the gauge as the flight line would have already checked this. The fault could be anywhere from the fuel tank transmitters (capacitances), power supply or anywhere in the cable runs right up to the gauge. If the gauge indicates a full scale deflection, the continuity check using the test kit will prove the fault to be the break up of the insulation block connection (at the bottom of the fuel tank) caused by water seeping into it. It is then replaced.

For the number two (the engine fire system) the circuit breaker, relay and the current limiter are checked using a fluke multimeter. If all these are good and the continuity check of the wiring up to the Fire Detection Control Unit (FDCU) is satisfactory, the FDCU is replaced and a functional test is carried out.

AVIONICS. This team is responsible for the aircraft avionics equipment such as the radio and radar. The work carried out on a minor and minor star servicing includes the removal and replacement of the HF radio aerial cables, inspection and testing of all the avionic equipment, any outstanding modifications and the rectification of any unserviceabilities.

The tradesmen will often remove the equipment "black boxes" to provide access to the areas that other tradesmen (propulsion, airframe and electrical) need to work on. One of these jobs is concerned with a corrosion check of a bulkhead and necessitates the removal of all the under flight deck avionic boxes and their mounting trays, these include radio, navigation and auto pilot. This in itself can cause problems, as the aircraft is over 28 years old and the soldered wiring does not take kindly to being disturbed.

Any long history of avionics problems is investigated using the specialised test equipment

Performing an STI to the brake control valve (pilot's side)

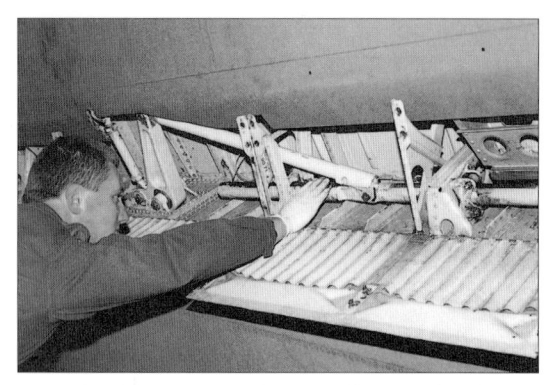

Applying grease to the port aileron push rod

Left technician servicing flight deck CAU. Right side, elevator booster assembly

Technician pointing to the elevator torque output lever

NDT checks on engine longeron bolts

Adjusting the flap track roller bearings

Bleeding the brakes

Inspecting the rear Lord mount

I think I've got it!

Working in confined space

Independent check on engine controls. Note the tensionmeter

Changing the starter solenoid

Safety wiring the fuel heater and strainer

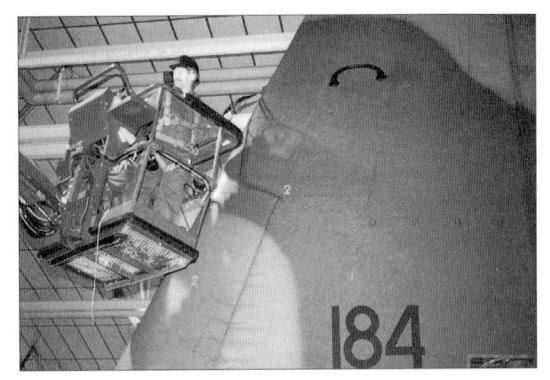

Changing HF aerials. Note the hangar roof!

Replacing damaged wiring

Checking wiring diagram

Replacing a fuel gauge

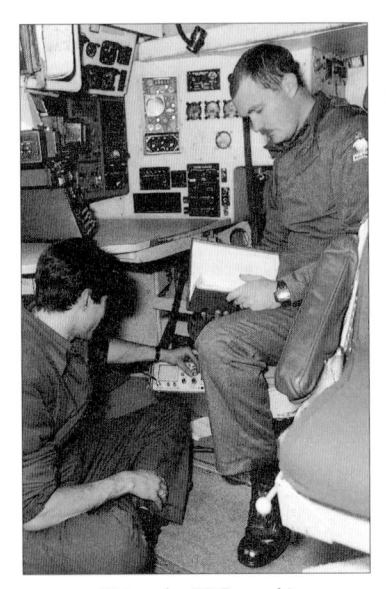

Using the TDR test kit

Checking the wiring inside a circuit breaker panel

Airframe chiefs! working on the forward pressure bulkhead

Vertical fin about to be re-fitted

Aircraft is moved under fin for final alignment

Crane in position to lift fin

Replacing the aft sloping aileron

Preparing the fin base before fitment

Technician removing corrosion on aft sloping aileron

Engine removed from aircraft by crane

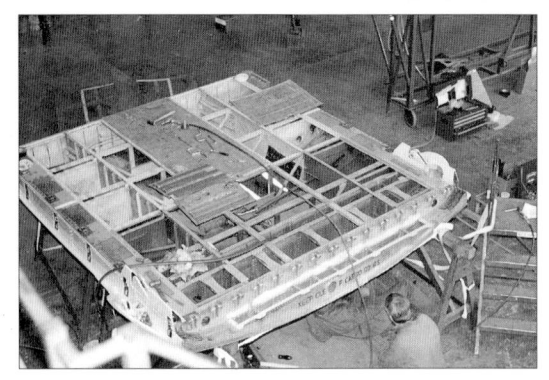

Ramp with panels removed

Replacing upper skin panel by Marshall Aerospace technician

Stripping the "D" panels

Tightening the BASOV

Re-fitting panel at rear of FS245

View of nose of the aircraft (radome removed)

Removing the engine driven hydraulic pump

Tug pushing the aircraft

View from inside the hangar

View of flight deck with crew seats removed

View of staging. No 2 engine removed

Leading edge and other panels removed

Aircraft kept rigid by belly trestles

such as the Combined Comms Test Set and the Time Domain Reflectometer (TDR). The TDR uses an electronic pulse which is timed and measured for its reflected energy, this enables the technician to determine exactly where the wiring is broken or damaged.

One problem encountered by the avionics team is caused by 'rolling robs'. If there is a shortage of equipment, for instance a radar scanner, then one is 'robbed' from an unserviceable aircraft to make another serviceable. This leads to another rob if one cannot be found in time for its air test and return to the line and so the cycle continues. Other work can be caused by the servicing carried out by other trades, such as the airframes replacement of a flying control booster pack, this means a full auto pilot functional and independent check.

At the end of the servicing the radar and HF radio require functional checks outside of the hangar, because of the radiated power of these equipments. The HF for instance gives out the equivalent of half a single bar electric fire and it can burn if you get to close to the aerial!

Two examples of the servicing required by the F700 are:

1. Port Compass Detector Unit needs replacing.

2. Pilots Windscreen cracked.

The Detector Unit provides magnetic information to the compass system and when it is replaced a compass swing is required to complete the job. This entails the aircraft being taken to a certified compass swing bay at the far side of the airfield, accurately aligned with various headings and the compass system adjusted accordingly. It is a time consuming job and can often take more than a day to carry out successfully.

The pilot's windscreen can only be removed after the ADI and HSI, amongst other indicators, have been removed to allow the airframe trades access. This requires functional checks to be carried out on the disturbed equipment when all work in the area has been completed.

MINOR STAR

This servicing is carried out every 2000 flying hours or every 36 months. It involves all of the servicings of the MINOR plus a further 4 days for additional work, such as:

a. **Airframe.** The MLG screwjacks and the shock strut oleos (if needed) are removed and sent to the components bay for servicing. The track shoes (upper and lower) and the drag pin bush are checked for wear and tear and a deeper NDT inspection is carried out. On the NLG, the jacking plug is removed, inspected and re–fitted or replaced. On each of the elevators, the leading edge is removed to inspect the anti–icing ducts and clamps for any damage. The port and starboard trailing edges are removed for deeper inspection, including the components of the trim tab section. The flaps are removed and inspected. The flap tracks, screwjacks and all associated components are checked and greased.

b. **Propulsion.** The engine generators are removed and their drives are inspected and lubricated. The engine throttle cables are checked for wear and tear and their tension adjusted, using a cable tension meter. On the AAR probe the NRVs, and on the centre dry bay, the fuel manifold's fuel clamps are checked for leaks.

c. **Electrics.** The two invertors and the four TRUs under the flight deck floor are removed and sent for bay servicing. The serviceable ones are then fitted and tested during the post engine ground run.

d. **Avionics.** The integrity of all the aerials are checked.

PAINTERS AND FINISHERS

Responsibility for the maintenance of all Hercules Aircraft, at Royal Air Force Lyneham is controlled by Engineering Wing. Aircraft Engineering Squadron operate three second line Servicing Flights, oneof which is Aircraft Support Flight (ASF). This is divided into two sections, Component Servicing and Painters and Finishers, who are responsible for the refurbishment on all off aircraft components. ASF is the Head Quarters for some 44 Painting and Finishing personnel, responsible for the refurbishment of all Surface Finishes on Hercules Aircraft, MT and Ground Support Equipment, dispersed throughout the Station.

Unlike normal painting requirements, ie your car or house, the Hercules aircraft requires a surface finish to perform in extreme weather conditions, and most importantly to protect the aircraft from corrosion for the longest possible period between

FS assessing damage

major rework, and at the same time meet the optimum operational performance, making this is a tall order. However, this has been achieved by the Aviation finishing world who have over the past 20 years given us the Paint Finishes to meet all modern day requirements, such as flexible and light weight two–pack paints.

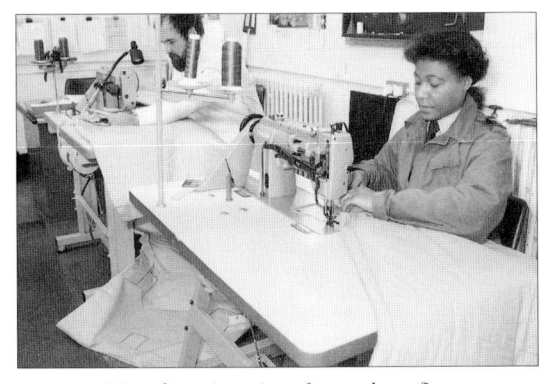

Manufacturing aircraft soundproofing

The majority of work carried out by almost 40 Painters and Finishers at Lyneham, is within Aircraft Engineering Squadron, particularly on the 4 aircraft Minor servicing teams. Here they carry out all surface finish requirements, from underbody protection to external and internal paint finishes. Overall there are some 10 different paint schemes on the Hercules aircraft. Our work also includes the painting requirements on first line and aircraft primary servicing, along with special tasks. One such task was the painting of Hercules aircraft to commemorate the 25th anniversary and the 75th anniversary of the Royal Air Force.

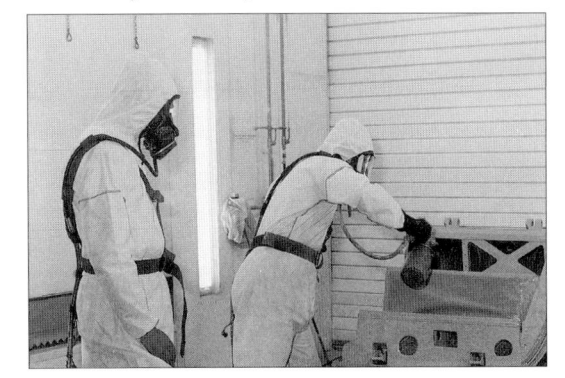

Refurbishing the steps of crew entrance door

They are also responsible for the internal refurbishment of the aircraft sound proofing, with some 1,200 panels per aircraft, and this is carried out in the trim bay within Aircraft Support Flight. Internal Safety markings are also manufactured on base, with 150 per aircraft. Again all decals are manufactured on base by the painter and finisher trade.

Painter and Finishers are a unique trade within the engineering frame work, as everyone can see at a glance what they've accomplished.

COMPONENT SERVICING SECTION

The role of the Component Servicing Section at Lyneham is to afford a second line maintenance facility for the Hercules fleet. The section is sub divided into 7 separate bays, each of which have a significant function in the type of specialist engineering support provided. The role of each bay is best outlined in separate paragraphs.

HYDRAULIC BAY This bay services some 80 hydraulic components, ranging from a complex flying control booster pack to a simple non return valve. The depth of servicing depends on the type of rectification required. The component may require a complete overhaul because it has consumed all its flying hours, or it may require simple fault diagnosis and replacement of piece parts before testing and returning to stock. The bay also carries out pre–issue checks on components serviced by 4th line contractors.

AIR CONDITIONING BAY Here they carry out routine overhaul and repair to some 36 components that are fitted in the aircraft's air conditioning system. A large proportion of the work is a direct result of a system failure, requiring fault diagnosis and piece part replacement.

ACCESSORIES BAY In the Accessories Bay various mechanical components from the aircraft's flying control and undercarriage systems are routinely overhauled or rectified if failure should occur during service. Included in the maintenance of some components is the use of magnetic particle non–destructive testing, used to identify flaws in component parts. The bay also carries out routine servicing to the in–flight refuelling probe, nozzle and basket. In addition to the maintenance work there is a requirement to manufacture wire rope control cables and the rigid and flexible pipes that are used in the aircraft's hydraulic, fuel and engine lubrication systems.

STRUCTURES BAY The Structures Bay carries out in–depth skin repairs to major components such as flaps, ailerons, elevators, cargo ramps and doors. It is normal for these items to crack from fatigue or sustain bird strike damage. Repairs to these can be very complex and take in excess of 3 weeks to complete. Much skill of hand and attention to detail is required for this type of work, and it is considered a specialist part of the airframe trade.

SEAT BAY Work in the Seat Bay involves routine 2nd line maintenance to the aircrew seats, crew door, fire extinguishers and water flasks. Some structural repair work is required on the door and seats.

TYRE BAY Situated in J3 Hangar, this Bay carries out routine 2nd line maintenance to Hercules wheels and brake units. It is a busy section with a high turn round of components.

OXYGEN BAY This Bay carries out several maintenance tasks, including routine overhaul and repair to oxygen regulators, lox converters and portable oxygen sets. Additionally, the Bay provides gaseous oxygen to all user sections on the unit. It also calibrates all oxygen gauges and NBC test equipment.

Routine bay service on flight deck water seperator

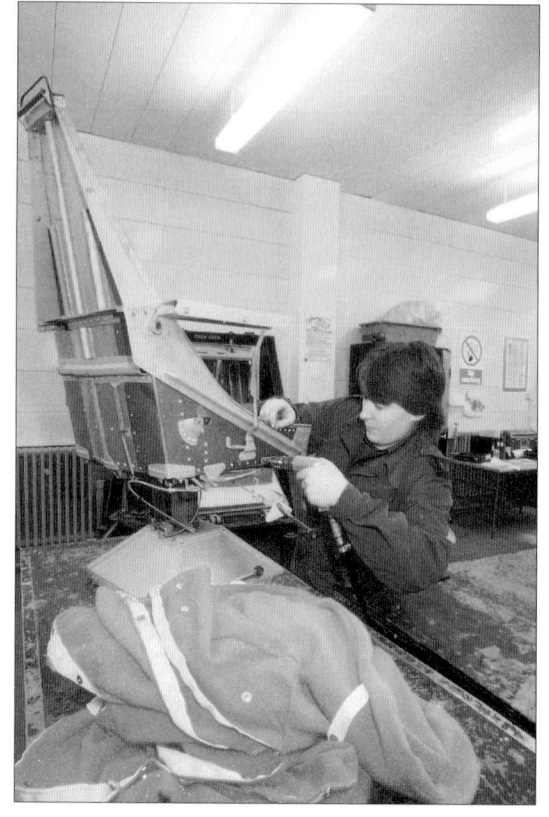

Bay service on crew seat

Assessories bay – routine bay servicing of flap and undercarriage components

Repair to the leading edge. Floor panel repair (background)

Assembling main wheels

Hydraulic pressure test on nose wheel steering cylinder

ORGANIZATION LINE DIAGRAM – MES

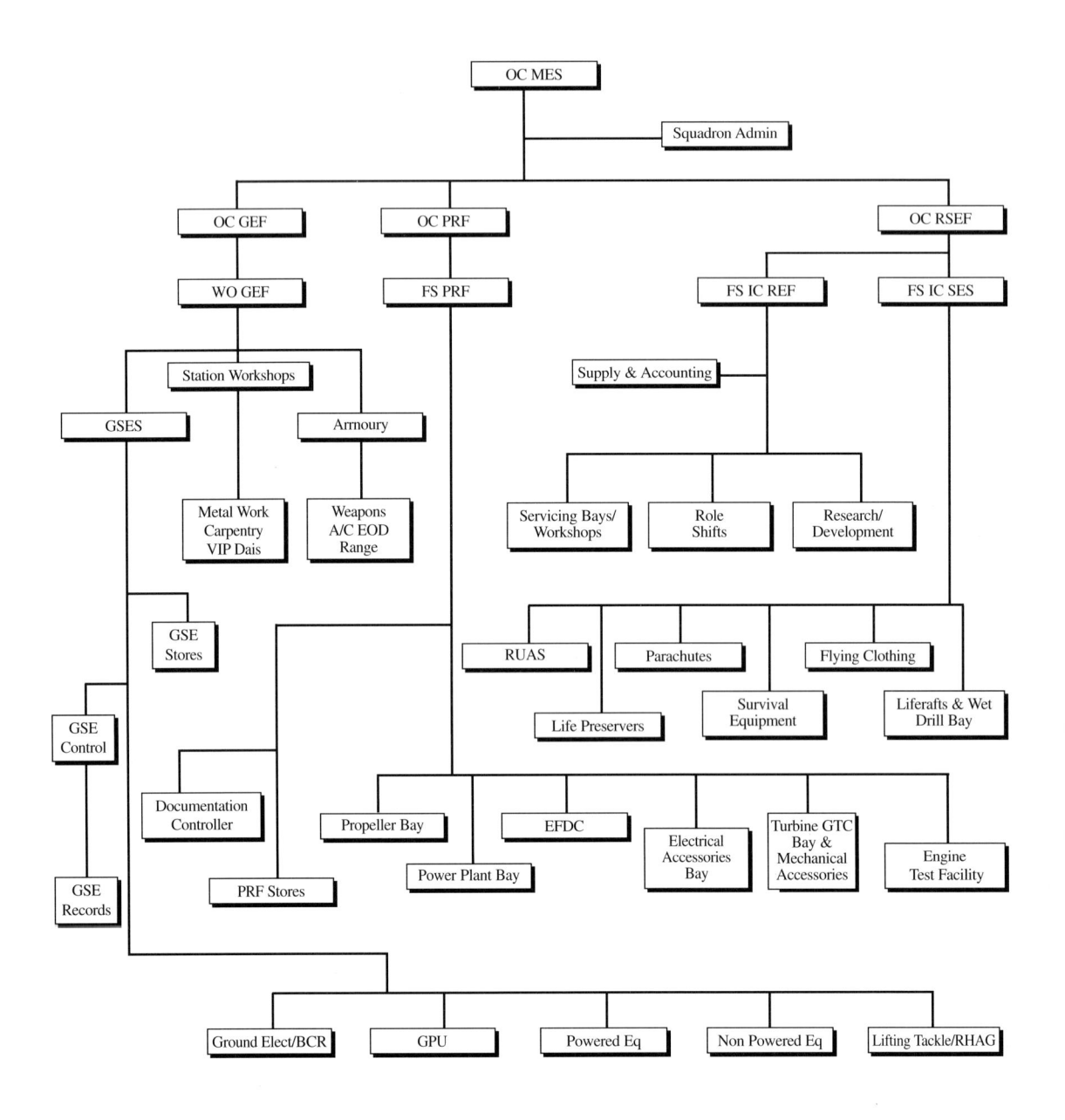

- OC MES
  - Squadron Admin
  - OC GEF
    - WO GEF
      - Station Workshops
        - Metal Work / Carpentry / VIP Dais
      - Armoury
        - Weapons / A/C EOD Range
      - GSES
        - GSE Stores
        - GSE Control
        - GSE Records
        - Ground Elect/BCR
        - GPU
        - Powered Eq
        - Non Powered Eq
        - Lifting Tackle/RHAG
  - OC PRF
    - FS PRF
      - Documentation Controller
      - PRF Stores
      - Propeller Bay
      - Power Plant Bay
      - EFDC
      - Electrical Accessories Bay
      - Turbine GTC Bay & Mechanical Accessories
      - Engine Test Facility
  - OC RSEF
    - FS IC REF
      - Supply & Accounting
        - Servicing Bays/Workshops
        - Role Shifts
        - Research/Development
    - FS IC SES
      - RUAS
      - Life Preservers
      - Parachutes
      - Survival Equipment
      - Flying Clothing
      - Liferafts & Wet Drill Bay

CHAPTER SIX

MECHANICAL ENGINEERING SQUADRON (MES)

The various flights belonging to MES are scattered around the Station, on the Domestic, A, B and D sites. The General Engineering Flight (GEF) is on the domestic site. The Propulsion Flight (PRF) is on D Site, whilst the Role Equipment and Support Flight (RSEF) is on the C and domestic sites.

PROPULSION REPAIR FLIGHT (PRF)

SERVICING CONTROL. The servicing controller is responsible for maintaining accurate records via the Documentation Controller. When an unserviceable engine arrives for rectification, it is also given a bay servicing if it has done more than 150 flying hours after its previous servicing. Sometimes, only major components need to be changed. Either way, Eng records send a complete set of log cards which also have the serial numbers of the components. The engine arrives from AES or LSS's with MOD Form 731 for components that are unserviceable. These are then noted and transferred to another folder and kept in the office. The U/S engine with the MOD F731 is sent to the Power Plant Bay – Engine 'BUILD' section and is moved to the engine "grave yard". From there, when its turn arrives, the engine is collected, dismantled and sent to various sections where they raise the necessary paper work as and when the components are serviced/replaced. They then transfer this information to the new cards held at the Servicing Control. Daily, this information is also fed into the computer. At the end of the Servicing period, about 98% of the records would already have been in the computer. When the cards are completed these are then checked against the records in the computer. As all the independent and quality control checks have been completed by now, the finished engine is sent to the Engine Test Facility for testing. When it is serviceable, it is returned to PRF where the engine and propeller are stored separately by their stores. When this engine is issued, the log cards pack–up goes to Eng Records and the record of items changed is noted on MOD 750A. The F750A accompanies the engine and the user squadron transfer these details on to the F700. The record kept in the computer is not destroyed.

The graveyard

POWER PLANT BAY (PPB) – 'BUILD' SECTION. The PPB carries out everything from routine bay servicing to full strip of the engine for Compressor, Combustion Module (CCM) change. The U/S engine, sometimes complete with its propeller, is wheeled in on its high stand to the PPB from the "grave yard". As the components are dismantled, the necessary paperwork is raised and accompanies them to the various bays in PRF. If an engine has flown for more than 150 hrs since its last servicing, or it comes with some unserviceabilities, it is also given a routine bay servicing. Other engines arrive for 'minor' servicing. Life expired CCM is replaced by new CCM and other new components fitted.

The stages of dismantling for a life expired CCM are as follows:

a. The propeller's spinner is removed followed by the dome assembly with its hydraulic fluid. Then the pitch lock regulator assembly and finally the nut securing the propeller assembly are removed from the propeller shaft. The propeller is then removed, complete with the propeller control assembly, by a hoist on to a stand and sent to the propeller bay.

b. The bottom tray which houses the oil cooler and oil cooler flap is then removed. The tray is, in effect, a large shallow pan which houses all the pipework for drainage such as leaks from the Reduction Gearbox (RGB) or oil tank. Next, the fairing which houses the air intake scoop is removed.

c. The air intake is then removed.

d. The nacelle unit, which houses the power section is called the Quick Engine Change (QEC). It is then lifted by a hoist on to a build up truck. The truck's front end secures the RGB and the aft end the CCM. The QEC nacelle is then removed from the power section (RGB and CCM) on to a low stand.

ASSEMBLING THE ENGINE

This is a workable stand providing access to all components.

e. The CCM is removed from the RGB, allowing access to the safety coupling and the torque shaft. The drive shaft of the tacho generator, EDP, starter and the generator are examined. The starter motor is removed and if the drive is worn, a new RGB is called for.

Between the processes from a. to e. numerous electrical cable plugs, hydraulic, fuel, bleed air, hoses and pipes and mechanical cables and rods have to be removed meticulously in stages. The 'build up' of the new power section begins separately with the CCM on the roll over stand and the RGB on its stand. In stages, the reverse e. to a. process takes place. After completion, an independent check is called for as the throttle cables have been removed and serviceable ones fitted. The servicing control section completes the paperwork and instructs the UETF section to test the power section before certifying it 'serviceable'. If an engine comes in for a minor bay service or with a problem such as 'smelly air conditioner', the process from stages a. to e. still applies. The 'build' section has a mammoth task on the bay service to locate the fault, strip and rebuild.

CCM arrives in container

CCM removed from container

CCM hoisted to the roll over stand

Roll over stand enables CCM to be turned to any angle

Building the RGB

RGB hoisted on to build up stand

RGB and CCM in their respective stands

CCM hoisted from roll over stand on to build up truck

RGB and CCM about to be joined

Close up of air inlet housing accessory drive housing, and ancillary equipment

RGB and CCM joined – forming the power section

Building – adding more ancillary equipment

Engine nacelle on stand

Nacelle hoisted on to power section – not an easy task!

Power section is fitted into nacelle – QEC

Fitting air intake scoop assembly

Tray built up and added behind the air intake on to the lower half of nacelle

Adding further ancillary equipment

Propeller assembly arrives on stand

Propeller hoisted out of stand and prepared prior to fitment

Alignng the propeller

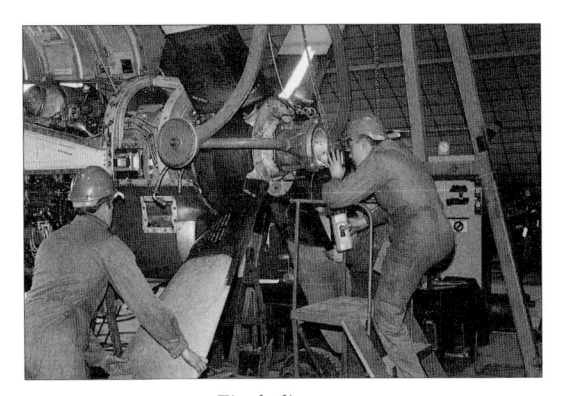

Final alignment

Torqueing

Propeller and QEC joined

Adding more components

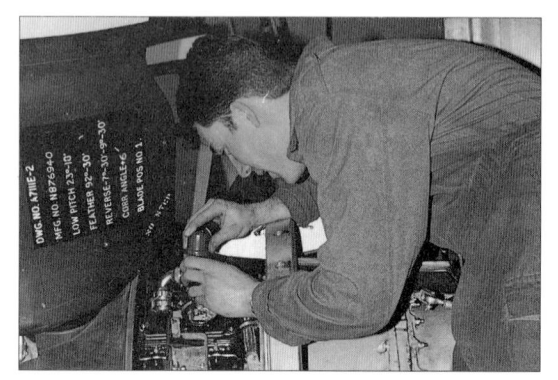

Adjusting the Beta schedule in the valve housing

Nearly there! Final preparation for test bed

Final engine run on UETF

BUILD'S PICTURE GALLERY

TURBINE, GTC AND MECHANICAL ACCESSORIES BAY. This bay deals mainly with mechanical components. From the 'build' section an array of mechanical equipment and components arrive for routine bay servicing, minor service or for rectification. Some of the major work they undertake is as follows:

a. STARTER MOTOR. If it has been used for more than 150 flying hours a bay minor service is given. The outer casing is removed to check the wear on the turbine. The oil is drained, flushed and replenished with a general look for particles. A full service which includes the inspection of the quill drive and, if damaged, it is changed.

b. TURBINE CHANGE. If an engine has a turbine problem which cannot be rectified, or is life expired, it is replaced with a new one. But for one that comes for example with damaged stator blades, the sequence of stripping and further inspection is as follows: The 18 pairs of thermocouples, the 6 combustion liners, the 2 light houses (oil transfer tubes) and lastly the bearings are removed. After stripping the damaged first stage stator, the blades are replaced individually. If on further inspection the first or second stage rotor blades are damaged, the turbine unit is re–assembled and sent to the manufacturer who has the capability of rectifying it.

c. GAS TURBINE COMPRESSOR (GTC). For a routine service, the GTC is run on a test bed to determine its state. It is then brought back to the bay and the outer casing is removed. The plenum chamber, combustion chamber and igniter are inspected and replaced if necessary. After draining the oil, the fuel filter is changed and the system flushed and replenished. Routine service is at 500 hours and replacement at 750 hours. If a GTC arrives from the flight line with a problem like 'oil mist from the breather' – noticeable during the GTC start cycle, the fault diagnosis is done on the test bed which will lead to which seal they have to change in the cluster. But, if an internal oil seal is leaking, the GTC is sent to the manufacturer where the seal is replaced.

Turbine build

d. ENGINE CONTROL ASSEMBLY. The cables, pulleys and gimbals that connect from the Quick Release Bulkhead (QRB) to the FCU and the Co–ordinator are stripped. The cables are cleaned, worn parts replaced and re–built. The short rod that connects the Co–ordinator to the bell crank on the

Servicing condition lever and throttle control assembly

CCM and the long rod from the CCM to the RGB bell crank and a fruther linkage to the valve housing, are sent to RAF Brize Norton for NDT checks.

e.   **LORD MOUNTS.** The two on the front and the one on the rear which holds the engine on to the engine frame (QEC) are stripped and re–assembled using new parts.

EARLY FAILURE DETECTION CENTRE (EFDC). The ability to determine the state of the engine is the function of the EFDC. The 'build' section will remove the two magnetic plugs from the bottom of the accessory drive housing and the compressor, and the one from the RGB. These are sent here for analysing. Each plug will have a certain amount of dirt, oil and metal stuck to it. It is given an ultrasonic bath, which removes everything except the ferrous metal. The ferrous metal is then transferred to a clear transparent tape and measured in units on a Debris tester. If the measurement is at an acceptable level it is stored in a record folder against its own aircraft and engine number. For example XV 222 engine number will have 4 pages for the engine and 4 pages for the RGB position. There are spaces left to record the date the sample was taken, the airframe hours and debris measured

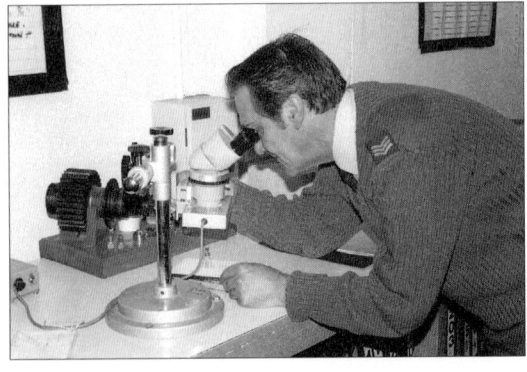

Looking through microscope to identify debris on magnetic plug

units. From this the state of the engines can be monitored. If the debris' units increases, the frequency of the magnetic plug checks are increased for closer monitoring. Eventually, if it is excessive, an engine change is called for. The 12 magnetic plugs for each aircraft are cleaned, stored in a box and issued to the flight line, where it travels with the aircraft. Magnetic plug checks are due every 65 ± 10 flying hours. There is one person on call for RAF Mount Pleasant Airfield in the Falkland Islands.

SHOP FLOOR – PROPELLER BAY. The propeller assembly, whether for normal bay servicing/maintenance or rectification, can come from the 'build' section or directly from AES or 'A' or 'B' Lines. The propeller control unit (valve housing and pump housing) is separated from the assembly and sent to the pump housing bay. For a normal bay maintenance an internal and external leak rate test is carried out on the propeller by connecting an hydraulic hose to the propeller assembly via a test piece. Using warmed pressurised hydraulic fluid, the blade angle movement is checked from full reverse to fully feathered position. To remove the large mechanical pitch stop at the flight idle blade angle position of 23º–24º, a break through pressure of 240–280 psi is introduced. This allows the 3 wedges in the low pitch assembly to move inwards causing the cam assembly to ride over and reduce the blade angle below 23º. The pressure required to unfeather the blades shall not be less than 180 psi. When this pressure is applied in the fully feathered position it removes the feather latches to enable the blades to move to a finer blade angle. Each of the four blades is checked on a test rig for the blade angle and the leading edge to the trailing edge is inspected. The mark 1 eyeball then looks for 'spots' on the blades. After fitting new seals, it is then assembled. The dynamic balance of the propeller is checked at the UETF. If the blades are pitted or damaged they are replaced. Blending is achieved if a blade is gouged.

PUMP HOUSING BAY. The propeller control unit (CU) has a life cycle of 4500 hours, after which it is reconditioned by Dowty Rotol. During this life, any that come in complete with the propeller from AES or the lines with suspected oil leaks, are bay serviced. The CU is made up of the valve housing (VH) and the pump housing (PH).

The maintenance mainly consists of removing the anti and de–icing brush pack and sending it to the electrical bay. The VH which is attached to the top

Bay maintenance of valve housing

Pressure testing of the propeller control unit

Torqueing of the propeller hub bolts

Preparing propeller for hydraulic test

Fitting control unit

Supervisor's Inspection

Marking up of Teflon strip position

of the PH is removed and sent to the VH bay. The Low Oil Level float switch is removed, tested and re–fitted provided it is serviceable, otherwise replaced. A bay serviced VH is fitted and the CU is then pressure tested. This is done by fitting a test fixture which simulates the propeller tail shaft. A hoist is attached to the CU bracket, an airline hose is fitted to the atmospheric breather and pressurised to 3 psi. It is then lowered into a container filled with white spirit which will show up any leaks. If a leak is found from the rear Gitz seal, for example, it is replaced and the CU is re–tested. A serviceable brush pack is then fitted. The CU is now ready awaiting fitment to a serviceable propeller.

VALVE HOUSING BAY. The bay servicing of the valve housing involves mounting it on a test rig where the correct voltage and resistance from the throttle anticipation potentiometer and speed bias servo motor (balances the fly weights) are checked. It is then moved to the work bench where the supply and standby filter is changed. On the 'alpha' shaft, the condition of the mechanical cams and the cam and pin assembly, are examined. Any worn or damaged components are changed and a full functional test is carried out electrically and hydraulically. On the test rig, the 'beta' shaft range of movement is checked for correct blade angle movement as the beta shaft controls the propeller in the ground range, for example during ground taxying. The valve housing in this bay is known as the 'mechanical brain' as there are numerous mechanical moving parts on this unit. They control the propeller on the ground 'beta' range from providing the correct blade angle for starting the engine to controlling the blades to a maximum of minus 7° blade angle during full reverse. This mechanical brain was born in 1954 and is still going strong and is testimony to the successful number of sorties during conflicts and peace times, every hour of the day (over 50 countries operate the C130).

ELECTRICAL ACCESSORIES BAY. The routine servicing of some of the equipment is as follows:

a. The anti and de–icing brush pack assembly is cleaned. The complete soldering of the new four pairs of electrical cables ('spider') to the terminals, connectors and carbon brushes takes place on the test bench. The polarity on the synchrophaser magnet connections are checked. The serviced complete contact assembly which has slip rings, two carbon

Assessing the condition of the slip rings

brushes, springs and their housing are then given an insulation check.

b. The TD amplifier is given a standard serviceability check, using a locally manufactured test set. The TD valve is inside the test set. The TD amplifiers four potentiometers' parameters are set up in accordance with the AP schedule in relation to the position of the TD valve. However, as no two TD valves are the same, the flight lines makes minor adjustments to a new TD amplifier when it is fitted to their aircraft. The four adjustment screws are at the rear of the TD amplifier.

c. The 18 pairs of thermocouples are checked to see if the top and side orifices are enlarged, elongated or cracked. Finally a resistance and current check is given on the terminals.

d. On the co–ordinator an electrical static check is done by moving the scale (shows throttle position) in fixed increments. This simulates the movement of the throttle and the readings are checked on a comparison chart. The 'cross–over' point micro switch is checked that it is within its limits of $66° \pm 2°$.

e. The disconnect unit is removed from the generator. It is then stripped, overhauled, checked and re–assembled.

When electrical problems arise on engines that are tested at the UETF, the bay's technicians will do a continuity check on the components and cables and replace any that are damaged. In PRF the bay is responsible for all electrical problems, checks and rectification of many components, either in its bay or 'in situ' on the engine during servicing or during the CCM build up. An assortment of locally manufactured and other test equipment is used. The FLUKE BM8 is the modern equivalent of the old AVO meter!

UNINSTALLED ENGINE TEST FACILITY (UETF). After an unserviceable engine has been rebuilt, the independent and quality checks are carried out. When this engine is to be tested, it is sent to the UETF. The complete unit (QEC) arrives on its stand and the QEC is lifted and secured on the test facility. Electrical, hydraulic, fuel and bleed air connections are made to the QEC. The bleed air comes from the GTC, positioned close by. However, the fuel tank is some 50 feet away. As usual, all safety precautions are taken. The safety man is positioned with the fire extinguisher at a safe distance from the propeller. The other two operators sit side by side inside the test cabin which is about the size of a bathroom. Inside the cabin is the test bench with a host of gauges and one throttle and condition lever which are connected to the engine electrically. One set of engine instruments (similar to the ones in the aircraft) are there for the third operator to note the figures.

There are other gauges on the test bench of which the digital RPM and fuel flow ones are used frequently for accuracy. All the three operators will be on intercom.

A pre test is done on the engine for any leaks. If this is satisfactory, a fault diagnosis is carried out and any faults rectified. The engine is then started, warmed and when it is within limits, it is run to full power of 1050°C or 19600 in lbs torque. Further runs are then done from full reverse to take–off position and all the figures noted in the following throttle positions: full reverse, ground idle, flight idle, cross–over (66°) and maximum power. The test is complete when a minimum of 98% efficiency is reached at 1050°C or 19600 in lbs torque and could take up to 2 hours or longer if there are any faults. Some faults can be rectified here, however, there are times when the engine will not become serviceable, even after hours of fault diagnosis. In this case the engine is returned to the 'builds' section for in depth rectification.

UETF are also responsible for many things, including the following:

a. Fault diagnosis, testing and rectifying the T56 Allison engine.

b. Vibration monitoring and propeller dynamic balancing.

c. Compressor cleaning which involves loading a hopper with coarse grit such as crushed walnuts, is introduced to the air intake by pipes. This cleans all the stages (stators and rotor blades) of the CCM.

UETF's test facility

MECHANICAL ENGINEERING SQUADRON (MES)

GENERAL ENGINEERING FLIGHT. The WO IC GEF is responsible to the Officer IC for the day to day operation of the flights, including discipline and welfare. There are two trade managers of the rank of Chf Tech. One is responsible for all mechanical aspect and the other of all electrical aspects of all support equipment, such as the ground power unit (GPU) and the MK 16 hydraulic servicing trolley. The GSE control maintains the records for servicing for Lyneham and satellite stations such as Hullavington and Rudloe Manor. When equipment is brought in for repair, the fault is assessed by the bay and the GSE control enters the data and produces the necessary paperwork. The inventory for all ground equipment is kept here.

MAINTENANCE BAYS GPU BAY. This bay maintains the much loved Houchin – 60 KVA trolley. This provides 115V, 3 phase 400 Hz AC or 28V DC if required. In addition, it has sockets which provide power for movable external lights to illuminate the surrounding areas. It has a six cylinder engine similar to the London bus and has been known to

Adjusting the fuel injection pump on the 'Houchin'

operate with one damaged cylinder. Ask the technicians about this faithful machine and they will tell you many true stories. All ground equipment parked on the flight line is given a daily inspection. The GPU has a 200, 400 and an 800 hours servicing cycle. It is also serviced annually or when it is unserviceable. In the annual inspection the mechanical servicing includes de–coke, top cylinder head gasket change. The electrical servicings include the re–wiring, soldering and fault finding with the capability to overhaul. This power set has been at Lyneham from the early 60's and is soon to be replaced by a new one early this year.

Servicing the IKW portable generator

Powered Equipment Bay service and maintain the following equipment:

a. MK16 Hydraulic servicing trolley.

b. Universal fuel tank replenishment trolley.

c. Aircraft maintenance self–propelled platform.

d. Air Start Trolley (provides air for starting if the aircraft's GTC is unserviceable).

e. Service general purpose forklifts and maintain other miscellaneous equipment, such as the parachutists' balloon platform. Of these, the universal fuel tank replenishment trolley takes a longer time for servicing and rectification as it involves three separate sub systems. Firstly, this multi use trolley is used for curing the sealant when the aircraft's leaking fuel tank is repaired. Secondly, it can pressurise an empty fuel tank to locate the leak area and lastly, it has breathing apparatus and connections to work inside a fuel tank safely.

Fault rectification on access platform self propelled. Servicing the Warwick Steam cleaner

The Non–powered Bay is responsible for the servicing and rectification of all non motorised equipment, such as bottle (nitrogen, oxygen and air) trolleys, safety raisers, highway staging, tow bars, LOX trolley, small hydraulic test bench, breathing apparatus for painters, Risbridger fluid replenishment gun and jacks from 2 to 35 tons and crash trolleys up to 75 tons. The 2 ton jack is for MT vehicles, the 75 ton crash trolley is for the movement of the Hercules (crash and salvage) and the 25 and 35 ton jacks for lifting the aircraft. Most equipment is serviced quarterly but the annual one involves a thorough deep servicing.

Lifting Tackle Section holds stocks of lifting slings and tackles for all operations, be it for the aircraft or for other uses around the station. For example, if the outer wing needs to be removed from the aircraft, a lifting beam with attaching cables is used. All tackles are given a six monthly maintenance and all replaced if a few strands are broken from the wire rope cable. The regularly used light weight propeller sling is stripped, examined, rectified and re–assembled. The Runway Hook Arrester Gear (RHAG) is inspected every 24 hours. Its 3 monthly in–depth maintenance involves replenishment of anti–freeze, gear box oil, restoration and examination. Lyneham is an MDA hence the RHAG is not for the Hercules but for visiting aircraft like the Tornado with hydraulic problems.

Assembling the nitrogen bottle trolley

Selecting a 'Disbury' mini hoist component

Located in the **Battery Charging Bay building** are the Battery Charging Room (BCR) offices and the Ground Electrical Section.

Battery Charging Bay is responsible for the servicing of aircraft and MT vehicle batteries for Lyneham and the satellite stations. A 24V 31 AH

Checking the output voltage (aircraft battery)

battery is fitted to the Hercules. It is serviced every 3 months and depending on the 3 types it takes 3 days to check, charge and measure at intervals the voltage, SG and charge drop rate. It can take up to 14 days if it fails the first and subsequent second and third tests. A fully charged new battery is issued if the old battery fails the three tests. Visiting aircraft, particularly light aircraft and second world war aircraft, like the Spitfire utilise the accumulator trolley (trolley acc). This consists 4 x 6V batteries secured on to a movable trolley which is charged from a convenient point outside the bay. The electrolyte level is checked and plugged in to the point which charges it automatically until required for use by VASS. Distilled water, spare batteries and safety equipment such as face masks and gloves, are stored inside the building but the sulphuric acid is stored externally in a safe room.

The Ground Electrical Section is tasked with the maintenance and servicing of all items of minor electrical equipment, portable appliances and temporary electrical installations in use on the station. They also undertake repairs of vacuum cleaners, kettles and irons belonging to the married quarters. When a new item is received it is checked, given a unique number and registered in the computer. Items like the microwave oven is checked for radiation leaks in situ and the data recorded. The section utilises a locally built test bench with test equipment and operates on the Electrical Hazard Area (EHA) safely.

Registering the minor electrical equipment

ARMOURY

"Everything that goes with a bang is the responsibility of the Armoury".

The Armoury is located within a purpose built building in the Technical Site and manned by a Chf Tech and two Sgts with a baker's dozen (JNCOs and below). The building conforms to all safety regulations and there are specially built rooms with metal external doors for safety and security. For instance, when the two aircraft fire bottles (aircraft fire extinguisher system) containing bromochrodifluro methane agent arrive for servicing, they are taken into one of these rooms to disarm them.

If an armed aircraft like a Tornado GR1 or GR3 diverts to Lyneham, it has to be parked at the designated area with the supervision of the Armoury personnel. This ensures that the high category explosive is parked away from buildings and personnel, and pointing in a safe direction. This section looks after the storage of ammunition and explosives. All the small arms, such as rifles and pistols, are located here within a highly secure storage room and all issues and receipts (on exercises and during the normal course of duty) are done through the small hatch outside the building. The Armourers check, record meticulously and maintain the entire stock and store them in a logical sequence on racks secured by cables and locks. They also record and safeguard guns and rifles belonging to visiting personnel (official weapons) and to station personnel (private weapons).

Returning weapon – ENDEX!

When armament equipment like the Varey pistol is removed from the aircraft for maintenance, it is returned to the Armoury. Also, when the aircraft bomb release (parachute release unit) rack is sent here, it involves not only maintenance but is stripped and new electrical and mechanical components fitted. Chaff and flares are prepared and inserted into their containers. These are then taken when a task is called for and fitted to the aircraft as a routine job. During station exercises they provide Explosive Ordnance Disposal (EOD) support and have to recover the station from post attack. This is an arduous and mentally demanding job. Due to the sensitivity and hazardous nature of explosive components, all explosive servicing has to be carried out in specially designated rooms. The volume of books pertaining to the many jobs of the Armourer far exceeds that of the servicing publications of the mighty Hercules aircraft!

Servicing BCF fire bottles.
Note the flare container (foreground)

Loading flare container to the Hercules

Lastly, in addition to the 'on' station tasks, they are responsible for parenting several other units and Air Training Corps (ATC). The ATC could be as far afield as Jersey, where checks of their armament procedures are carried out. Due to the sensitive nature of the armament world, not even the tip of the iceberg has been covered in this book.

ROLE EQUIPMENT SECTION

The Role Equipment Section of Engineering Wing, comprises of four shifts of 15 personnel each, made up of two SNCOs, three JNCOs and nine tradesmen, normally of the Airframe trade, plus one JNCO and two tradesmen of the Supply trade, providing 24 hours, 365 days a year coverage, supported by a dayshift workshop, supply and administration staff totalling approximately twenty personnel of various trades.

Maintaining the ageing side guidance

The section's task, under the direct control of Engineering control, is to prepare all aircraft to meet the daily flying requirements of the station, be they on training, exercise or departing overseas, in any one of approximately 65 different variants of the twenty basic Hercules roles, ranging from the aircraft being stripped of all role equipment for servicing purposes, to the most complex of fits such as the para–wedge role, enabling the deployment of ninety plus paratroops concurrently with the air despatch of supplies (normally one–ton containers of armaments) from the wedge platform mounted on the aircraft ramp, or the air–dropping of medium–stressed platforms (MSP) containing landrovers and trailers, where attention to detail is paramount to ensure the safety of personnel and aircraft. As can be imagined, the importance of the Role Equipment Section and its experienced tradesmen to the operation of the Hercules fleet, cannot be over–stressed.

Fitting the centre passenger seats

The actual tasks are generally carried out by teams of four tradesmen, including a Corporal or Sergeant supervisor where the aircraft are roled or re–roled to the fit that is required. This can sometimes take the form of the worst possible scenario, ie taking the aircraft from the full paratrooping role to a full air dropping role, which can take anything up to four hours per aircraft with an experienced team of fitters. This situation usually occurs when working in close harmony with the fifth airborne brigade during their major exercise, when up to fifteen aircraft have to be roled for initial deployment and then re–roled for re–supply tasks.

However, this is not always the case, for some tasks require only one or two tradesmen to check the existing aircraft role for correctness so that the aircraft can be used again in the same role, when the engineering operations and plans section are able to task the aircraft in this manner.

Shift control office

To assist with the workload of the section, the SNCOs in charge of each of the shifts liaise closely with the Engineering plans personnel whilst the flying programme is being written in an attempt to minimise role changes, or hopefully make the changes as easy as possible (for example changing from one roller conveyor fit to a similar role, or one paratrooping role to a slightly different fit). Included in this communication chain are the line servicing

Finishing a roller conveyor fit

shift controllers to ensure that the subject aircraft are capable of fulfilling their intended tasks.

Frequently, when aircraft are away from Lyneham, a role change may be called for, ie the outgoing load may be palletised with the aircraft in a roller conveyor fit and the incoming load could well be a wheeled load, where a clear–floor role is required. In these instances personnel of Role Equipment Section travel with the aircraft, as supernumerary crew, in order to expedite the role change in as short a time as possible, so that there is no delay to the aircraft schedule.

During such times as Operation Bushel, (bringing famine relief to the people of Ethiopia) and Operation Granby (the support of Allied Troops following the invasion of Kuwait by Iraq) Role Equipment personnel were included as an integral part of the RAF Lyneham Engineering detachment to those areas where they carried out role changes in sometimes difficult and/or hostile conditions. These are just two instances of this type of operation where Role Equipment personnel have played their full part.

Also during the Gulf crisis, it was decided that all aircraft would be prepared so that they would have the capability to be quickly converted to "casevac" (casualty evacuation) use, no matter what the existing in–use role was. This meant that litter (stretcher) strops were permanently fitted in their correct positions and then stowed, so that they could be utilised in as quick a time as possible. However, with the extensive modification of the Hercules fleet during its long and distinguished service career, the "full" stretcher role was not possible on any of the aircraft. To circumvent this problem SNCOs of Role Equipment Section, in consultation with some senior Air–Loadmasters, came up with a modified "casevac" role to make the best possible use of the aircraft. Fortunately, as everyone knows, our casualty numbers were very low and these "air–ambulances" were not called into service. This is just one such case where personnel of Role Equipment have assisted in the solving of problems concerned with aircraft loads. These problems can occur at any time, especially when differing loads are carried on the same aircraft at the same time, ie when carrying palletised loads and wheeled loads, when communication between Air–Loadmasters, the UKMAMS section and Role Equipment section is necessary to Role and load the aircraft in the required manner.

As can be understood, the Role Equipment section, although sometimes regarded as the "poor relation" within Engineering Wing, is a very important cog of the machine that is RAF Lyneham, and the operation of the Hercules fleet.

SURVIVAL EQUIPMENT – TRADE FUNCTION – HERCULES

The main function of Survival Equipment (SE) is to support the Airborne Life Support Equipment for all aircrew.

The SE Team at Lyneham comprises 31 from the rank of SAC to FS. The practical skills can be divided into four main areas in direct support of the Hercules:

a. Aircrew Equipment Assemblies (AEA) which includes both protection and communication equipment.

b. Liferafts and Survival Aids, including the 33 seat Liferaft, the largest being used in the Royal Air Force. Each life raft is equipped with inflation equipment and highly specialised Survival Aids necessary for the survival of passengers and crew under all climatic conditions.

c. Parachutes, Safety Harness Systems, Specialist Strops, Hung–up Parachute Release

Routine 15 weekly servicing on the Atlantic headset

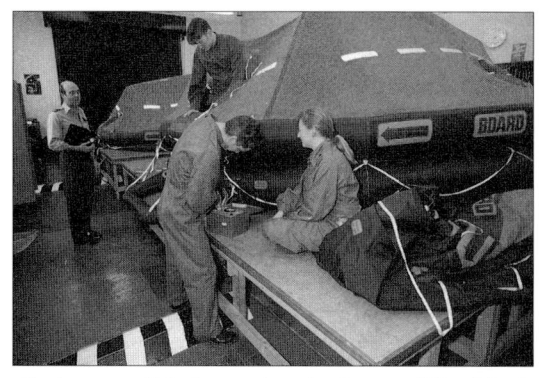

Testing a sea light battery location beacon (liferaft bay)

Systems to support the dropping of loads and troops with the Hercules. In addition, this area maintains all crew and passenger seat Safety Harness Systems.

d. The maintenance of Operational and Practice Air Sea Rescue Apparatus (ASRA) adapted to be carried and deployed by the Hercules.

Included in the AEA facility is the maintenance of the specialized aircrew Nuclear Biological Contamination (NBC) protective AEA and the specialist Night Vision Systems.

Sizing and fitting of LSJ Mk25

The Survival Equipment skills are many and very varied. They include:

a. Parachute packing.
b. Liferaft packing.
c. Tailoring and general sewing repair skills
d. Gas charging.
e. Basic engineering.
f. Basic electronics/electrical
g. Instructional skills.

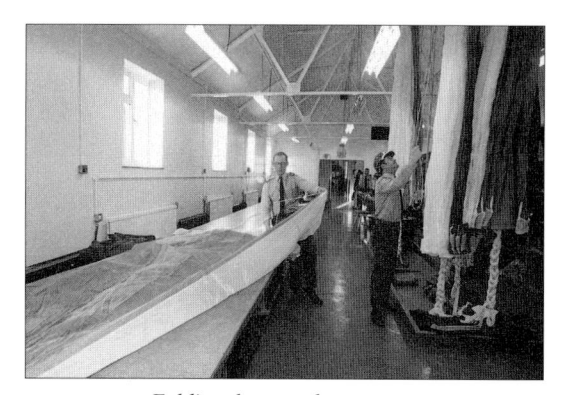

Demonstration of night vision goggles

Many of the maintenance personnel hold special skills, including:

a. The training of aircrew in the donning and doffing of the aircrew NBC equipment.

b. Size, fit and adjust AEA which includes protective helmets, Aircrew Respirator Mk 5 (AR5) hoods and oxygen masks to individual aircrew.

c. Assist in the training of aircrew in dry and survival drills in the pool.

Folding the parachute canopy

STATION WORKSHOPS (SWS)

The SWS is made up of General Workshop Technicians (GWT) and a team of carpenters.

The GWT's trade covers the three main fields of Engineering: Welding, Sheetmetal Fabrication and Machining. The tradesmen are responsible for providing all aspects of ground support engineering on the station in tasks ranging from manufacturing and cut repairs to items of ground support equipment, vital to the continual smooth operation of the fleet. On the other extreme, they produce items such as "NO ENTRY" signs and knife edge barriers for the Police Flight.

Technician completing an aircraft component on the milling machine

Rip saw machine with a 3 foot circular saw

Tungsten Inert Gas (TIG) welding on a Hercules tail pipe

Gas cutting profile for ground equipment trolley

All the tradesmen have completed further courses of advanced training which allow them to carry out repairs, modifications or manufacture components for use on the aircraft. During the 1982 Falklands conflict the SWS were involved in the conversion of aircraft for air–to–air refuelling purposes. During the recent 1990–1991 Gulf conflict, a flight deck ventilation system was manufactured which was installed to each aircraft.

Most of the aircraft work now tends to be small 'one off' manufacture of a component to be replaced and found to be corroded or damaged during servicing. Any welding required on the aircraft engines is done in the SWS if time permits. Otherwise it is done "in situ" on the aircraft in the hangar. A team for this kind of emergency is available 24 hours a day, including weekends.

The carpenters' team consists of service and civilian personnel. They provide ground engineering support through the unit. There is not one section that has not utilised this, from Ops to the Police Dog Section.

The days of wooden fuselages are a thing of the past, but inside the fuselage there are many items still to be maintained, such as the Nav's table and galley panels. All are manufactured to exacting standards using approved aircraft materials. Other aircraft related tasks are the preparation of wooden pallet loads for dropping, and the never ending stream of tactical chocks carried on board.

On a more ceremonious note, the Royal Dias is looked after by a Sgt in Workshops, who ensures it is in a condition befitting Royalty treading on it! He goes with it to various parades and functions to make sure it is assembled and used in the correct manner at all times.

CHAPTER SEVEN

ELECTRICAL ENGINEERING SQUADRON (EES)

ORGANIZATION LINE DIAGRAM – EES

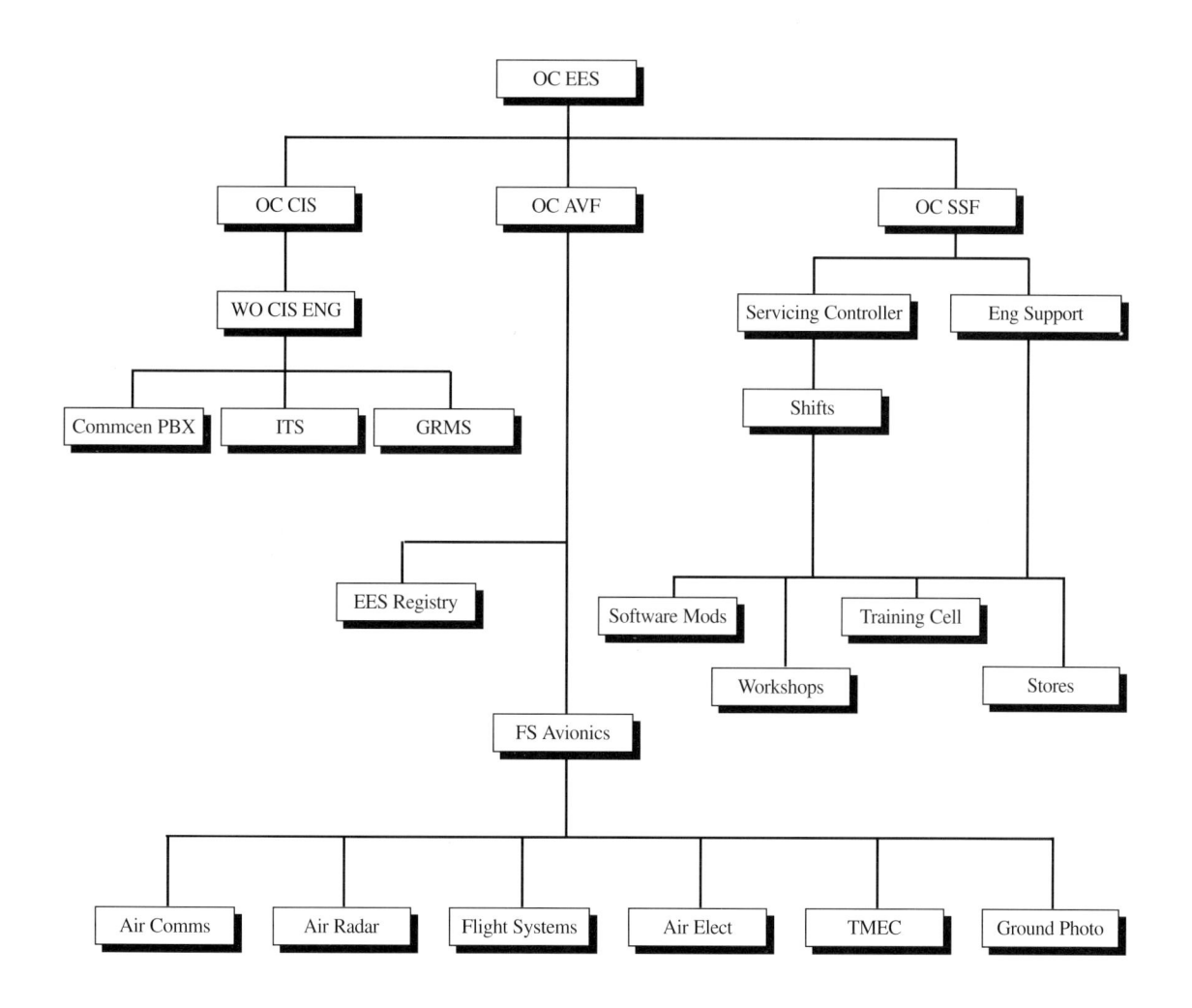

```
                              OC EES
                                │
        ┌───────────────────────┼───────────────────────┐
      OC CIS                  OC AVF                  OC SSF
        │                       │                       │
    WO CIS ENG                  │              ┌────────┴────────┐
        │                       │        Servicing Controller  Eng Support
  ┌─────┼─────┐                 │              │
Commcen PBX  ITS  GRMS          │            Shifts
                                │
                   ┌────────────┤
              EES Registry      │
                                │         ┌─────────┬─────────┬─────────┐
                                │   Software Mods        Training Cell
                                │           │                 │
                                │       Workshops           Stores
                                │
                          FS Avionics
                                │
   ┌──────────┬──────────┬──────┴──────┬──────────┬──────────┐
 Air Comms  Air Radar  Flight Systems  Air Elect  TMEC   Ground Photo
```

AVIONICS BAY. The Avionics Bay is made up of 6 sections. The first 3 consist of Air Communications, Air Radar and Flight Systems.

The 'immaculate' avionics flight bays

The personnel employed here are cross–trained on the above trades. About 95% of the controls and indicators operated by the 2 pilots and the navigator ends up here for rectification. Although most of the test equipment is archaic, the standard of servicing is second to none. This is reflected in the successful sorties by the fleet in peace time and during conflicts, as in the Falklands (1982) and the Gulf (1990–1991).

The Air Communications Section do not repair and service only headsets, but also the latest UHF/VHF, UHF and VHF radios. The older HF sets may need replacement of resistors, capacitors and transistors using the traditional method of using portable AVO type equipment, prods and the mark one eyeball. For the latest V/UHF receivers tests may reveal the faulty components on one of the integrated circuits boards, in which case the board is changed.

Servicing headsets

The Air Radar Section looks after all the radar equipment, such as the CCWR (Cloud Collision Warning Radar) and the radar altimeter as used by the pilots and most of the equipment in the Navigator's instrument panel. The test equipment in this bay includes many black boxes found in the aircraft. For example for the navigator's Decca Doppler 62M2 control panel to function involves inputs from the aerials, control unit, tracker and a T/R unit. If a fault such as "Doppler does not lock on" appears on an aircraft prior to start up, the line tradesman knows which black box is unserviceable. A 'flash' demand is requested and a new box arrives from ESG (Electronic Supply Group) which he replaces. The unserviceable box goes to ESG stores where it is sent to the Air Radar Section and a functional check is carried out by the test equipment oscilloscope and Fluke spectrum analyzer. However, all the equipment used in the aircraft for the function of the Doppler are here. The unserviceable unit is connected to them before any checks. The tradesman then follows the AP schedule subsequently and narrows it down to where the fault could occur. Using the circuit diagram and a lot of patience, he will pinpoint accurately to a particular module board which will then be changed. After a functional check, it is labelled and sent to the ESG store for storage. Should any new equipment arrive from the MU or the manufacturer, the bay does a functional test and returns to ESG store. But certain equipment, such as an unserviceable Radar altimeter, is functionally checked and tested for the fault but is not repaired in the bay, but sent to a civilian company.

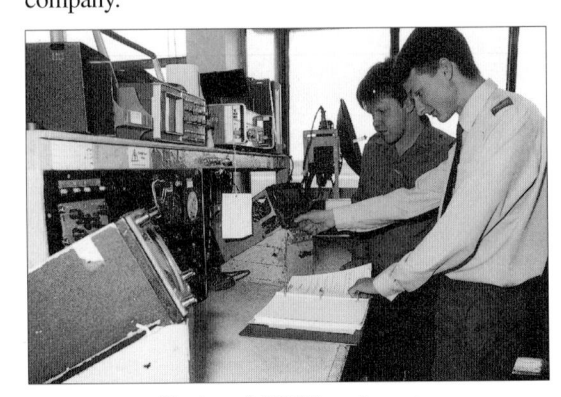

Testing of CCWR equipment

The Flight Systems bay services some of the most important instruments and systems used by the pilots and the navigator. Some of these are: the ADIs, HSIs, C–12 compasses and their associated gyros and the auto–pilot. Items such as the auto–pilot servomotor has a 4000 hours life after which they are categorised and sent to the MU at Sealand. The slave motors and clutches are re–conditioned, replaced and tested on the rig. Many parts, black boxes and the gyro platform make up the components needed for the function of the auto–pilot. In the bay, this equipment plus the test sets and the rig, are available to confirm whether any unserviceable auto–pilot component can be repaired or adjusted up to second line servicing level. If the platform unit comes in with a cracked dome, it is replaced and then given a functional test. This involves introducing similar conditions, as though it is fitted to the aircraft. For example, the platform is tilted as in a climb, and a circle disc with a painted Hercules aircraft moves showing it is climbing. Any problems with the gyros of the C–12 compass are put on a tilt rig and run for four hours to exercise its bearing and afterwards minor adjustments are done. However, other complicated unserviceabilities on the ADI and the C–12 compass could end up with circuit board changes on their associated black boxes.

AIRCRAFT ELECTRICAL SECTION

This section, located within AVF, is further sub–divided into six sections. A C/T, 2 Sgts and 13 NCOs and airmen are responsible for the bay servicing, calibration, fault diagnosis and rectifications of over 500 gauges, warning lights, thermostats, thermal switches and heavy equipment, such as the generator and synchrophaser. 50% of these are visible to the naked eye and located on the flight deck and cargo compartment of the aircraft. In addition, they look after the calibration of the test equipment used by other flights like the GTC test panel, used by PRF.

Servicing the oil quantity transmitter

The main bay is some 1500 square feet with many test benches built locally. Most test and calibration equipment built by Service personnel since 1968 is secured to the benches. Some American built test equipment are also utilised. However, modifications have been carried out to modernise all test equipment. All non–radio transmitters and receivers fitted to the aircraft, such as torquemeter gauges, generator frequency and voltmeter gauges, are serviced here excluding the oxygen and hydraulics, whose indicators only are checked by AES. Regulated AC 115V, single and three phases, 400 Hz and DC are available on the test benches and so is the compressed air and vacuum for the checking of items like the altimeters and the vertical speed indicators. It is impossible to describe all the work carried out from this section but a few are mentioned here. When a faulty altimeter arrives, a thorough service is given after the component has been replaced. It is then tested, in accordance with the schedule, using suction, and the results and tolerance are checked against electronic test equipment with a digital scale.

The fuel pressure gauge check involves introducing fluid to one side of the diaphragm which moves a worm gear on the other side. This drives a potentiometer and the test equipment displays the reading digitally.

In addition to all the indicators and transmitters tested here, they also rectify and test components like the synchrophaser, safety valve (for pressurisation), speed sensitive control (controls engine start sequence) and all the lights such as anti–collision and landing lamps. The synchrophaser 'black' box rectification consists of tracing the fault to an integrated circuit board, which is then replaced. It is sometimes frustrating as one cannot see with the eye what is wrong with the faulty portion of the black box, but has to rely on the test equipment and precise location by using the probes.

Generator Bay performs routine servicing rectification and replacement and refurbished of life expired components on items such as the main and ATM generators, voltage regulators, TRUs, invertors, relays, ATM and recirculating fans.

On the main aircraft generator during a 2000 hours life expired servicing, the outer casing of the generator is removed. A full servicing, including an overhaul, is then given to the rotors with a continuity check (electrically) and a balance check on the rig. Any weights to be added are done by SWS. it is then re–assembled, checked, tested and then returned to the ESG bay. However, if a generator arrives from the line with a failed bearing, the rectification takes a longer time. If the outer casing containing the stators is not damaged, only the rotors need changing. This involves removing the old damaged section (rotor). The new rotor has to be fitted with additional components before testing it. The rotor 'build' consists of balancing with new fitted bearings and bearing inserts. This rotor is then fitted to the stator assembly via a bell plate, which retains and positions the rotor in relation to the stator. The stub shaft assembly is fitted and then hand cranked to check the clearance, torque other retaining screws and wire locked. On the opposite side the air adaptor is fitted. The whole unit is then tested on the 'generator rotax' rig. The rotor is turned at 6000 RPM the same as the aircraft. The output voltage, frequency and phase rotation is monitored on a variety of gauges on the test panel.

Servicing the main aircraft generator

CABLE BAY. The Cable section manufactures and repairs the looms of aircraft axial and co–axial cables. Numerous tools, one manufacturing machine and highly trained personnel make this possible. The non co–axial cable drum is loaded one side of the cable identing machine. The operator then programmes firstly the 'batch', the 'dwell' – how bold the imprint on the cable, the 'end length' – spaces between each ident and the 'wire length' – actual length of cables in centimetres. For co–axial cables this machine cannot be used, but ident labels made from a labelling machine, are manually attached to the cable. Examples of co–axial cables are the screened cables used on the UA 60 intercom boxes and the fuel compensator (capacitance) from the fuel tank to the indicator on the flight deck and the SPR. The majority of the cables are attached to the aircraft electrical plugs, as looms, and are found throughout the aircraft. Hence the identification of cables is paramount.

ACTUATOR AND DOMESTIC EQUIPMENT BAY. The actuator section looks after servicing and rectification of the actuators which move linearly to either open or close doors such as GTC and air deflector doors or to control the cooler flaps, aileron and rudder trim tabs and the static line retrievers. When an item becomes unserviceable, rectification is carried out up to fourth line servicing. The GTC and the static line retriever actuators are sent to another unit if they cannot be repaired. All unserviceable items are repaired, serviced and tested for tensile and compression checks using weights. For a suspected actuator an initial test is carried out. It is then overhauled and if no further fault is found, a post repair test is given. As the Hercules fleet is now over 28 years old, the frequency of repair and servicing has increased. The Domestic Section occupies half of the actuator room and is responsible for the aircraft oven, 2 gallon water containers and in–flight heated flash (keeps the food containers warm). Using a small test bench, the unserviceable equipment is cleaned before servicings commence. Maintenance is up to fourth line servicing. The thermostats used in the oven are sent to the 'T' stat bay.

Testing of the rudder actuator

THERMOSTAT BAY ('T' STAT BAY). Facilities here provide accurate test equipment and cleaning facilities not only to check the domestic oven bay but also the thermocouples found in the turbine section of the Allison T56 engine and the air conditioning and pressurisation system.

GENERATOR RUNNING BAY. The assembled generators are tested in this section on the appropriate rig and test equipment for checking and adjusting the voltage and frequency.

Manufacturing a marking, using the cable identification machine

Generator test facility

SIMULATOR SERVICING FLIGHT (SSF)

There has been a Simulator Servicing Flight at Lyneham since the late 60s when Simulator No 1 was installed. Servicing was carried out by a team of donor tradesmen taken from List 1 and List 2 electrical trades and added to, in the mid seventies, by direct entry tradesmen who were trained at Locking to replace the donors and take over the Simulator servicing within the Royal Air Force as a whole. In the early 90s a new trade came on the scene (L Mech ST) trained at Cosford in all aspects of simulation to carry out maintenance tasks in situ on the simulator and in the maintenance areas off simulator. In the late 1980s a number of Simulator Technicians (L Tech ST) were selected to work on the Advanced Simulation Techniques (AST) Hercules simulators. The 3(AST) Hercules Simulators were installed at the cost of approximately £15 million each, between 1982 and 1985 on the new site across the road from Sim No 1. After some 20 plus years of operation Sim No 1 was finally decommissioned in 1991, by which time the 3 AST simulators were now fully established.

SSF is a flight within the control of Electrical Engineering Squadron (EES). The flight has a manning level of 38 personnel, ranging from WO to ST Mechanics at SAC level. SSF consistently reaches a performance figure better than 90%. Each of the Simulators currently has a flying task every day Monday to Friday of 12 hours. The remaining time every day is by the servicing and maintenance to keep the Simulators running at maximum efficiency.

Situated within the Simulator complex are the Simulator Squadron aircrew training offices under the control of Hercules OCU 57 Sqn. The Squadron Leader in charge of the Simulator Squadron organises the flying programme for Squadron aircrew (5 sqns), Squadron groundcrew, Foreign Air Forces, Ground training school, Hercules Maintenance school, Simulator trade training, and if time allows any visits of which there are many.

SSF consists of four work areas and three simulators. The work areas being:

Administration area – manned by 6 personnel controlling the day to day management, Engineering Support, Engineering servicing software and Modification and shift control.

Course Design and Training Cell – manned by two SNCOs tasked with updating current in Service trade training courses as new equipment is installed and then carrying out the training task as new personnel arrive within the flight.

Workshops – consisting of a mechanical workshop for carrying out hydraulic, pneumatic and general mechanical servicing, an electronic workshop for pcb, instrument and peripheral servicing, a visual flight attachment room where servicing to any of the visual system components can be carried out and a stand alone 8/32 computer system for various software management operations, all under the control of an SNCO.

Visual repair facility – carrying out a set up

Stores – manned by a supplier, who is their link with the supply network.

The three simulators have their own associated equipment and operating rooms, thus making the whole complex fairly large.

A typical day's flying starts with a handover between the shift bosses at 0630 hrs, the offgoing shift having already prepared the Simulators as far as possible with Before Flights, making the simulators ready for the day's sorties. If any simulator is not ready for the first sortie, the necessary paperwork is

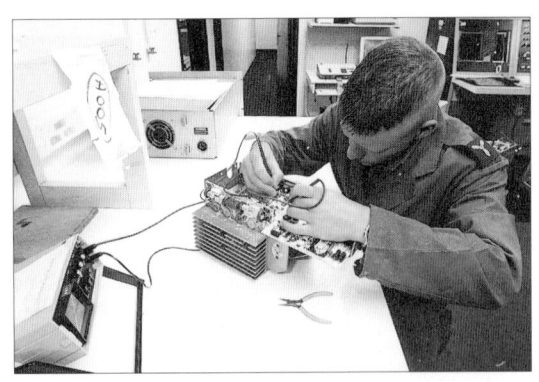

Component checking on a visual deflection amplifier

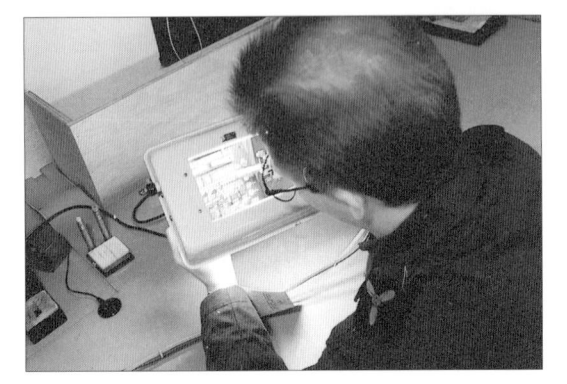

Inspecting a circuit board for damage

Checking out the Instructor's Operating Station

Corporal technician flying at 1200ft. 153 knots – normal before flight checks performed daily

raised in the F700 in the same manner as for an aircraft thus advising the aircrew of any limitations or deferred faults. The Simulators are ready for flying at 0800 hrs and a sortie normally lasts for 2 hrs. When completed the aircrew informs the simulator groundcrew of any faults that may have occurred and enters them in the F700. The groundcrew then rectify any faults and carry out a turn round servicing and annotate the F700 accordingly. At 1500 hrs the next shift take over at the end of the days flying an After Flight is carried out, then any outstanding rectification, scheduled and progressive servicing is carried out. At 2300 hrs the next shift takeover and the on coming shift then carries out the necessary outstanding maintenance including the B/F ready for the following days flying programme.

COMMUNICATION AND INFORMATION SYSTEMS ENGINEERING FLIGHT (CIS)

This flight is commanded by a Flt Lt. The WO is responsible to him for the day to day running of the flight. PBX is the telecommunication section responsible for operating the British Telecom (BT) service exchange and all the telephones and faxes around the station. It also handles other external and emergency calls. The equipment utilised by this section has been modernised and computerised. The communication centre (COMMCEN) processes incoming and outgoing signal messages having direct lines to switching centres. Incoming signals are distributed via respective registries. Voice communication is possible over the HF network to PWHQ and they also have the capability to speak to the Hercules aircraft.

GROUND RADIO MAINTENANCE SECTION (GRMS). By far the most important section that is not directly connected with the Hercules aircraft. But, with the UK's notorious weather and the many kinds of aircraft that could land at this Master Emergency Diversion Airfield (MEDA), this section provides many kinds of radio and radar Navigational Aids (NAVAIDS) cover. On the airfield they maintain ground radar cover such as Precision Approach Radar (PAR), Watchman Radar (Primary Radar) whose Transmitters (TX) are located on the airfield. Their Receivers (RX) are co-located with the TX. The information from these units is received in Air Traffic control (ATC) on the "radar hands".

The Instrument Landing System (ILS) signal produces "beams" to guide the aircraft on to the ground. This ILS information can be picked up by the Hercules aircraft and displayed on the ADI. The PAR and the Primary Radar information is transmitted audibly from ATC and these contain information such as height, distance, bearing and position of other aircraft in the vicinity of the airfield and so on, and can be received by the VHF/UHF radios. Other NAVAIDS such as Digital Resolution Direction Finder (DRDF), NDB and TACAN transmit only the position of the transmitter (Here I am, you find me!) which the receivers in the aircraft can tune to and follow, for navigational purposes. On a foggy day a combination of all the above are used by the aircraft, from cruise height right down to the Minimum Descent Height (MDH). The MDH is the height at which the pilot must see the runway lights. In addition to daily maintenance and routine servicing of these equipment scattered around the airfield, they also maintain all the radar equipment including the management Radio in the ATC building. As ATC, Operations (Ops) and the GDCC cannot look at all the aircraft parked on the pan, closed circuit TV (CCTV) receivers are utilised with the cameras positioned in strategic places on the aircraft pan. Due to their sheer size, each Hercules occupies about half an acre of space on the pan. The GRMS with its large workshop and variety of test equipment also looks after other satellite stations, such as Wroughton.

Changing tapes (records all ATC ground fair communications)

ORGANIZATION LINE DIAGRAM – EOPS

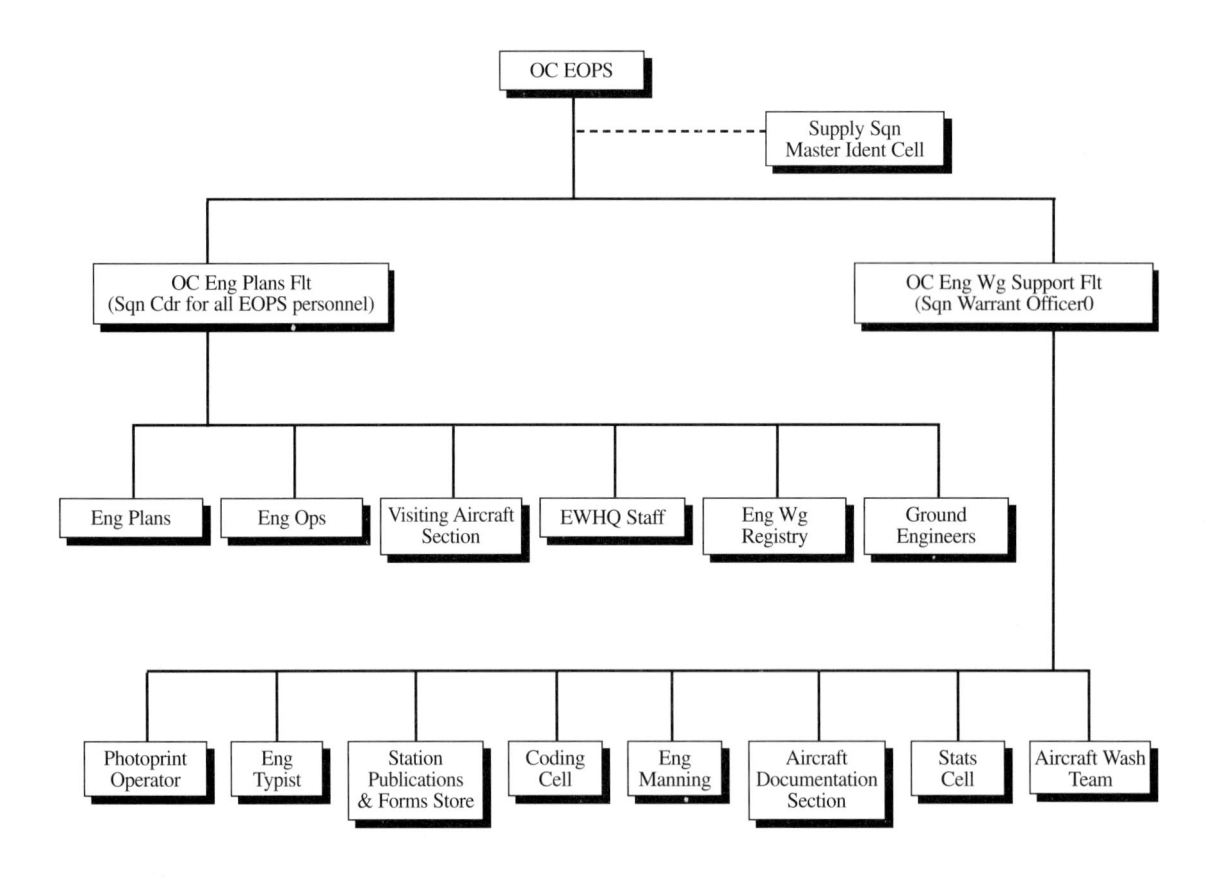

```
                              ┌──────────┐
                              │ OC EOPS  │
                              └────┬─────┘─────────────┐
                                   │          ┌────────┴────────┐
                                   │          │   Supply Sqn    │
                                   │          │ Master Ident Cell│
                                   │          └─────────────────┘
                 ┌─────────────────┴──────────────────┐
       ┌─────────┴──────────────┐         ┌───────────┴──────────────┐
       │   OC Eng Plans Flt     │         │  OC Eng Wg Support Flt   │
       │(Sqn Cdr for all EOPS   │         │  (Sqn Warrant Officer0)  │
       │      personnel)        │         │                          │
       └────────────┬───────────┘         └───────────┬──────────────┘
```

Under OC Eng Plans Flt:
- Eng Plans
- Eng Ops
- Visiting Aircraft Section
- EWHQ Staff
- Eng Wg Registry
- Ground Engineers

Under OC Eng Wg Support Flt:
- Photoprint Operator
- Eng Typist
- Station Publications & Forms Store
- Coding Cell
- Eng Manning
- Aircraft Documentation Section
- Stats Cell
- Aircraft Wash Team

CHAPTER EIGHT

ENGINEERING PLANS FLIGHT

Eng Plans? ... Surely the nearest thing to an oxymoron since the term Intelligence Officer was coined to describe those who arranged Allied losses in the 1st World War!

ENG PLANS – short and long term planning in progress

But, Eng Plans it is, although most of the time within the Flight is spent planning how to stay afloat in a world of rapidly crumbling C130s, diminishing resources and over optimistic tasking.

The Flight itself is split into three sections. The first section consists of two parts. There is a two–man planning cell working days to produce "the plan" (known as the programme or dream sheet), scheduling maintenance and producing colourful management aids and data. There is also a ten strong team providing twenty–four hour coverage to control the plan that the planners have produced. Because of the difficulty of producing the daily programme and managing the long term servicing schedule, the planners are often compared to jugglers, attempting to keep all their balls in the air, but not having enough balls to start with. One reason for this ball shortage is that the C130 fleet has been modified into a variety of mini fleets, very few of which have similar equipment fitted. As the C130 Operators naturally work on the principle that the smallest mini fleet is the most desirable, many requests for aircraft with "this and that fitted" but "very few of them attached" and "certainly none of those at all on board" will regrettably be rejected (but always with an air of genuine concern and words of comfort for the unlucky applicants). Another related reason for the difficulty in achieving accurate planning of the daily flying is the necessity of using aircraft that return late at night (probably unserviceable) to make up the next days' task. The shift working Eng Controllers (DEOCs and Eng Co–ords) are responsible for turning the aspirations of the programme into aircraft for the next days flying. They are also there to provide support and spares back–up for the next section from within Eng Plans.

Station Operations in action – Compulsion Control

Aircraft Ground Engineers (AGE) This section is the valiant team of Ground Engineers (GEs) who stop at nothing in their quest to keep the C130 serviceable down route, or at least till it staggers to a more conducive location! They are admired even by the vastly overpaid Aircrew, both for the size of their wallets and their unfailing ability to always arrive at the Party Room after the rest of the crew have drunk all the beer and gone out on the town. GEs are renowned for their suntans in winter, exotic cars and long–winded tales. Led by the venerable SAGE (Senior Aircraft Ground Engineer), a man respected for his even more amazing stories of legendary lands, fabulous fortunes, and, of course, his whale-sized wallet, they emulate James T Kirk, visiting places where none have gone before (provided there is no accommodation on base).

Hercules aircraft departing RAF Lyneham on most route taskings have an Aircraft Ground Engineer (AGE) allocated to them. The AGE is an aircraft technician who has undergone specialist training encompassing all the aircraft trades. This training enables him to work completely independently on all systems whenever the aircraft is away from base. The allocation of AGEs to route tasking is basically on a "who is available" basis and this results in an extremely varied and interesting life-style. AGEs spending, on average, 200 days a year enclosed in a metal tube – the freight bay of a Hercules on route.

An AGE becomes part of the crew for the particular task for which he is nominated. His role in flight is that of a passenger; consequently AGEs become very adept at sleeping in the most obscure places within the freight bay of the aircraft. When the aircraft reaches its destination the AGE, after a pleasant flight being waited on hand and foot, commences work.

The amount of time being spent on the ground depends on the work that has to be undertaken. Sometimes the aircraft lands mainly to pick up fuel. Usually, however, a night stop is involved in which case servicing is required.

On the odd occasion, when the aircraft has landed in a serviceable condition, the AGE will carry out an after-flight servicing, any out of phase servicings and all replenishments necessary before joining the rest of the crew at the hotel or on-base accommodation. Invariably though, various problems have developed throughout the flight and after being debriefed, usually by the Flight Engineer, the AGE will carry out any rectification necessary. This is not always that simple, the amount of spares carried can vary from next to nothing to at best a limited amount. Resourcefulness, ingenuity, the infamous yellow tool box and whatever is hidden in the bottom of the bag are called upon in many situations. In most cases a "fix" of some form can be effected that will enable the aircraft to continue safely on task the next day. The time spent reaching this point depends on the amount of work to be done, if it takes all night so be it, but usually a few hours will see the aircraft fully serviceable and ready to go again.

Should a fault with the Hercules prove to be beyond the capabilities of the AGE then spares have to be requested from base. The AGE is responsible for liaising with the local handling agents (who may not speak English and not many AGEs can converse in many other languages) and for requesting the correct spares. Once the spares are received, after successfully negotiating the Customs bureaucracy, the AGE will, hopefully be able to make the aircraft serviceable so that it can continue on its way. As soon as the aircraft is airborne the AGE assumes his usual position, curled up somewhere fast asleep. Normally he dreams of another night spent on an airfield trying to fix some obscure fault.

Visiting Aircraft Section (VAS). The third arm of the mighty Eng Plans empire comprises the airmen and airwomen of the Visiting Aircraft Section (VAS). They operate from an elegant corrugated iron and plasterboard building, next to the high power ground running bays and are far away from the corridors of power (and the pleasures of doubleglazing). As well as moving all the powersets and major ground equipment around the airfield and delivering engines and propellers to sections, this gallant band also have responsibility for handling all visiting aircraft. For many visiting VIPs, their first sight of Lyneham (and their most enduring memory) will be the sight of the rain drenched VAS handling team, right dressed in whites and attempting to stand to attention in a howling gale and 24 hours a day they provide crash coverage – a job they hope never to perform.

"Bones" marshalling the Gazelle helicopter

This then, is Eng Plans Flight and, as is traditional in these matters, it is headed by two Officers who move massive amounts of paper.

134

AIRCRAFT GROUND ENGINEERS (AGE) ON INTERNATIONAL FLIGHTS

Smudge and Gary – replenishing the LOX system at Goose Bay, Canada

Supervising the de-icing of the frozen airframe (-25°C) at Gander, New Foundland

John and the author having a NAAFI break at Al Jubail, Saudi Arabia during the Gulf crisis (1991)

Refuelling at the "Rock" – Gibraltar

Stumpy and Gregsy (SVC) with a first class baggage transport

Nige Butland removing water from the fuel tanks, Belize

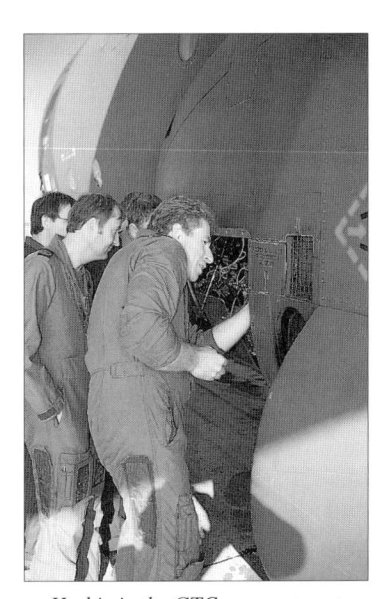

Herbie in the GTC compartment surrounded by supervision

ORGANIZATION LINE DIAGRAM – MTS

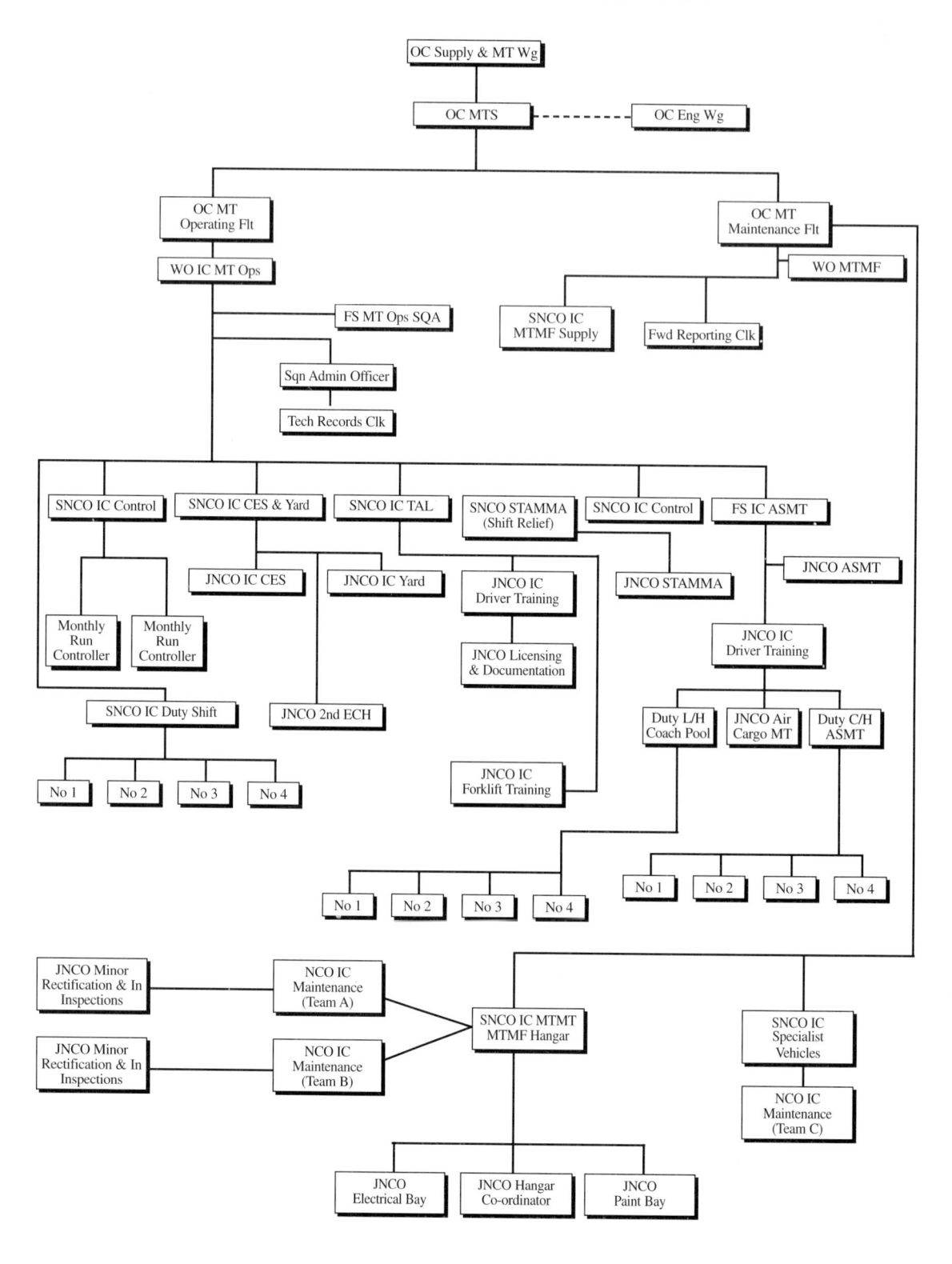

CHAPTER NINE

MECHANICAL TRANSPORT (MT) SQN

Although MT Sqn belonged to Engineering Wing in the past, it now forms part of Supply Wing. The author has included MT Sqn in this book as without their support no Hercules servicings or operations can take place. Aircrew need transportation from the terminal building, ground technicians need a large towing vehicle to tow the aircraft from the hangar and specialist vehicles like those used by the Defence Fire Service (DFS) are needed to provide fire cover. All these are serviced by MT Maintenance Flight (MTMF) and operated by MT Operating Flight (MTOF).

The OC MT Sqn is of the rank of Sqn Ldr and commands the 2 flights. The OCs of MTMF and MTOF are normally of the rank of Fg Off or Flt Lt. As the MT Sqn is large, it is located on A, C and D Sites and only a short description is given of most of the sections.

MTMF specialist line (one of the oldest WWII building)

MTMF. The Flight is located on 'A' site and is the vehicle servicing element of the MT Sqn. The servicing responsibility is for over 520 vehicles ranging from fire fighting trucks to Vauxhall Corsa cars as well as specialist vehicles for lifting freight and loading it on to any aircraft by adjusting its platform height. The second line routine maintenance plus random rectifications are carried out on an eight to five (day shift), 5 days a week basis. There is also a duty shift to provide emergency servicing and breakdown support 24 hours a day, 365 days a year. There are some 47 members of staff which also includes 4 suppliers, 2 painters and 6 ground electricians. The flight is sub–divided into A, B and C line teams who are responsible to the WO trade manager.

The servicings carried out are similar to civilian garages. There are 6 and 12 monthly servicings. The documentation, for example the landrover used by AES, starts from the MT control MTOF. The vehicle is handed to MTMF (the paper work is received via the computer printer). A job card is raised here and is left in slots to await manpower. During servicing certain components are replaced, as necessary. The stores can get the supplies within a short space of time. However, during random rectification if a new engine is required, the unserviceable one is removed and packed. The stores then send it to the army depot, where a serviceable one is issued to complete the job on time. However, certain vehicles carry priority. If the fire vehicle turns up with problems on the vehicle or its specialist equipment, the investigation commences immediately, whilst the paperwork arrives via MT control. This flight is very busy and the servicing bays mechanical and electrical sections, offices, spray paint building, brake and vehicle testing facilities are neatly spaced inside and outside the hangar.

MTOF. They keep a record of all the vehicles in their computer system, whose information is available to MTMF and the Air Cargo MT section. The SNCO IC control looks after the monthly run. For example, the coach as used daily by personnel from the guard room to ATC. The duty run controller receives the F658 from sections for duty runs to locations outside Lyneham. He does the necessary paperwork and issues this to the SNCO IC Duty Shift, who runs the

Leyland DAF 4 tonner during daily inspection (DI)

DI on a Vauxhall Corsa

3 day and one duty night shift, thus providing transportation 24 hours throughout the year. If an aircraft diverts to another station, or during emergency, this section is kept busy.

The Combined Equipment Services (CES) is responsible for the first line servicing. This also involves the installation of number plates, fitting and issuing when a new vehicle arrives. They also ensure that the Daily Inspection (DI) areas are clean and that replenishment materials such as air, water and oil are available.

Fitting number plates

The Training and Licensing (TAL) Section is responsible for issuing the F600 (licence to drive service vehicles like the landrover) and to renew such licences annually. They investigate accidents which involve Service vehicles inside and outside the Lyneham area. There is also a civilian instructor and examiner who issues licences to those personnel who wish to drive the fork lift.

The STAMA is the main computer room, and keeps the records of over 520 plus vehicles, prime movers and transporters. This system is linked to RAF Brampton in addition to MTMF and Air Cargo. All paperwork, including job cards, starts from here.

AIRCRAFT SUPPORT MT (ASMT)

The ASMT is one section that works closely with the Hercules aircraft and consists mainly of civilians. The duty leading hand IC Coach Pool, runs a 4 shift pattern to provide transport 24 hours a day for aircrew and groundcrew from the married quarters and from any part of the station to the flight line or to their respective aircraft. They also provide transport for foreign aircrew and maintain a backup for emergencies, such as collecting spares from the stores to the aircraft when unserviceabilities arise during the start up of the aircraft. The JNCO IC Air Cargo MT Section, has the responsibility for a few specialist vehicles, such as the Atlas (Condec) freight loader and transporter and large fork lifts. They are kept busy day and night as the main function of the Hercules is "freight" transportation. The last section is the ASMT itself. They provide a 4 shift pattern 24 hours a day and possess numerous specialist vehicles. When a propeller or the QEC is to be removed or installed on the aircraft, a crane is called for. The refuelling bowser is doubled up as a snow plough vehicle by fitting a plough to the front of the vehicle. On very cold days the Trump de-icing vehicle is used to melt the ice impinged on the airframe. The Symonds hoist vehicle is used to lift the tradesmen to change the anti-collision light filament from the tip of the empennage and also to service the HF aerials and so on. For the contaminated runway (ice and snow) the de-icing vehicles are kept busy. However, when information of an impending bad weather report is received, crystals with anti-icing property are sprayed on the runway. There are many more specialist vehicles maintained by AMST. The experienced and matured FS IC AMST maintains a high standard in executing the normal and unexpected duties. This is only achieved by a close working relationship with the majority of civilian staff.

MTMF

Bird Control Unit Landrover – discussing the snag

Re-tuning the ambulance vehicle

Removing the gearbox from the Leyland DAF 4 tonner

The 3 dwarfs on the DAF!

Checking the brakes on a "roller brake tester"

Major servicing on the Leyland refueller (bowser)

AMST

Atlas aircraft loader in "raised position"

Loader in aircraft loading position

Apart from the fire trucks, AMST drivers operate these vehicles

Crew coach

KONSIN Sprayer (Runway de-icer)

Snow plough and UREA spreader (Runway anti-icer)

CHAPTER TEN

DEFENSIVE EQUIPMENT

AN/ALQ – 57. The capability to use the Infra-Red Counter Measures (IRCM) is incorporated on approximately 30 Hercules. The system is an airborne IRCM designed to protect the aircraft from heat-seeking missiles. It radiates controlled, pulsed, high-intensity Infra-Red (IR) energy from two IR transmitters. After attaining the correct operating temperature, each transmitter radiates a jamming code which consists of a repeating series of IR pulses designed to disrupt the IR guidance system(s) of approaching missiles. The IR transmitters become extremely hot when operating and if the system is tested on the ground they should not be touched for 45 minutes after they have been switched off. Additionally while operating on the ground there is a very serious danger to the eyes from the radiated IR transmitter.

RADAR WARNING RECEIVERS (RWR). There are 3 variations of RWR systems currently fitted to the Hercules fleet. They are similar in that they can detect and identify radar transmissions within a 360 degree azimuth region about the aircraft on which it is installed. Built in test equipment (BITE) is provided on each system to check the operation and assist in the location of a faulty component.

ORANGE CROP (MAROC) ESM This is the first of the three variants fitted to the Hercules and can be found on the CMk1K (tanker aircraft). The system consists of sensitive receiving equipment designed to analyse various radar transmissions and present the findings on a display. There are separate aerial assemblies which provide the RF components and the system operates over a frequency range of 600MHz to 18Hz.

Orange Crop is capable of providing the following functions:-

(1)   A primary sensor for the identification and location of surface vessels by detection of their radar transmissions.

(2)   A complementary system to the existing aircraft radar for the location and identification of surface vessels.

(3)   A radar homing facility to enable the aircraft to approach within visual range of a surface vessel or other sources, for identification purposes.

(4)   A proximity warning of surface-to-air missiles or radar controlled guns, by detecting their high data rate radar emissions.

(5)   A general radar reconnaissance facility in any tactical situation in which the aircraft may be involved.

(6)   Detection of emissions of submarines radars.

AN/ALR–66(VC). This RWR system is available on many Hercules and is an airborne defence and RWR which automatically detects and identifies emitters in the C – J bands. It is capable of presenting a display that designates both the identity of the emitters and the azimuthal angle of arrival of each displayed emitters, again utilising a system of aerials in the wing tips.

Sky Guardian. This is the most recent RWR fit on 4 Hercules aircraft and is a wide band crystal video RWR. The system provides audio and visual information when illuminated by either pulse, pulse modulated, continuous wave radio signals. It detects and identifies radar emitters in the frequency range 0.7 – 18GHz (C – J) and presents the information on 2 indicators on the flight deck.

AN/AAR 47. This is a passive Missile Warning System (MWS) fitted to some Hercules aircraft which can be combined with AN/ALE – 40 (Chaff and Flare system) to provide protection against missile attack. The AN/ALE 40 Counter Measures dispensing system (CMDS) is fitted to some aircraft and provides the capability to dispense countermeasure chaff and/or flares.

Currently each of the Hercules has dispensers under each wing root, with a payload of 15 in each dispenser. There is in progress a programme of modification to increase the number of dispensers. The setting up of the system is done by the navigator who will (depending on the perceived threat) program the system either for manual or automatic initiation of dispensing operation.

Manual initiation is achieved by operating a remote dispense switch and will cause the system to eject flare cartridges in accordance with the settings of the programmer. The remote dispense switch is a pistol grip type requiring operation of both thumb and trigger finger to initiate a dispense signal. There are 3 such switches – 1 at the navigator's station, 1 at each of the two paratroop doors. Automatic initiation is achieved when the MAWS triggers and provides a signal to the ALE 40 system, via the automatic release switch and will cause the system to eject flares in accordance with the settings on the programmer.

The AN/AAR 47 Missile Warning System transmitter/receiver (centre of picture)

Fitting flares (port side) to the Counter Measures dispensing system

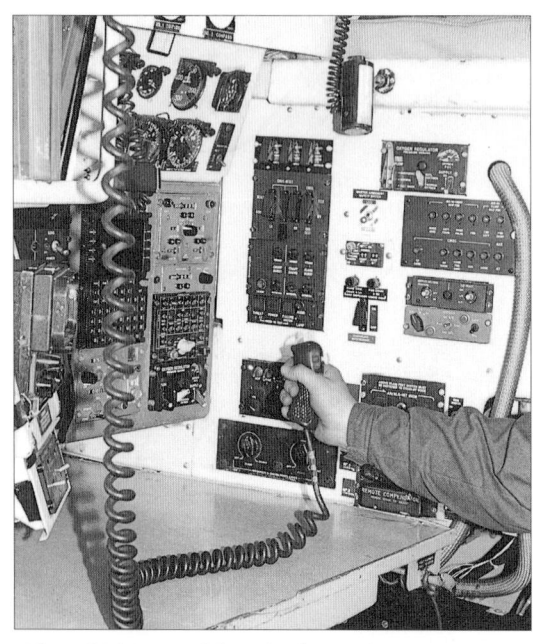

Manual initiation of flares by the pistol grip type switch from the navigator's station

Flares ejecting from dispenser (near Sarajevo airfield, Bosnia)

The Hercules does possess one offensive weapon – IT'S SHEER SIZE!

Receiver warning aerials (port wing tip)

AN/ALR-66, display and control unit (extreme left) at navigator's station

AN/ALQ-57, technician cleaning the port IRCM transmitter on a B/F servicing (rear of port main wheel)

The faithful Orange Crop (MAROC) elctronic counter measure receiver (port wing tip)

Operational success (using the MAROC) interception of an Argentine Navy vessel within the Falkland Island Protection Zone (FIPZ). Note the guns and the EXOCET missile launchers (rear). One of the author's many operational missions

Hercules near Lyneham

Hercules on low level para drop over Belize, Central America

XV 292 over RAF Lyneham (Silver Jubilee paint scheme 1993)

Hercules CMk3P (foreground) and a CMk1P

Watching the weather with Snoopy! the unique WMk2

CMk1P over "Great How", Cumbria

WMk2 about to land

Rear view of a CMk1K

CMk3 conversion at Marshall Aerospace

The 2000th Hercules being assembled at Lockheed, Georgia (January 1993)

View of the basket (only 3ft away!). Note the 80ft AAR hose from the CMk1K (tanker) aircraft

View of the receiver aircraft from the rear of the tanker over the Falkland Islands

Front instrument panel

The same panel and also the engineer's overhead panel illuminated for night flying, but in the Link – Miles simulator

Engineer's overhead panel

The navigator's station on the CMk1K. Note the HDU control panel (beside the curtain)

Khe Sanh "steep" approach at Lyneham

XV206 – Khe Sanh approach over Sarajevo, Bosnia 1995

Releasing the flares (defensive material prior to landing)

XV206 at Sarajevo airport

An unsurfaced runway (UR)

One of the landing zones (LZ) in Northern Saudi Arabia during the Gulf conflict in 1991

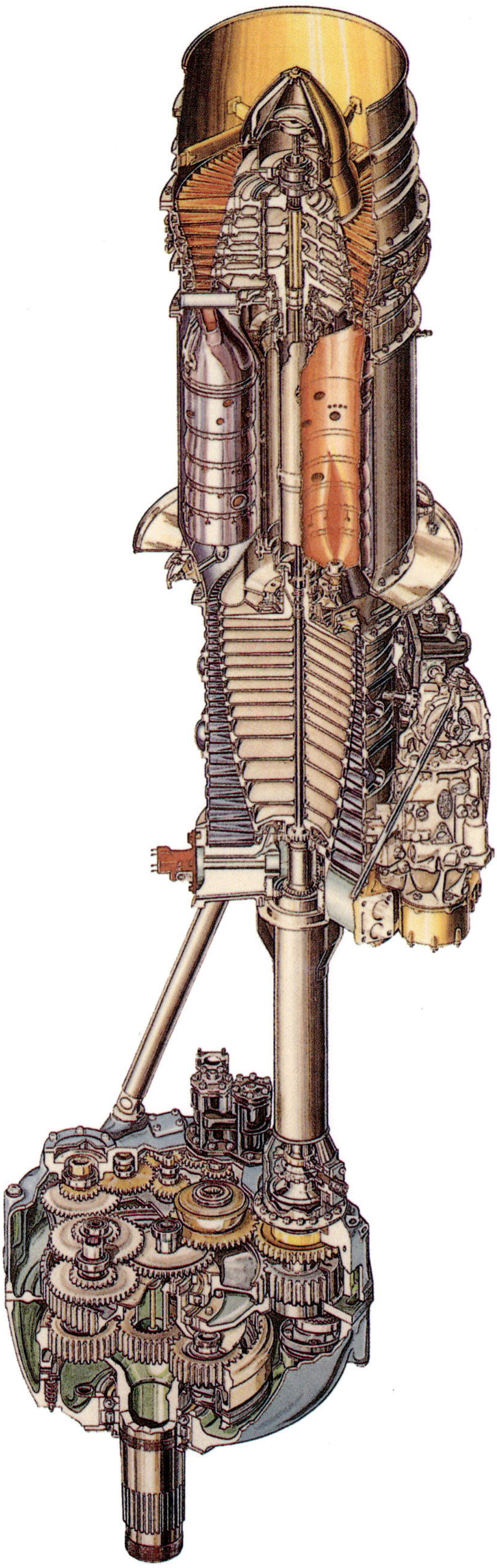

*Rear view showing the cargo door locked up and the ramp lowered on the support stand.
The inset photograph shows a light tank exiting over the lowered ramp*

Assembling the Allison T56-A-15 engine (PRF)

Adding more ancillary equipment on to the QEC (PRF)

PMS in use to strip paint from the crew door

Aircraft undergoing the "minor" servicing (AES)

XV292 was painted in the "silver jubilee" livery in 1992 by ASF (painters and finishers)

Aircraft in full passenger fit

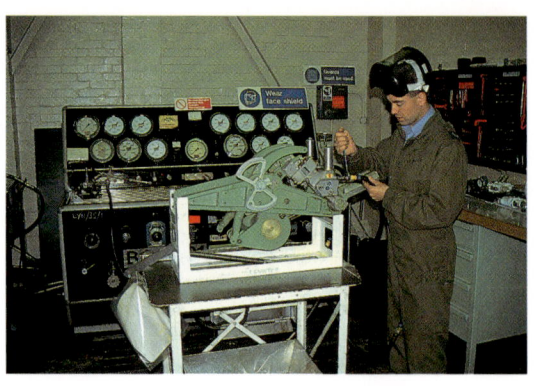

Hydraulic pressure testing (ASF)

Aircraft kept rigid by belly trestles (ALSS)

Inside the test cabin (UETF)

The engine test facility (UETF)

Servicing the HDU's (BLSS)

Rectifying the fault on the GTC after "minor servicing" (AES)

Propeller change at Riyadh, Saudi Arabia (1991)

Aircraft wash bay

Minor servicing (AES)

Testing the auto-pilot platform (EES) Inset – sunset at Lyneham

ACKNOWLEDGEMENTS

This book would not have been possible without the kind assistance of Wg Cdr T Kirby MBE,RAF, Officer Commanding Engineering Wing(Nov 1992 - 1995)

All the Co-operation from the personnel of Engineering Wing.

It is difficult to single out each and everyone but the following have had a special hand in the production of this book by giving support and investing valuable time and effort.

SQN LDR D Ellis
FLT LTs D Saunders, G Parker
WOs Gore, M Kelly, RE McKleish, Wilson
FSs E Botham, RI Ogden(oggy), D Stoddart, D Williams
C/Ts Gerrard, Jones, Packham
SGTs K Breeze, M Daykin, B Gillian, 'Geordie'Hunn, DA Keal, B Logan,
MC Marmoy, D Rose, N Pryor, WGJ Worthington
CPLs DJ Gosling, Wyatt, A Pollard, DB Brown, J Files, T Gill, RC Lock,
M Glenn, B Bond, 'Tiny' Draper, JA 'Ozzy' Osborough, Gage, D Sheffield,
Angie Powell, Jeff Gibbings, RG O'Brien,
SACs JG Holdom, Andy Brown, PA Cobbett, P McDermott, A Craggs, R Mahon

Entire personnel of PRF and especially, Karen Holness, Rosa, Larry,
MJ Jacobs, Taff(Marshall Aerospace), Tom Thomas, N Brittain

Mr GL Couzens, Mr G Thomas, Kelvin Patterson, John Savigor, Jacho Johnson, 'Baldrick'Thorpe, Bense Hedges, SM Clayton, Simon French, AR Welsby, P Bond, Andy Whittle, Paul Rowland, Karen Evans. Roy Cozens

Special thanks to Cpl Glen Iverson(ex-RAF Chivenor), now Sgt at RAF Cosford, who made 3 visits to take approximately 30% of the photographs for this book.

PRINCIPAL PHOTOGRAPHERS- Andy Muniandy, Sgt Glen Iverson, Mr Jeremy Flack(Aviation Photographs International).

Photograph credits:

Lockheed	page Nos... 1, 147b
Marshall Aerospace	148T
Allison Gas Turbines	154
Sgt Andy Whittle	5T, 152BR &TR
Cpl Paul Rowland	145, 166, 168
SAC(W) Karen Evans	138TR, 162, 167, 172,174B
Cpl JA Osborough	80, 134, 173T
Sgt Simpson(Elmo)	152BL, 142BR
Brian Logan	86, 146B
Sqn Ldr E Le Count RAF(retd)	144B
Dave Fry	153, 168
Alan Bainbridge	147, 162
Tom Langridge	5BR

The rest of the photographs by the Principal photographers

Hercules CMk3 over Dunmail Rais, Wales

Under belly and rear view of Hercules CMk1K (tanker version)

Front view of XV192

Three Hercules during Primary servicing, inside the large hangar

XV292 painted in the 25th anniversary scheme (Silver Jubilee livery) in 1992

CMk3 XV199 over the pan at RAF Chivenor, North Devon

Hercules CMk1 over the Arabian desert, during the Gulf conflict in 1991

It's sunny and I'm heavy too!

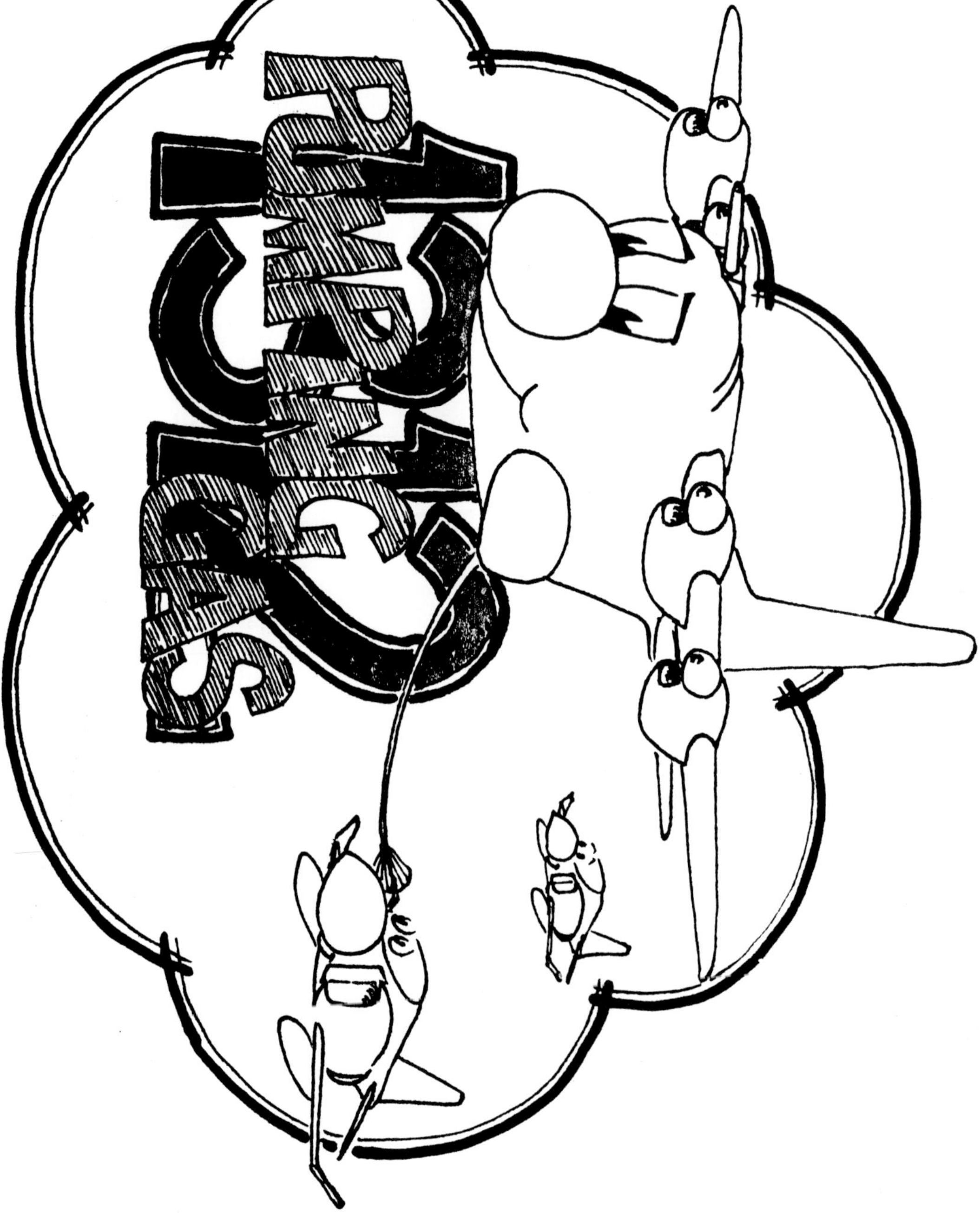
PUMPING GAS

I just wiggled these wires and it started (illustration by Sgt N Brittain – PRF)

ULTRA LOW LEVEL AIRDROP

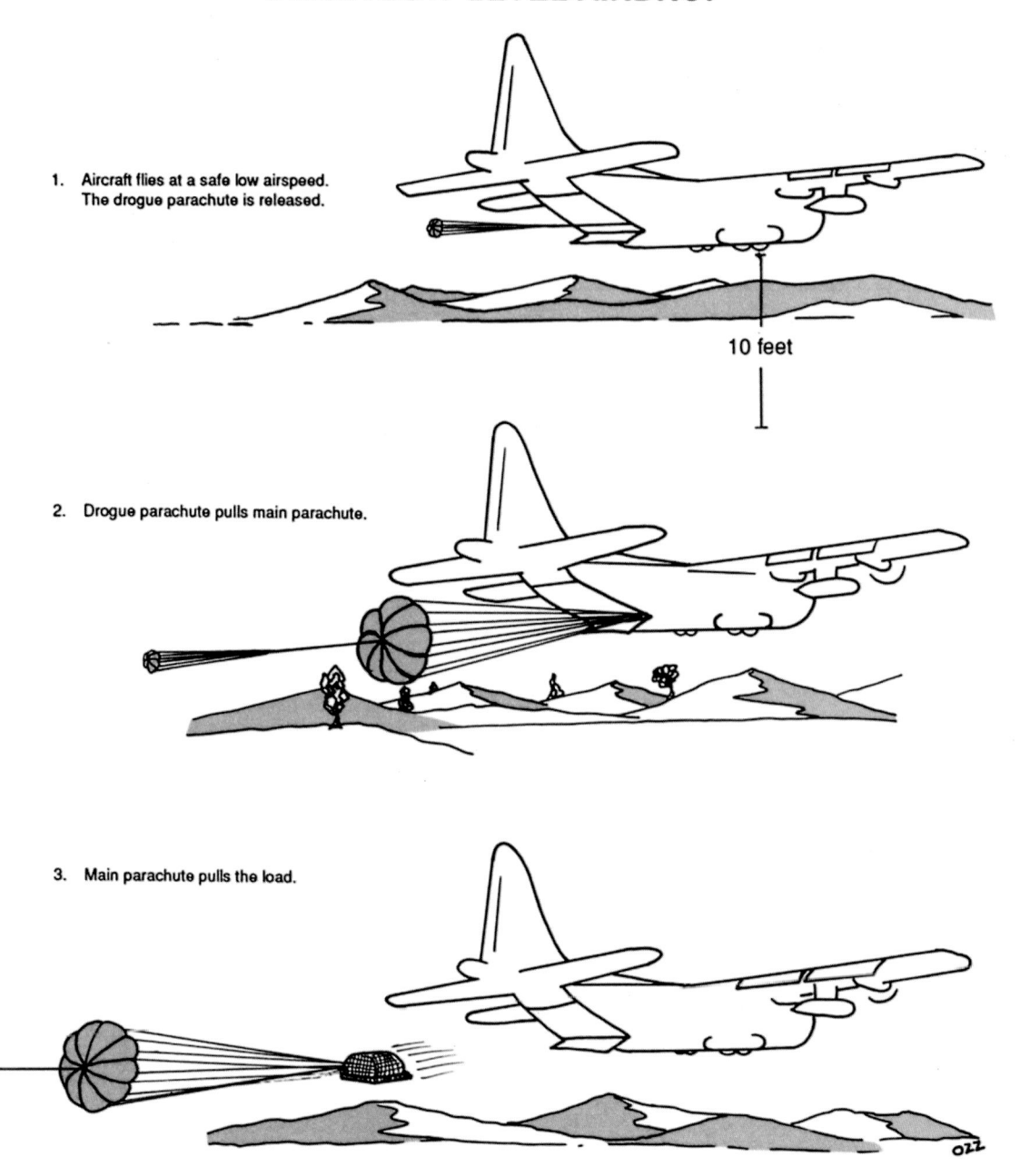

1. Aircraft flies at a safe low airspeed. The drogue parachute is released.

10 feet

2. Drogue parachute pulls main parachute.

3. Main parachute pulls the load.

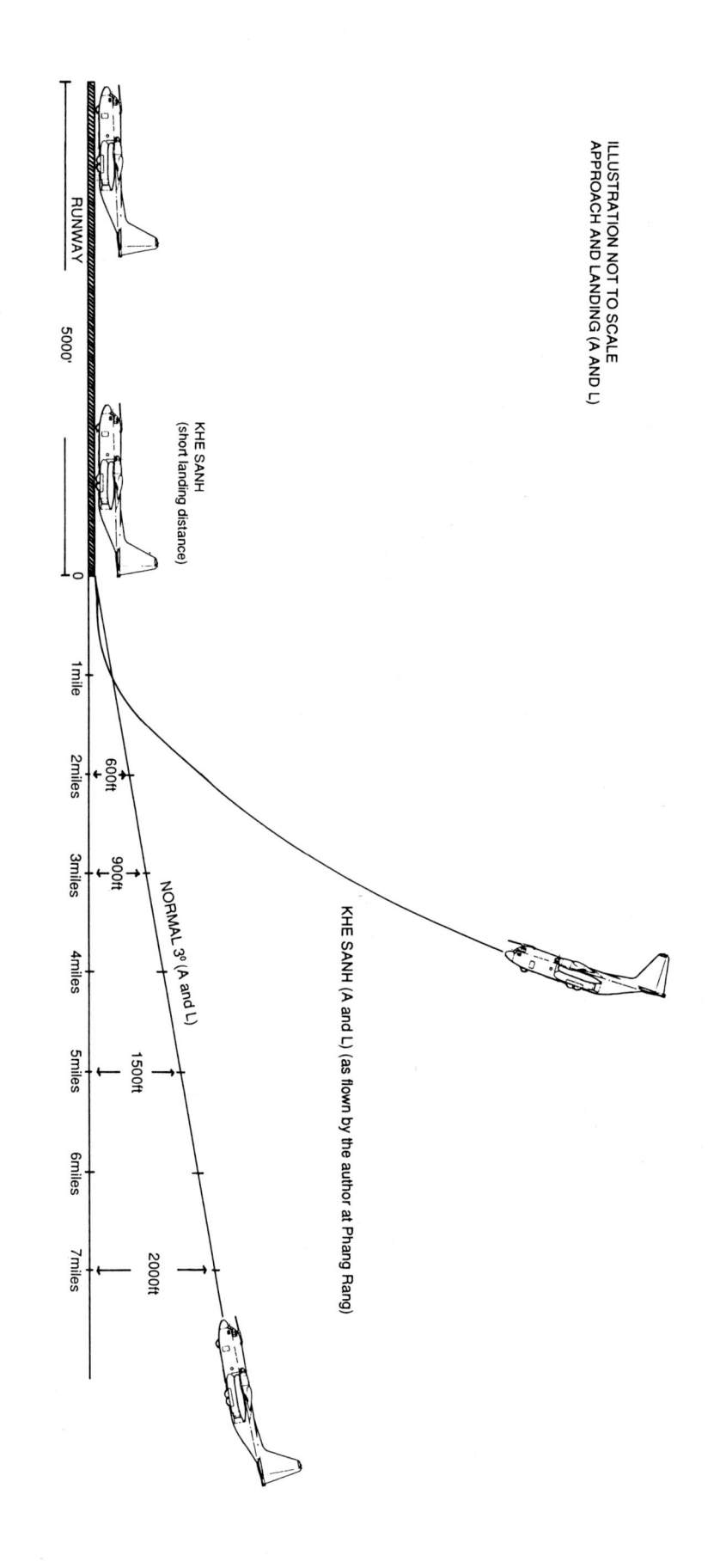

ILLUSTRATION NOT TO SCALE
APPROACH AND LANDING (A AND L)

RUNWAY

5000'

KHE SANH
(short landing distance)

1 mile

2 miles — 600ft

3 miles — 900ft

NORMAL 3° (A and L)

4 miles

5 miles — 1500ft

KHE SANH (A and L) (as flown by the author at Phang Rang)

6 miles

7 miles — 2000ft

Tactical (A and L) as used by Nos 47 and 70 squadron in Bosnia to avoid small arms fire and missiles

173

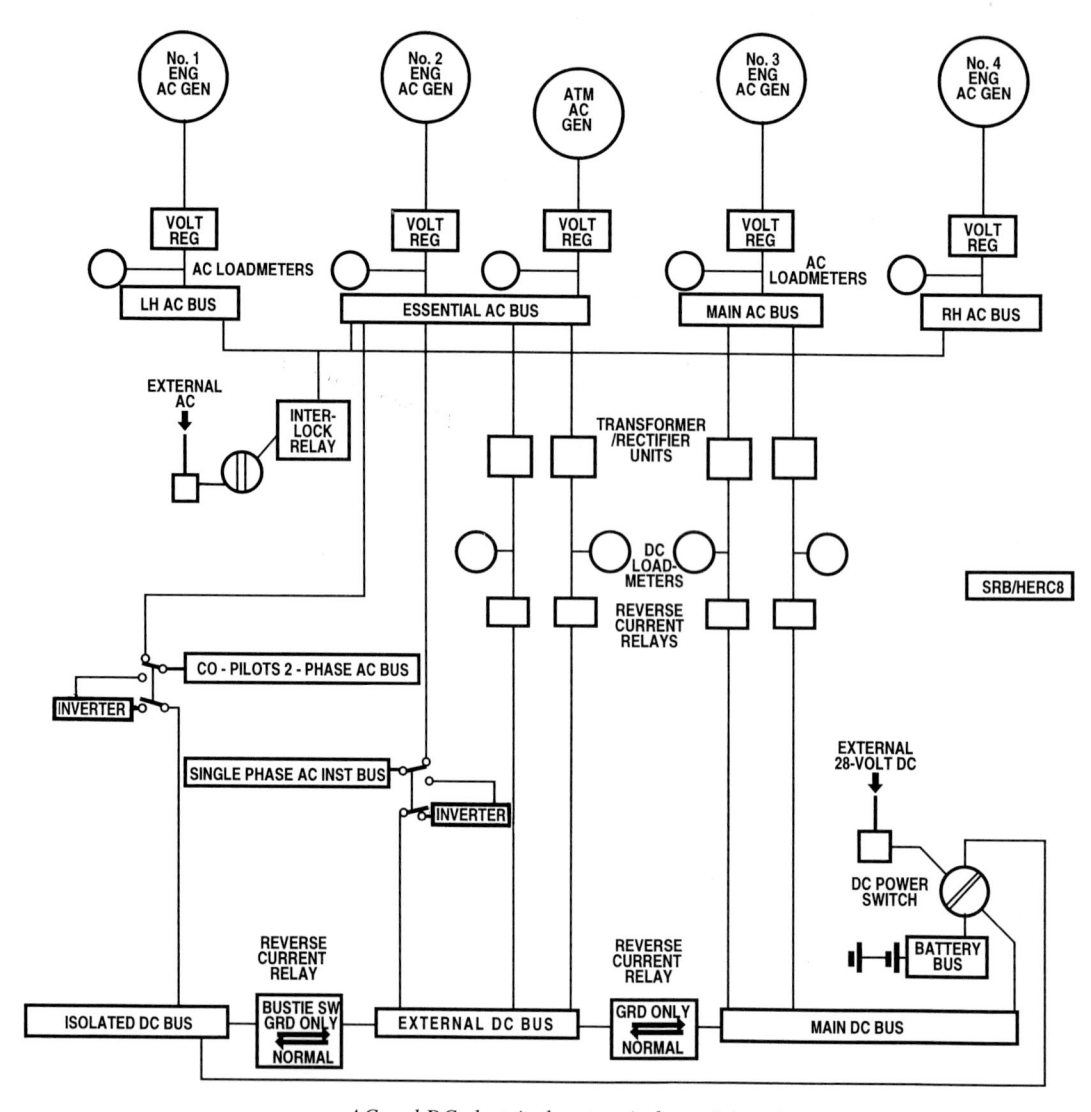

AC and DC electrical system (schematic)

Engine component locations

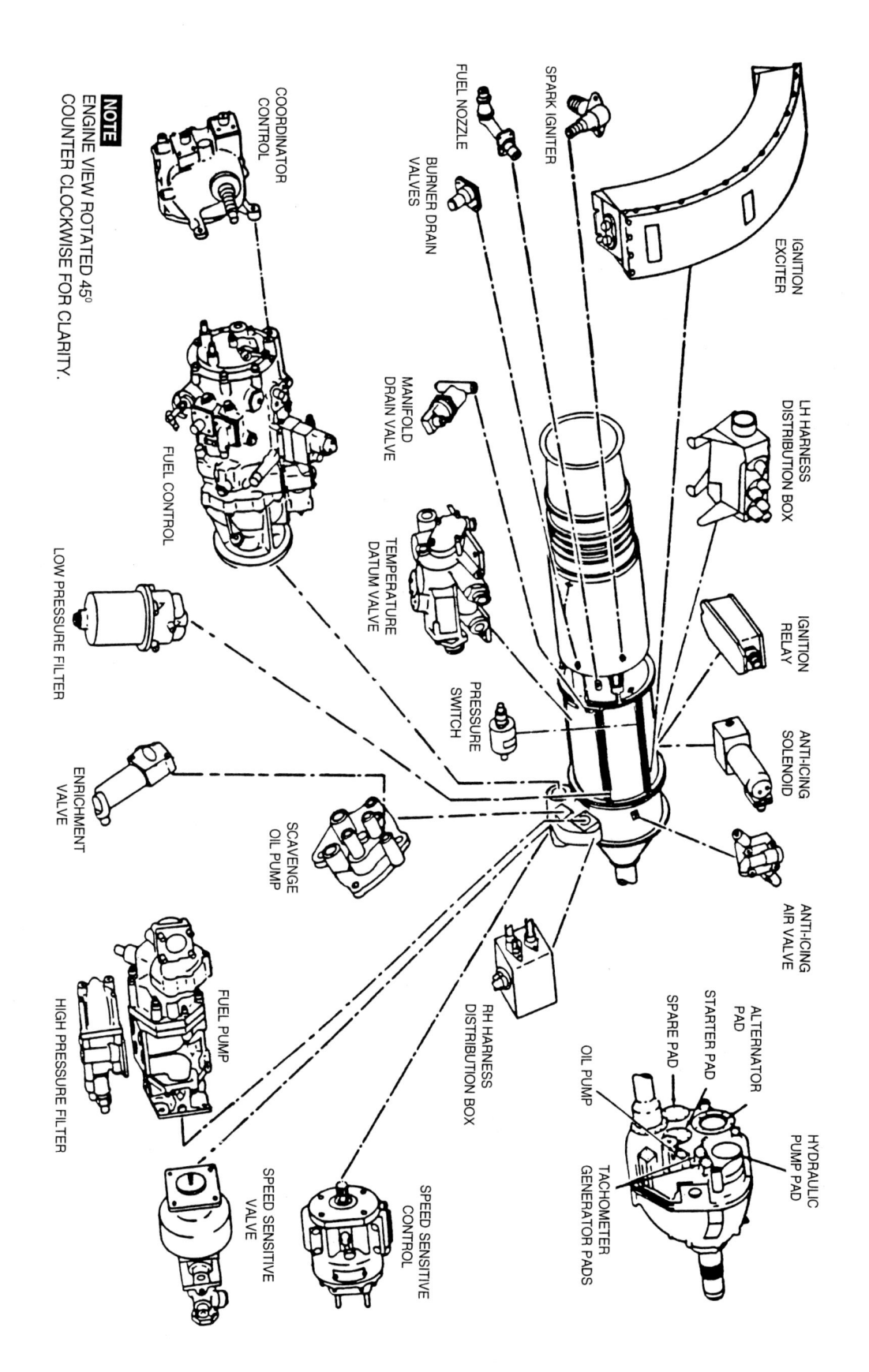

ROBO-FLM
FLight Line Mechanic

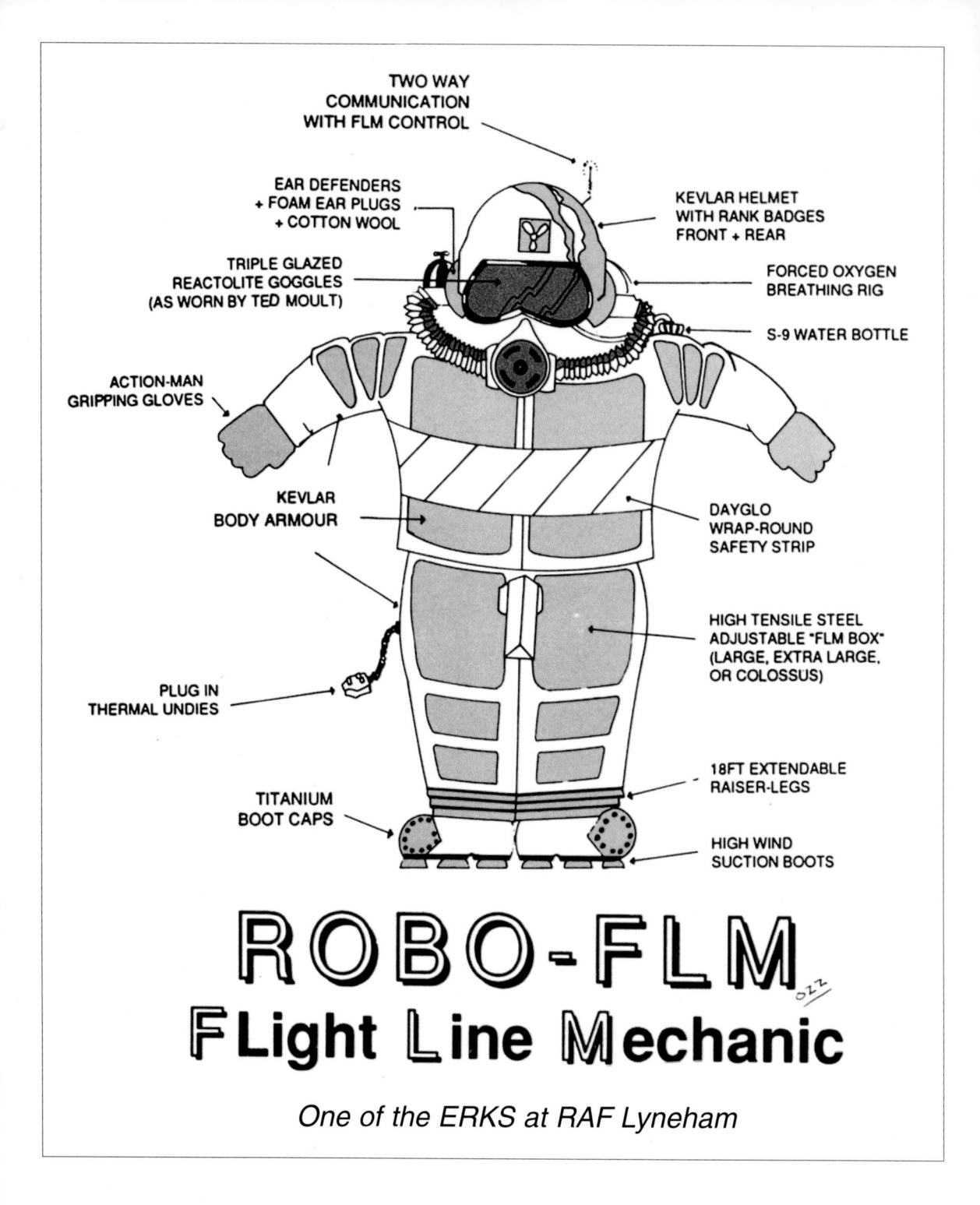

One of the ERKS at RAF Lyneham

- TWO WAY COMMUNICATION WITH FLM CONTROL
- EAR DEFENDERS + FOAM EAR PLUGS + COTTON WOOL
- KEVLAR HELMET WITH RANK BADGES FRONT + REAR
- TRIPLE GLAZED REACTOLITE GOGGLES (AS WORN BY TED MOULT)
- FORCED OXYGEN BREATHING RIG
- S-9 WATER BOTTLE
- ACTION-MAN GRIPPING GLOVES
- KEVLAR BODY ARMOUR
- DAYGLO WRAP-ROUND SAFETY STRIP
- HIGH TENSILE STEEL ADJUSTABLE "FLM BOX" (LARGE, EXTRA LARGE, OR COLOSSUS)
- PLUG IN THERMAL UNDIES
- 18FT EXTENDABLE RAISER-LEGS
- TITANIUM BOOT CAPS
- HIGH WIND SUCTION BOOTS

The author's last award winning book: Hercules – The RAF Workhorse, and this book are available from "Hercules Publishing House" 18, St. Mary's Close, Bradenstoke, Chippenham, WILTS. SN15 4ET. Price £14.95 (incl. of P & P).